SUGAR BUST
For Life!
...WITH THE BRENNANS
COOKBOOK AND COMPANION GUIDE

Based on the diet principles found in
SUGAR BUSTERS!™ Cut Sugar To Trim Fat.

ELLEN C. BRENNAN

Consultant, Editor, Publisher, Sales and Marketing
Director for the original, best-selling

SUGAR BUSTERS!™ Cut Sugar To Trim Fat

THEODORE M. BRENNAN

Co-owner of Brennan's Restaurant in New Orleans
and Co-author of the internationally acclaimed cookbook...

BREAKFAST AT BRENNAN'S®...AND DINNER, TOO!

Over 400 Recipes, Menus, Red Wine List, Brand Names and more...

for weight loss, energy, diabetes and cholesterol control
and an easy, healthful lifestyle.

The validity of Sugar Busters, L.L.C.'s claim of federal trademark rights in the term
"Sugar Busters!™" is acknowledged.

Published by Shamrock Publishing Inc.
P.O. Box 15439
New Orleans, Louisiana 70175-5439

Printed in the United States of America
Quebecor Printing Book Group

ISBN 0-9663519-0-8
Typography by Sir Speedy
Second Edition

Table of Contents

NEW!

Sugar Bust For Life!...With The Brennans, Part II

Acknowledgments

We wish to acknowledge and extend our heartfelt thanks to the following significant contributors:

To H. Leighton Steward for sharing with us in 1993 his new low sugar way of life in a gift of Michel Montignac's *Dine Out and Lose Weight*. Leighton's vision of an easy interpretation of Montignac's concept and, as a result, his spearheading the *SUGAR BUSTERS!™ Cut Sugar to Trim Fat* project provided a means to good health for countless individuals.

To our daughter, Alana, for relentlessly devoting hours of overtime to ensure the production of *Sugar Bust For Life!* We could not have done it without her.

To Barbara C. Heim for her immeasurable creativity and organization especially at a time when we were not very creative or organized.

To the talented cooks in the kitchen who have tasted, tested and assured the "home" friendliness of our scrumptious recipes:

Chef Michael Roussel	Sous Chef Lazone Randolph
Alana M. Brennan	Barbara C. Heim
Maria Ceron	Nicolle S. Hoy
Rose F. Cohen	Sally S. Johnston
Mildred Crouere	Monique S. McConnell
Pat and Dene Denechaud	Bertha Williams

To the following special individuals for their invaluable contributions to the *Sugar Bust For Life!* project:

Bridget R. Brennan	Elmer Hemphill
James C. Brennan	Harry Hill
Theodore M. Brennan, Jr.	Eleanor C. Joseph
Wayne Chambless	Jane W. McCall
Billie M. Cox, Jr.	Mary P. Nass
George Frazier	Eliana Oda
Alan H. Goodman	Chad A. Ventola
Anne M. Grace	Bonnie Warren

Introduction

*E*llen C. Brennan was initially a consultant to the authors of *SUGAR BUSTERS!™ Cut Sugar to Trim Fat* as an editor and publisher. She endorsed the concept through her Foreword for the book at the authors' request. Ellen's belief in this new way of eating was the basis for her commitment to the promotion as well as to the distribution and sales of over 200,000 copies. On behalf of the authors, she became a counselor to hundreds of you who, after reading the book, asked for clarification or further explanation of various aspects of changing your eating habits.

Sugar Bust For Life! is the response to those many phone calls and faxes requesting recipes, menus, brand names and tips for success. It was obvious to Ellen that those who had read *SUGAR BUSTERS!™ Cut Sugar to Trim Fat* or just understood its basic guidelines still needed help in following this low sugar dietary concept and guidance in maintaining a new and healthy way of life.

These hundreds of readers primarily were asking for "more information," details and simple explanations to basic questions — of which the answers were not always obvious to everyone. *Sugar Bust For Life!* addresses the most prevalent and recurring topics to clarify what has appeared confusing for some.

Sugar Bust For Life! is not a medical guide, nor do its authors offer any medical advice. If you have medical questions or concerns, you should always check with your physician. If, however, you are looking for an easy guide to support your change in eating habits, *Sugar Bust For Life!*, written by the Brennans from firsthand knowledge of the popular low sugar way of life, is the book for you.

Through research and experience, the Brennans realize that there are various interpretations and opinions of how to maintain successfully a life in which sugar is taboo. In the forthcoming pages, they share the exact approach that has worked for them and how they believe others can enjoy the same success. Most important, the Brennans hope to eliminate confusion with a comprehensive format rich in detail and consistency.

Why a companion guide for a healthy meal plan? *Easy* is the key word. In the "Big Easy" — a city with a rich heritage of fine dining and just plain good eating — following a healthy meal plan can be a challenge.

Ellen and Ted Brennan understand the challenge. Surrounded by dining opportunities, Ellen and Ted have wisely adjusted their eating habits to maintain their good health, to feel good and to look good. The Brennans do so without sacrificing recipes that create three scrumptious meals and satisfying snacks every day. As a result, they do not feel hungry nor do they experience cravings for "forbidden" foods.

Now, the Brennans have put all their acquired knowledge into a guide to make it easy to follow a healthy meal plan. *Sugar Bust For Life!* is a guide that provides an easy way of eating without having to rely on counting calories or fat grams. They have taken the guesswork out of making wise choices. They have compiled a list of brand names from which to choose. The book also includes recipes that delight and satisfy the most discriminating palates. There are easy menu plans from "soups to nuts," tasty desserts as well as a suggested red wine list to complement your meal.

So, what makes this style of eating healthy? First and foremost is the realization that foods that spike your insulin level, known as high glycemic carbohydrates, are harmful to your health. This low sugar dietary concept can improve cholesterol, triglycerides, blood sugar levels, blood pressure, digestive disorders, help attain that desired weight while diminishing the symptoms of diabetes and restoring strength and stamina. You will discover a way to eat right while eating well. *Sugar Bust For Life!* unfolds an easy road to a healthful life for you.

Food Guide

Sugar Bust For Life! reveals everything you will need to achieve an easy, low sugar lifestyle. Simply know that there are foods you can eat, foods you cannot eat and foods to be eaten in moderation. Let the following lists be your easy guide as you *Sugar Bust For Life!*

Foods for Feasting

Low Glycemic Foods
0–40 Index

Meats and Fowl, lean and skinless

Alligator	Pork
Beef	Quail
Chicken	Rabbit
Cornish Hens	Squab
Duck	Turkey
Goose	Veal
Lamb	Venison
Liver	Other Wild Game

Seafood

Abalone	Mussels
Anchovies	Oysters
Catfish	Pompano
Caviar	Prawns
Clams	Redfish
Cod	Red Snapper
Crabmeat	Salmon
Crawfish	Sardines
Drum	Scallops
Eel	Sea Bass
Flounder	Shark
Grouper	Shrimp
Haddock	Snails
Halibut	Sole
Herring	Squid
Lemon Fish	Swordfish
Mackeral	Trout
Lobster	Tuna
Mahi Mahi	Turbot

Dairy Products

Butter	Eggs
Cheeses, assorted	Margarine
Cottage Cheese	Milk, all types
Cream	Sour Cream
Cream Cheese	Yogurt

Note: The sugar found in milk is a natural sugar called lactose which is acceptable.

Vegetables

Alfalfa Sprouts	Kale
Artichokes	Kidney or Red Beans
Arugula	Leeks
Asparagus	Lettuce
Avocado	Lima Beans
Bamboo Shoots	Mint
Bean Sprouts	Mirliton
Black Beans	Mushrooms
Broccoli	Mustard Greens
Brussel Sprouts	Okra
Butter Beans	Onions
Cabbage	Parsley
Cauliflower	Radicchio
Celery	Radishes
Chick Peas	Red Bell Peppers
Chili Peppers	Red Peppers
Collard Greens	Scallions
Cucumbers	Shallots
Eggplant	Soy Beans
Endives	Spinach
Escarole	Squash, Yellow
Garbanzo Beans	Tomatoes
Garlic	Turnips
Green Beans	Turnip Greens
Green Onions	Watercress
Green Bell Peppers	Water Chestnuts
Hearts of Palm	Yellow Bell Peppers
Jalapeno Peppers	Zucchini

Miscellaneous

Beverages (free of sugar or other unacceptable ingredients)
Brown Rice Cakes
Chocolate
(60% or greater cocoa content)
Coffee
Cooking Oils (Canola, Corn, Olive, Peanut, Safflower, Soybean, etc.)
Dill Pickles
Hot Sauces
Mustards
Nuts
Olives
Peanut Butter
Seasonings and Spices
Sauerkraut
Soy Milk
Soy Sauce
Tea
Tofu, fresh (read label)
Vinegar

Fresh Fruit

The glycemic index of each fruit listed ranges from low to moderate.

Apples
Apricots
Blackberries
Blueberries
Boysenberries
Cantaloupe
Cherries
Cranberries
Figs
Grapefruit
Grapes
Honeydew Melon
Lemons
Limes
Manderin Oranges
Nectarines
Oranges
Papaya
Peaches
Pears
Persimmon
Plantains
Pomegranate
Plums
Raspberries
Satsumas
Strawberries
Tangerines

The sugar found in fruit is a natural sugar called fructose. It is only detrimental to the low sugar way of life when eaten at the wrong time or with other food groups.

- The rule to apply with no exception is the following: Fruit must be consumed alone at least 30 minutes prior to eating anything else or at least 2 hours after eating.

- Natural whole fruit preserves with no sugar added should be eaten the same way as fresh fruit. However, an occasional treat of an acceptable cracker with sugarless whole fruit preserves is not harmful.

- Fruit juice, even unsweetened, is quickly absorbed when consumed. The minimum pulp content of fruit juice as compared to the rich pulp content in a piece of fruit can create an intense glycemic response — that is, fruit juice can elevate blood sugar levels. We believe that fruit juice, even unsweetened, should be avoided for weight reduction or for blood sugar level maintenance. Once desired weight is attained and if glycemic response is not a serious concern, the consumption of fruit juice should follow the same rule applied to fruit — that is at least 30 minutes prior to a meal or at least 2 hours after.

- Sugar free desserts containing fruit are not included in the "Just Dessert" recipe section. A sugar free fruit dessert should follow the same rule for consumption as any fresh fruit — that is 30 minutes before a meal or at least 2 hours after. The demand for desserts with such a restriction is limited. In addition, a sugar free fruit dessert should consist only of the fruit itself and should not include other ingredients such as cereal, cottage cheese, cream, cream cheese, eggs, ice cream, nuts, ricotta cheese, sour cream, whipped toppings, pie crusts (even whole grain), yogurt, etc.

- We believe the use of lemon and lime juice in our recipes to be insignificant and the rule for fruit consumption to be non-applicable.

Foods for Moderation

Moderate Glycemic Foods
40 – 60 Index

Whole Grain Breads, Flours and Pasta

Mixed Whole Grain Breads
Oat Bran Bread
Pumpernickel Bread
Rye Bread
Stone Ground Whole Wheat Pasta
100% Whole Durum Wheat Semolina Pasta
Stone Ground Whole Wheat Bread
Stone Ground Whole Wheat Pita Bread
Whole Grain Flours (Barley, Brown Rice, Oat, Rye,
Stone Ground Whole Wheat, etc.)

Vegetables

Black-eyed Peas	Pinto Beans
Green Peas	Split Peas
Lentils	Sweet Potatoes
Navy Beans	Yams

Whole Grains

Barley	Oat Bran
Brown Basmati Rice	Oatmeal
Brown Rice	Wheat Bran
Buckwheat	Wheat Germ
Bulgar	Whole Grain Cereal
Cracked Wheat	Wild Rice

7

Forbidden Foods

High Glycemic Foods
60 and greater index

Fruits & Vegetables

Bananas
Beets
Carrots
Corn
Dates
Kiwi, very ripe
Mango
Parsnips
Pineapple
Potatoes, Red and White
Prunes
Raisins
Taro
Watermelon

Snacks

Candy
Chee Wheez
Chocolate (less than 60% cocoa content)
Corn Chips
Cornnuts
French Fries
Granola Bars
Ice Cream (most), Ice Milk, Sherbet, Sorbets and Other Frozen Desserts
Museli Bars
Popcorn
Potato Chips and Sticks
Pretzels
Rice Cakes

Baked Goods, Flours & Grains

Bagels, Wheat and White	French Bread
Biscuits, Wheat and White	Gingerbread
Bread, Wheat and White	Grits
Bread Crumbs	Hamburger and Hot Dog Buns
Breadsticks	Kaiser Rolls
Bread Stuffing	Melba Toast
Cakes	Millet
Cereals, Refined	Muffins
Cookies	Pancakes
Corn Bread	Pastries
Corn Flour	Pies
Cornmeal	Pita Bread
Couscous	Pizza
Cracker Meal	Refined White Pasta
Crackers, Wheat and White	Rice, Basmati White
Cream of Wheat	Rice, Instant (Even Brown)
Croissants	Rice, White
Croutons	Shortbread
Donuts	Taco Shells
English Muffin	Tapioca
Flour, Enriched Wheat† and White	Waffles

 BEWARE: Many sugar free baked goods are unacceptable because they are made with refined wheat flour and not stone ground whole wheat flour.

†Do not confuse wheat flour with stone ground whole wheat flour. However, as noted on the label most brand name stone ground whole wheat breads are laced with "hidden sugars" such as honey.

Beverages

Beer (Includes Ale and Lite Beer)
Chocolate and Malted Milk Drinks
Colas and Drinks: bottled, canned and packaged mixtures (containing sugar, hidden sugars or other unacceptable ingredients)
Liqueurs
Tonic Water

Miscellaneous

Barbecue Sauce
Breakfast Bars, Drinks and Pastries
Chili Sauce
Coffee Creamers
Condensed Milk
Fruit Jams, Jellies and Preserves
Gelatin Mixes, Flavored and Sweetened
Gravy (Canned and Packaged)
Hamburger Mix
Ketchup (Most)
Marshmallows
Meal Supplements
Meat spreads, canned
Pot Pies, Frozen
Prepared Meals (Canned, Frozen and Packaged)
Pudding Mixes
Salad Dressings (Many Bottled and Most Packaged)
Soups (Most Canned and Packaged)
Tofu (read label for unacceptable ingredients)

Hidden Sugar & Other Unacceptable Ingredients

Barley Malt	Honey
Beet Juice	Malted Barley
Beet Sugar	Maltodextrin
Brown Rice Syrup	Maltose
Brown Sugar	Maple Syrup
Cane Juice	Modified Food Starch
Cane Syrup	Modified Tapioca Starch
Cornstarch	Molasses
Corn Syrup	Potato Starch
Dextrose	Raisin Juice
Flour: Corn, Enriched Wheat and White	Sugar, Raw and Refined
Glucose	Sucrose
High Fructose Corn Syrup	

Food For Thought with Fourteen Daily Menus

Compiled by Monique S. McConnell, R.D., L.D., Clinical Dietitian, specializing in cardiology

The fourteen daily menus, compiled by clinical dietitian Monique S. McConnell, R.D., L.D. for *Sugar Bust For Life!*, will help you maintain your new lifestyle with very little guesswork. Just keep in mind that these are only suggested menus. Substitution at any meal of a different recipe or one of your own creation is acceptable, luncheon and dinner items are interchangeable and changing the order in any way or eliminating an item altogether is also acceptable.

In the menus to follow, Monique will show you that eating well is what *Sugar Bust For Life!* is all about. It is a new and healthy way of life, not just a diet. Monique's menus display the versatility and creativity made possible when you *Sugar Bust For Life!* This lifestyle plan is the answer to less than satisfying meals and restrictive low calorie diets that for some people can even create a fear of food. Such deprivation is unhealthy.

Sugar Bust For Life! will show you how to enjoy eating and be healthy! This new way of eating will help you lose weight and keep it off without feeling hungry or craving food for long periods of time. There are just a few medically acknowledged facts that, once understood, will make changing your lifestyle of eating easy to do.

First and foremost is the fact that refined or simple sugar and certain complex carbohydrates referred to as high glycemic carbohydrates, such as a

11

white potato, can stimulate the pancreas to secrete high levels of insulin. Insulin regulates blood sugar levels and high levels of insulin cause storage of excess sugar, not used for energy, as fat, inducing the liver to produce cholesterol. Also excessive consumption of refined sugar and certain complex carbohydrates can effect the immune system and create risk of disease.

The *Sugar Bust For Life!* way of eating is not about counting fat grams or calories but about simply avoiding refined sugar and other high glycemic carbohydrates. It's not a quick weight loss concept. Yet, weight loss should be steady and consistent by eating from all food groups in moderation.

Some people have realized that weight loss is expedited by eating protein alone. Interestingly, eating protein alone has the directly opposite effect of eating the high glycemic carbohydrates that are stored as fat. Therefore, eating just a sirloin strip, a grilled chicken breast or Trout Meuniere will signal the pancreas, instead, to secrete an enzyme called glucagon which, actually, will break down stored fat. In addition, eating low glycemic foods leaves you feeling full for longer periods of time compared to high glycemic foods

Remember the key words — **Moderation** and **Portion Control** — coupled with the fact that no two people are exactly alike. Following the guidelines set forth here and recognizing that you are different from anybody else will start you on your way. Telling you to eat only a certain number of calories or fat grams daily is not the answer. Reasonably sized servings are a "must." There is no set formula for everyone; there are simple guidelines of "Do's" and "Don'ts" to be modified by the individual. Also keep in mind that although Monique's fourteen daily menus offer a variety of choices, it is still necessary to exercise caution in the quantity of food you consume despite the fact your mother may have taught you to eat everything on your plate.

There is no question that lunch is a difficult meal to arrange for the person "on the go." Forethought and advance preparation of this midday meal is most helpful for achieving set goals. This is especially critical in avoiding the classic pitfalls of "fast foods" or other comparable, readily available, unhealthy choices. Packing a lunch bag of fruit and cheese with a chicken breast, a container of tuna salad atop mixed greens or half of a sandwich are just a few ideas for viable substitutes for any menu lunch item.

The only suggestion to exercise with caution is the sandwich. More than one slice of whole grain bread a day can inhibit weight loss for some. Also, if convenient, any of the suggested dinner menus may be eaten midday instead. Some people may prefer the luncheon items as a light evening fare.

As you can see, finding what is exactly right for you is accomplished by trial and error. Once your desired weight is attained, a maintenance plan should be easily determined by the same trial and error method.

Many people are guilty of overeating the "right" foods! Especially, the over-consumption of moderate glycemic carbohydrates, such as whole grain pasta, brown rice, beans, sweet potatoes and whole grain breads, can cause weight loss to stop or slow down. If this happens, try restricting yourself to protein and green vegetables for a while to achieve better results and cautiously ease in the moderate glycemic carbohydrates once weight loss resumes.

Women sometimes complain that they don't lose weight as easily as men. Again, this is where trial and error methods may come into place. Women may need to be more aware than men of portion control and more cautious about carbohydrate consumption, especially those moderate glycemic carbohydrates. Once again, the elimination of such carbohydrates at certain meals and a regimen of protein and green vegetables only should expedite weight loss. Perhaps, eating protein alone at lunch or dinner for a period of time would be beneficial. Weight loss in women also can be stymied by hormones or birth control pills. So, if you are a woman who is taking this type of medication, by all means, check with your physician.

It is never wise to eat right before going to bed. Be sure to eat no later than three hours before bedtime. Most cholesterol is produced at night and a late night meal can cause indigestion.

Meals should be well-balanced with all food groups eaten in moderation and that includes fat. Beware, however, that some fats are bad and others are not! Saturated fats can increase your blood cholesterol level or low density lipoproteins (LDL), known as "bad" cholesterol. On the other hand, monounsaturated fats such as olive, canola and fish oils can be good for you as they should not adversely effect your high density lipoproteins(HDL) or "good" cholesterol and can actually elevate HDL levels. In addition, this lifestyle promotes the consumption of the necessary 20-25 grams of fiber daily which also reduces cholesterol levels.

In our recipes, there is opportunity for you to modify your fat intake by choosing skim milk over cream, margarine over butter, olive oil over other oils. This is not a high fat diet as some might think. All food groups are to be eaten in moderation. You control what and how much you eat. *Sugar Bust For Life!* is about eating healthy with moderation as the key.

No meal plan is successful without including water. Eight glasses of water daily are very important. Limiting your sodium intake is also important. Drinking an adequate amount of water helps to eliminate excess sodium from your body. Further, drinking too much of anything during a meal interferes with digestion. Sugar free beverages with caffeine are acceptable in moderation. Just beware that caffeine is a stimulant and will cultivate your appetite.

Remember, too, that alcoholic beverages can inhibit any diet. If you choose to indulge, remember never do so on a empty stomach. A dry red wine is the drink of choice and, again, extreme moderation should be exercised in its consumption. Drinking a glass of red wine daily can actually benefit your cardiac health and can also be instrumental in lowering "bad" (LDL) cholesterol levels while raising the "good" (HDL) ones.

Sugar Bust For Life! also allows you to eat right when dining out. You can enjoy a meal at your favorite restaurant and still maintain a healthy lifestyle. Even if you fall prey to small amounts of "forbidden" foods, no permanent harm is done. You simply modify your next meals accordingly to get back on track. The best news is that after indulging in those "forbidden" foods over a weekend, Monday morning no longer means starving to compensate as it once did on low-cal diets. It simply means eating right while eating well.

Snacks during the day can actually be good for you because they keep your blood sugar from dropping too low and your metabolism from slowing down. Keeping a can of nuts or a box of acceptable crackers in your car can appease any hunger pangs.

Last, but not least is our recommendation that you exercise daily to benefit your overall health. Again, check with your physician as to the best type of exercise for you. Yes! You are eating adequate carbohydrates for exercise unless, that is, you are a marathon runner. Remember, fruit and vegetables have natural sugars and this is a low sugar dietary concept, not a no sugar dietary concept. Only strictly protein diets can cause ketosis.

So get yourself moving!!! Walking is probably the easiest form of good exercise. After all, the only equipment you need is a comfortable pair of walking shoes with proper support.

Easy is what *Sugar Bust For Life!* is about — an easy road to a healthful life for you. The fourteen daily menus that follow will help you on your way.

Week 1

MONDAY	BREAKFAST	LUNCH	DINNER
	½ Cantaloupe (Wait 30 minutes) Shredded Wheat with Skim Milk Sugar-free Yogurt Coffee or Tea	Black Bean Soup (page 68) Caesar Salad with Grilled Shrimp (page 112)	Mixed Green Salad with Classical French Dressing (page 135) Chicken Florentine (page 203) Grilled Tomatoes (page 266)
	Snack (page 20)	Snack (page 20)	Snack (page 20)
TUESDAY	BREAKFAST	LUNCH	DINNER
	Peach (Wait 30 minutes) Egg, sunny-side up or once over easy 1 strip crisp Bacon Stone Ground Whole Wheat Toast with Butter or Margarine Coffee or Tea	Spinach Salad (page 114) Rosemary Chicken (page 192)	Mixed Green Salad with Ranch Dressing (page 137) Red Snapper Provencale (page 178) Rice & Asparagus Au Gratin (page 276)
	Snack (page 20)	Snack (page 20)	Snack (page 20)
WEDNESDAY	BREAKFAST	LUNCH	DINNER
	Orange (Wait 30 minutes) Oatmeal Sugar-free Yogurt Coffee or Tea	Tuna Salad (page 126) on a bed of field greens with Tomato Vinaigrette (page 141)	Hearts of Palm (page 113) Chicken With Fresh Mushrooms (page 196) Wild Rice (page 276)
	Snack (page 20)	Snack (page 20)	Snack (page 20)
THURSDAY	BREAKFAST	LUNCH	DINNER
	½ Grapefruit (Wait 30 minutes) Scrambled Egg 1 Slice Canadian Bacon Stone Ground Whole Wheat Toast with Butter, Margarine or Cream Cheese Coffee or Tea Snack (page 20)	Tomato Basil Soup (page 58) Cobb Salad (page 111) Snack (page 20)	Spinach Salad (page 114) Roast Pork (page 205) Sweet Potatoes with Lime (page 270) Snack (page 20)

FRIDAY	BREAKFAST	LUNCH	DINNER
	Strawberries (Wait 30 minutes) Puffed Kashi with Skim Milk Sugar-free Yogurt Coffee or Tea	Cucumber and Onion Salad (page 122) Beef and Bean Chili (page 224)	Mixed Green Salad with Hazelnut Vinaigrette Dressing (page 140) Grilled Jumbo Shrimp (page 236) Green Beans with Dilled Havarti Cheese (page 259)
	Snack (page 20)	Snack (page 20)	Snack (page 20)
SATURDAY	BREAKFAST	LUNCH	DINNER
	Apple (Wait 30 minutes) Poached Egg atop Canadian Bacon and Stone Ground Whole Wheat Toast or Grillades (page 157) Coffee or Tea	Mixed Green Salad with Green Goddess Dressing (page 137) Lemon Baked Fish (page 175)	Jackson Salad (page 113) Roast Tenderloin of Beef (page 228) Cauliflower and Broccoli Casserole (page 255) Chocolate Mousse (page 292) or Cheesecake (page 296)
	Snack (page 20)	Snack (page 20)	Snack (page 20)
SUNDAY	BREAKFAST	LUNCH	DINNER
	Blackberries (Wait 30 minutes) Mame's Pancakes (page 154) with Butter or Margarine and Sugar-free Syrup 1 Strip of Crisp Bacon or Eggs Ellen (page 151) Bran Muffin (page 313) Coffee or Tea	Split Pea Soup (page 67) Chicken Salad with Curry (page 109)	Green Salad with Stilton Cheese and Walnuts (page 114) Grilled Double Veal Chops (page 241) Grilled Marinated Vegetables (page 245)
	Snack (page 20)	Snack (page 20)	Snack (page 20)

Week 2

	BREAKFAST	LUNCH	DINNER
MONDAY	Orange (Wait 30 minutes) Shredded Wheat with Skim Milk Sugar-free Yogurt Coffee or Tea Snack (page 20)	Gazpacho (page 52) Citrus Chicken (page 199) Snack (page 20)	Mixed Green Salad with Lemon-Soy Dressing (page 136) Barbecued Shrimp (page 169) Macaroni & Cheese Annie (page 274) Snack (page 20)
TUESDAY	½ Grapefruit (Wait 30 minutes) Poached Egg atop Stone Ground Whole Wheat Toast Sugarless Sausage Coffee or Tea Snack (page 20)	Mixed Green Salad with Ranch Dressing (page 137) Louisiana Hamburgers (page 218) Snack (page 20)	Spinach Salad (page 114) Baked Catfish Creole (page 176) Fiesta Rice Casserole (page 278) Snack (page 20)
WEDNESDAY	Strawberries (Wait 30 minutes) Oatmeal Sugar-free Yogurt Coffee or Tea Snack (page 20)	Lentil and Ham Soup (page 70) Crabmeat atop sliced Tomatoes and Onions (page 129) Snack (page 20)	Mixed Green Salad with Roquefort Dressing (page 134) Chicken with Chives (page 201) Eggplant Parmesan (page 258) Snack (page 20)
THURSDAY	Apple (Wait 30 minutes) Scrambled Egg Sugarless Turkey Sausage Mestemacher Toast with Butter or Margarine Coffee or Tea Snack (page 20)	French Onion Soup (page 65) Southwestern Chicken Salad (page 108) Snack (page 20)	Spinach Salad (page 114) Sautéed Lamp Chops (page 207) Skillet Sweet Potatoes (page 272) Snack (page 20)

FRIDAY	**BREAKFAST**	**LUNCH**	**DINNER**

	Plum
	   (Wait 30 minutes)
	Pumpernickel or Rye
	   Toast with Butter
	   or Margarine and
	   Melted Cheese
	Sugar-free Yogurt
	Coffee or Tea
	Snack (page 20)
		Seafood Salad
		   (page 129)
		
		Snack (page 20)
			Wild Rice Stuffed
			   Tomatoes
			   (page 118)
			Steak au Poivre
			   (page 229)
			Asparagus with
			   Mustard Sauce
			   (page 254)
			Snack (page 20)

SATURDAY	**BREAKFAST**	**LUNCH**	**DINNER**

	Blueberries
	   (Wait 30 minutes)
	Scrambled Egg with
	   Chopped Ham
	   and Cheese
	or Pecan Oatmeal
	   Waffle (page 154)
	   with
	Butter or Margarine
	   and Sugar-free
	   Syrup
	Canadian Bacon
	Coffee or Tea
	Snack (page 20)
		Broccoli and Cheese
		   Soup
		   (page 61)
		Chef Salad
		   (page 109)
		French Dressing
		   (page 135)
		
		Snack (page 20)
			Tomato and Onion
			   Salad
			   (page116)
			Marinated Shrimp
			   (page 169)
			Creamed Spinach
			   (page 262)
			Chocolate Mousse
			   Torte (page 296)
			   or Butterscotch
			   Custard (page 291)
			
			Snack (page 20)

SUNDAY	**BREAKFAST**	**LUNCH**	**DINNER**

	½ Cantaloupe
	   (Wait 30 minutes)
	French Toast
	   (page 153) or
	Crabmeat Omelette
	   (page 147)
	Bran Muffin
	   (page 313)
	Coffee or Tea
	
	Snack (page 20)
		Chicken Salad
		   Theodore
		   (page 107) atop
		   Mixed Greens
		   with Vinaigrette
		   Dressing
		   (page 138)
		
		Snack (page 20)
			Asparagus in
			   Mustard
			   Vinaigrette
			   (page 120)
			Grilled Butterflied
			   Leg of Lamb
			   (page 242)
			Tomato Zucchini Au
			   Gratin (page 266)
			
			Snack (page 20)

Suggested Snacks

Assorted Cheeses

Cheese and Crackers (See Brand Name Guide for acceptable crackers)

Cottage Cheese

Chocolate — a square of 60% or greater cocoa content
(with a few of your favorite nuts gives the taste of a candy bar!)

Creole Cream Cheese

Dill Pickles

Fruit (to be eaten 30 minutes before a meal or at least 2 hours after a meal)

Hot Chocolate (with 60% or greater cocoa)

Hummus

Nuts (plain, roasted or spiced, see recipe section)

Olives (black, green and stuffed)

Peanut Butter

Pickled Vegetables (cauliflower, green beans, okra, etc.)

Raw Vegetables
(plain, with cheese spread, cream cheese, peanut butter or
dip-see recipe section)

Sardines and Sliced Onions

Smoked Clams and Oysters

Sweet Potato Chips

Triscuit® Nachos (Triscuit® with melted cheese, salsa and jalapeno peppers)

Yogurt, Sugar-free

Recipes

Surrounded by dining opportunities, Ellen and Ted Brennan have mastered the easy, healthful lifestyle *Sugar Bust For Life!* affirms. They understand the challenge.

Whether entertaining friends at Brennan's Restaurant of New Orleans or dining casually at home, Ellen and Ted know how to apply their acquired knowledge in maintaining a low sugar lifestyle. They understand how to provide you with a healthy meal plan without sacrificing recipes that create three scrumptious meals every day.

Some recipes should be prepared in advance to facilitate this low sugar way of life. In particular, barbecue sauce, ketchup, mayonnaise, salad dressings and, even, ice cream are a few suggestions to be prepared ahead of time. Advance preparation of bread crumbs, marinades, certain sauces and stocks will also facilitate the preparation of many recipes. The extra time invested is worth ensuring the simplicity of your new lifestyle.

Sugar Bust For Life! allows creativity in your kitchen never imaginable on conventional, low calorie and low fat diets. For variety and flavor, keep in mind that many sauce recipes can be served with baked, broiled or grilled chicken, meat or seafood. Our pasta sauce section offers additional variety.

The Brennans chose Sweet 'N Low® to use in their recipes as it does not lose its sweetness with heat. This artificial sweetener added to a cold mixture as opposed to a hot one will create less of an aftertaste. They found that the aftertaste of any acceptable liquid artificial sweetener in a hot or cold mixture was minimal. The following Sweet 'N Low® equivalents to sugar can be helpful:

¼ cup sugar	*instead use*	3 packets, 1 teaspoon bulk or 1½ teaspoons liquid
⅓ cup sugar	*instead use*	4 packets, 1¼ teaspoon bulk or 2 teaspoons liquid
½ cup sugar	*instead use*	6 packets, 2 teaspoons bulk or 1 tablespoon liquid
1 cup sugar	*instead use*	12 packets, 4 teaspoons bulk or 2 tablespoons liquid

You will find that the recipe section includes various rice, pasta and sweet potato suggestions. Forever be cautious not to overeat the "right" foods. Although certain recipes call for brown rice, sweet potatoes, and whole grain pasta, over-consumption of these moderate glycemic carbohydrates can cause weight loss to stop or slow down. Unless your desired weight is attained, pasta and rice should not be your main meal but an occasional side dish. As always, moderation is key.

In the recipes, there is opportunity for you to modify your fat intake by choosing skim or low fat milk over cream, margarine over butter, canola or olive oil over other oils. *Exercise caution as many times low and no fat often equate to high sugar content.* However, this is not a high fat diet as some might think. Food groups are to be eaten in moderation with you controlling what you eat.

Just keep in mind that suggested low fat modifications will alter the consistency of soups and sauces making them thin in texture. Instead of using cream, white flour or cornstarch as a thickener, substitute 2 tablespoons of stone ground whole wheat flour, which is equivalent to the same amount of white flour or to 1 tablespoon of cornstarch. Be sure to strain the sauce before serving for a smoother consistency. The following guide will help you modify your fat intake if you so choose:

Low Fat Modifications

Whole Milk	*instead use*	Skim, Low fat, Buttermilk
Heavy Cream	*instead use*	Evaporated Skim Milk
Butter	*instead use*	Margarine, Olive or Canola Oil
Sour Cream	*instead use*	Low fat sour cream or Light Yogurt
Whipped Cream	*instead use*	Chilled & Whipped Evaporated Skim Milk with a dash of lemon juice
High Fat Cheese	*instead use*	Skim Milk Cheese
Cream Cheese	*instead use*	Neufchatel Cheese
Egg	*instead use*	2 Egg Whites or ¼ cup Egg Substitute
Mayonnaise	*instead use*	Light Yogurt
Bacon	*instead use*	Lean Ham or Canadian Bacon
Ice Cream	*instead use*	Sugar free Fruit Flavored Ice (see page 306)
Salad Dressing	*instead use*	Olive Oil with Vinegar or Lemon

The *Sugar Bust For Life!* recipe section envelopes a world of fine dining for your very own kitchen. The days of monotonous, unsatisfying dieting are over. For your culinary pleasure, the Brennans reveal in the pages to follow recipes of fine quality and flavor. You will eat healthy while satisfying the most discriminating palates.

CHAPTER FIVE

Appetizers, Hor d'Oeuvres, Snacks

Asparagus and Crabmeat Mousseline

64 fresh asparagus spears
2 cups cold water
½ teaspoon salt
2 lbs. lump crabmeat, picked over to remove any shell and cartilage
¼ cup (½ stick) butter or margarine
Mousseline sauce (see below)
Freshly grated Parmesan cheese for sprinkling

Serves eight

Rinse the asparagus spears thoroughly under cold running water, then trim the stems so that the spears are about 4 inches in length. Using a vegetable peeler or knife, scrape away the tough skin from just below the asparagus tip to the base of the stalk. Place the prepared asparagus in a large sauté pan along with 2 cups of cold water and the salt. Boil the spears gently over medium heat until tender, then remove them from the pan and blot dry on paper towels. Place the cooked asparagus on a warm plate while cooking the crabmeat. Melt the butter or margarine in a large skillet. Add the crabmeat and sauté for several minutes until the crabmeat is heated through. To serve, divide the asparagus spears between 8 plates. Top the asparagus spears with about ½ cup of crabmeat, then cover with mousseline sauce. Sprinkle with Parmesan cheese and serve hot.

Mousseline Sauce

½ cup heavy cream
Pinch of salt
Pinch of white pepper
1 teaspoon chopped fresh parsley
1 tablespoon dry white wine
2 cups hollandaise sauce (see Index)

In a medium bowl, combine the cream, salt, and pepper. Beat the mixture with a whisk until thick enough to form a ribbon trail, then add the parsley, wine, and hollandaise sauce. Fold until thoroughly blended.

Crabmeat Marinière

½ cup (1 stick) butter or margarine

1 cup scallions, finely chopped

3 tablespoons stone ground whole wheat flour

2 cups milk

½ teaspoon salt

½ teaspoon cayenne pepper

⅓ cup dry white wine

12 oz. lump crabmeat, picked over to remove any shell and cartilage

1 egg yolk, beaten

Paprika for sprinkling

Serves four

*M*elt the butter or margarine in a small skillet. Add the scallions to the pan and cook for a few minutes over medium heat until tender. Reduce the heat to low, then blend in the flour. Cook the mixture for 3 to 5 minutes, stirring constantly. Pour in the milk and stir until smooth, then add the salt, cayenne, and wine. Simmer 10 minutes, stirring occasionally, then fold in the crabmeat. When the crabmeat is heated through, quickly beat in the egg yolk.

Spoon the crabmeat mixture into four ¾ cup ovenproof molds or ramekins. Sprinkle with paprika, then broil until lightly browned, about 2 to 3 minutes. Serve piping hot.

Buster Crabs Béarnaise

4 baby soft-shell crabs

¼ cup (½ stick) butter or margarine

stone ground whole wheat flour for dusting

Salt and black pepper to taste

⅓ cup béarnaise sauce (see Index)

Serves four

*C*lean the crabs by removing the eyes and gills; trim the tails.

Melt the butter or margarine in a large sauté pan. Sprinkle the crabs on both sides with salt and pepper, then dust lightly with flour. Place the crabs in the pan and cook over moderately high heat for 3 minutes per side; the crabs are very delicate, so handle them gently during cooking. Place the cooked crabs on heated serving plates and top each with a heaping tablespoon of béarnaise sauce.

Shrimp Paradis

4 lbs. raw peeled shrimp

2 tablespoons garlic purée

1 cup green onions, finely chopped

½ cup celery, finely chopped

¼ cup parsley, finely chopped

⅓ cup green pepper, finely chopped

1½ sticks butter or margarine

2 tablespoons stone ground whole wheat flour

1 teaspoon salt

2 teaspoons pepper

2 tablespoons Worcestershire sauce

¼ cup dry white wine

Serves eight

*S*lowly melt butter or margarine in a large covered skillet. Add garlic purée, vegetables, salt, pepper, and Worcestershire sauce. Blend thoroughly, cover and simmer 30 minutes. Add flour, wine, and shrimp and blend into vegetables. Cover and simmer 10 minutes. Serve immediately.

Italian Barbecued Shrimp

15-20 (about 1lb.) large raw shrimp, peeled and deveined

½ cup (1 stick) butter or margarine

¼ cup water

2 garlic cloves, minced

1 tablespoon Italian seasoning

1 tablespoon thyme leaves

2 teaspoons chopped fresh parsley

1 teaspoon black pepper

Pinch of paprika

Pinch of salt

Pinch of white pepper

Preheat oven to 375° F.

Serves four

Slice the shrimp lengthwise down the back, being careful not to cut all the way through. Melt the butter or margarine in a large skillet and sauté the shrimp for 1 to 2 minutes. Stir in the remaining ingredients and ¼ cup water. Cook briefly, then transfer the shrimp and butter mixture to a shallow ovenproof dish. Bake in the hot oven for 3 to 4 minutes.

To serve, divide the shrimp between four plates, then pour some of the sauce over the shrimp.

Oysters Rockefeller

2 cups (4 sticks) butter or margarine

1 celery rib, finely chopped

2 bunches scallions, finely chopped

1 bunch parsley, finely chopped

3 tablespoons Worcestershire sauce

1 teaspoon Tabasco®

½ to ¾ cup Herbsaint or Pernod (use more or less according to taste)

¾ cup bread crumbs (see Index)

48 oysters in their shells

Rock salt

Preheat oven to 375° F.

Serves eight

Melt the butter or margarine in a large skillet and add the celery, scallions, and parsley. Sauté for 5 minutes, then add the Worcestershire and Tabasco®. Reduce the heat to medium and cook for 10 minutes. Add the Herbsaint or Pernod and bread crumbs and cook another 5 minutes. Remove the pan from the heat and transfer the mixture to a bowl. Chill in the refrigerator 1 hour until cold, but not firmly set.

Using an oyster knife, pry open the oyster shells, then remove the oysters. Discard the top shells; scrub and dry the bottom shells. Drain the oysters. Arrange 6 oyster shells on an ovenproof pan or tray lined with a layer of rock salt about an inch deep. Make 8 trays in all. Place 1 oyster in each of the shells.

Remove the chilled Rockefeller topping from the refrigerator and beat it with an electric mixer to evenly distribute the butter or margarine and infuse air into the mixture; transfer the mixture to a pastry bag fitted with a large plain tip.

Pipe a tablespoon of the mixture onto each oyster, then bake in the hot oven for 5 to 8 minutes. Serve each person one tray of piping hot oysters.

Mussels Vinaigrette

6 lbs. mussels in the shell

¼ cup red wine vinegar

¼ cup extra-virgin olive oil

1 teaspoon paprika

1 teaspoon sweet paprika

1 large seeded lemon, cut into extra thin slices

1 tablespoon salt

2 tablespoons fresh parsley, finely chopped

2 cloves garlic, minced

Serves four

*C*lean the mussels and remove and discard their beards. Rinse them under cold water and drain well. Pour the oil and vinegar into a large stock pot. Add the remaining ingredients and salt to taste. Bring to a boil and simmer for 1 minute. Add mussels, cover and cook for 3 to 4 minutes until the mussels open. Transfer the mussels and their liquid to a bowl, discarding any that have not opened. Let cool at room temperature and refrigerate 3 to 4 hours before serving.

Buffalo Wings

10 lbs. chicken wings

2 cups Gorgonzola dressing (see Index)

Celery sticks

Preheat oven to 425° F.

Serves four to six

Sauce:

2 sticks butter or margarine

1½ cups hot pepper sauce

*S*plit the wings at each joint and discard the tips; rinse then pat dry. On baking sheets place the wings and bake for 30 minutes. Turn and bake for an additional 30 minutes, until golden brown. Drain well and place in a large bowl. Melt the butter or margarine over medium-low heat and stir in the hot pepper sauce. Toss with the cooked chicken wings until thoroughly coated. Serve immediately with Gorgonzola dressing and celery sticks.

Steak Tartare Anastasia

3 egg yolks

2 tablespoons paprika

1 heaping tablespoon white onion, finely diced

1 heaping tablespoon capers, finely chopped (reserve 2 tablespoons of the brine)

1 heaping tablespoon dill relish, finely chopped

3 anchovies

1 heaping tablespoon scallions, finely chopped

1 tablespoon chopped parsley

2 tablespoons Worcestershire sauce

¼ teaspoon cayenne pepper

1 tablespoon ketchup (see Index)

1 clove garlic, minced

1 teaspoon red wine vinegar

⅛ teaspoon dry mustard

Salt to taste

¼ teaspoon black pepper

¼ teaspoon lemon juice

1 lb. prime sirloin, trimmed of fat and coarsely ground

Kale for garnish

Serves four

*I*n a mixing bowl, whisk the egg yolks with 1 tablespoon of the paprika. Stir in the onion, capers, caper brine, and dill relish. Chop the anchovies into a fine dice then, using the side of a chef's knife, smash the anchovies into a paste. Add the anchovy paste, along with the remaining ingredients (except the meat and garnish) to the caper mixture and whisk until well incorporated.

Place the ground sirloin in a glass or stainless steel bowl. Add half of the anchovy-caper mixture to the meat and mix thoroughly. Blend in the remaining tablespoon of paprika, then gradually stir in the rest of the anchovy-caper mixture. Mold the steak tartare on a platter lined with kale leaves; refrigerate for 1 to 2 hours. Serve immediately with pumpernickel, rye or acceptable cracker (see Brand Name Guide).

Chicken Liver Pâté

2 cups (4 sticks) butter or margarine

2 lbs. chicken livers

2 medium onions, quartered

1 teaspoon allspice

1 teaspoon paprika

¼ teaspoon salt

¼ teaspoon black pepper

1¼ cups sliced pimento-stuffed olives

Serves twenty

*M*elt ½ cup (1 stick) of the butter or margarine in a large saucepan. Add the chicken livers, onions, allspice, paprika, salt, and pepper. Cover the pan and simmer the mixture over low heat about 8 minutes.

Transfer the liver mixture to a food processor and purée with the remaining 3 sticks of butter or margarine. Place the purée in a bowl and chill in the refrigerator until partially set, about 30 minutes.

Mold the mixture into a loaf shape and stud the surface with the sliced olives. Return the pâté to the refrigerator and chill until firm, then slice and serve with an acceptable cracker (see Brand Name Guide).

Boiled Shrimp with Choice of Sauces

1 gallon water
3 large lemons, halved
2 large bay leaves
1½ teaspoons cayenne pepper
1½ teaspoons black pepper
5 tablespoons salt
2 garlic cloves
1   3 oz. bag of crab boil (optional)
3 lbs. medium raw shrimp

Serves six

Bring 1 gallon of water to a boil in a stock pot, then add the lemons, bay leaves, cayenne, black pepper, salt, garlic, and crab boil. When the water returns to a boil, add the shrimp. Boil the shrimp for 5 to 8 minutes, then drain in a colander; when cool enough to handle, peel and devein. Serve with any of these suggested sauces: Creole Mayonnaise, Creole Relish Remoulade, Horseradish Mustard Sauce, or New Orleans Remoulade, (see Index).

Spiced Shrimp Manchac

2½ lbs. peeled, boiled shrimp (see Index)

Dressing:

2½ tablespoons celery seeds
3 tablespoons capers
1½ tablespoons salt
¾ cup white vinegar
1½ cups olive oil
¼ teaspoon Tabasco®
2 cups sliced red onions

Serves four

Add shrimp to combined dressing ingredients and refrigerate at least one day.

Shrimp Royale

1 lb. boiled peeled shrimp (see Index)

1   8 oz. package cream cheese, room temperature

½ cup green onions, finely chopped

½ cup chopped celery

3 tablespoons lemon juice

2 tablespoons chopped fresh parsley

¾ cup mayonnaise (see Index)

½ teaspoon salt

3 dashes Tabasco®

Serves six

*D*ice shrimp into small pieces. In a bowl blend cream cheese with green onions, celery, lemon juice, parsley, salt, Tabasco®, and mayonnaise. Gently fold in shrimp. Cover and refrigerate for 6 hours. Serve with an acceptable cracker (see Brand Name Guide).

Shrimp Lafitte

1 lb. boiled peeled shrimp (see Index)

¼ teaspoon salt

⅛ teaspoon black pepper

½ teaspoon thyme

2 tablespoons onions, finely chopped

1 egg, beaten

⅔ cup dry white wine

6 tablespoons butter or margarine, room temperature

¼ teaspoon Tabasco®

Preheat oven to 350° F.

Serves six

*I*n a food processor finely grind the shrimp. Add salt, pepper, thyme, onions, egg, dry white wine, Tabasco®, and butter or margarine and mix well. Place the mixture in a baking dish and bake for 50 minutes. Refrigerate for 3 hours and serve with an acceptable cracker (see Brand Name Guide).

Crawfish Mold

2 lbs. blanched crawfish tails

1½ cups mayonnaise (see Index)

1   8 oz. package cream cheese, room temperature

1   2 oz. bottle capers, drained

½ cup celery, finely chopped

¼ cup fresh parsley, finely chopped

1 teaspoon garlic salt

½ teaspoon Tabasco®

½ teaspoon paprika

2 teaspoons Worchestershire sauce

2 teaspoons gelatin

1 cup water

Serves eight

Blend the mayonnaise and cream cheese. Add crawfish tails, parsley, celery, capers, paprika, garlic salt, Worchestershire sauce, and Tabasco®. Soften gelatin in water and heat until dissolved. When cooled add to the other ingredients and pour into a 6 cup mold. Refrigerate for 2 to 3 hours, then serve.

Sardine Mousse With Curry

8 canned sardines in olive oil, boned, skinned, drained and tails discarded

6 oz. cream cheese, room temperature

2 tablespoons fresh parsley, finely chopped

1 teaspoon curry powder

¼ cup capers, rinsed and well drained

Pinch of freshly grated lemon zest

1 tablespoon anchovy paste

Serves eight

In a food processor combine all ingredients. Process until smooth. Transfer to a bowl and serve at room temperature. May be served with hard boiled eggs, cherry tomatoes, or an acceptable cracker (see Brand Name Guide).

Creole Crabmeat Spread

2 cups fresh lump crabmeat

3 thinly sliced scallions

4 dashes Tabasco®

2 dashes Worcestershire sauce

¼ grated green pepper

¼ cup sour cream

½ cup mayonnaise (see Index)

1½ teaspoons fresh chives, finely chopped

⅛ teaspoon ground allspice

¼ teaspoon ground cumin

½ teaspoon lemon zest, finely grated

salt and pepper to taste

Serves four

Toss the crabmeat and scallions together in a bowl. In another bowl combine the sour cream, mayonnaise, Tabasco®, green pepper, chives, cumin, Worcestershire, lemon zest, and allspice. Gently fold the mixture into the crabmeat. Add salt and pepper. Cover and refrigerate until ready to use. Serve on acceptable crackers (see Brand Name Guide).

"Hot" Crabmeat

1 lb. lump crabmeat

1 cup grated sharp Cheddar cheese

2 green onions, finely chopped

6 tablespoons mayonnaise (see Index)

4 dashes Tabasco®

Triscuit®

Preheat oven to 450° F.

Serves eight

In a bowl, combine the crabmeat, cheese, onions, mayonnaise, and Tabasco® very gently. Place a heaping teaspoon of the crabmeat mixture on Triscuit® and place in the oven for 6 to 8 minutes, watch carefully. Serve immediately.

Smoked Salmon Mousse

7 oz. smoked salmon

1 lb. cream cheese, room temperature

½ cup butter or margarine, melted

juice of ½ lemon

¼ cup green onion, finely chopped

¼ cup heavy cream

4 tablespoons capers

2 teaspoons prepared horseradish

Pinch of white pepper

Serves six

Whip the cream cheese in a mixer until smooth. Slowly add the remaining ingredients. Continue whipping until consistency is very smooth. Refrigerate for 1 hour until firm. Serve with an acceptable cracker (see Brand Name Guide).

Cream Cheese and Salmon Spread

1   8 oz. package cream cheese, room temperature

½ cup diced smoked salmon

1 tablespoon mayonnaise (see Index)

Dash lime juice

Dash garlic powder

1 large shallot, white part only, finely chopped

½ teaspoon Worcestershire sauce

Dash Tabasco®

Serves four

Mix all ingredients together and chill. May be served with pumpernickel or an acceptable cracker (see Brand Name Guide).

Endive with Smoked Salmon

6 oz. chopped smoked salmon
1 tablespoon fresh lemon juice
2 tablespoons extra-virgin olive oil
2 tablespoons fresh chives, finely chopped
salt and pepper to taste
4 large Belgian Endives
1 oz. salmon roe

Serves eight to ten

*I*n a bowl, mix the smoked salmon, lemon juice, olive oil, chives, and salt and pepper. Blend well, cover and refrigerate for 1½ hours. Discard the outer leaves of the endives. Separate from the heart the tender leaves that are large enough for stuffing. Chill these leaves in the refrigerator. When ready to serve, gently fold the salmon roe into the smoked salmon mixture. Spoon the salmon mixture into the endive leaves and serve immediately.

Deviled Eggs

6 large eggs
4 dashes Tabasco®
1 teaspoon prepared yellow mustard
1 teaspoon Dijon mustard
salt to taste
1 tablespoon fresh chives, finely chopped
½ teaspoon black pepper
3 tablespoons mayonnaise (see Index)
Paprika, for garnish

Serves four

*I*n a pan cover the eggs with cold water, place the pan over medium-high heat and bring to a boil. Reduce the heat to a simmer and cook for 15 minutes. Rinse the eggs under cold water and peel. Allow the eggs to cool in a refrigerator for 15 minutes. Halve the eggs lengthwise and carefully scoop out the yolks. In a bowl mash the yolks with a fork and add the mustard, Tabasco®, salt, pepper, and chives. Fold in the mayonnaise. Fill the whites with the egg yolk mixture, and sprinkle the tops with paprika.

Cerviche

1¼ lbs. fish fillets

2 tomatoes, peeled, seeded and diced

1 small chopped pimento

1 chopped green onion

juice of 6 limes

6 tablespoons fresh cilantro, finely chopped

salt and pepper to taste

1 diced avocado

1 teaspoon dried oregano

10 pitted black olives

Serves six

Cut the fillets into ½ inch squares and place in a large bowl. Cover all the pieces with the lime juice and let stand for 4 hours. Drain the fish and pat dry on paper towels. Put the fish into a large bowl and add tomatoes, pimento, green onion, and cilantro. Add salt and pepper. Stir to blend and refrigerate for 4 hours. When serving add the avocado, olives and oregano to the fish mixture. Serve immediately.

Fresh Salsa

3 tomatoes, finely chopped

1 small onion, finely chopped

½ teaspoon salt

1 tablespoon lime juice

1 tablespoon fresh cilantro, finely chopped

1 jalapeno pepper, minced

2 tablespoons parsley, finely chopped

1 garlic clove, minced

1 teaspoon cooking oil

1   8 oz. canned tomato sauce

5 dashes of Tabasco®

Serves ten to twelve

Combine all ingredients in a bowl and mix well. Cover and chill for at least 3 hours. Serve at room temperature.

Mexican Layer Dip

1	16 oz. can refried beans

Chili powder

1   8 oz. container sour cream

1   8 oz. jar picante sauce; mild, medium, or hot

6 oz. guacamole (see Index)

3 Roma tomatoes, diced

1   8 oz. jar sliced jalapeno peppers (optional)

8 oz. finely grated sharp Cheddar cheese

1   8 oz. jar black olives, sliced

Serves ten

On a large platter or shallow dish lay refried beans, sprinkle chili powder, add sour cream and the remainder of ingredients in the order given. Serve with acceptable crackers (see Brand Name Guide).

Guacamole

4 ripe avocados

2 plum tomatoes, peeled, seeded and chopped

1 tablespoon onions, finely chopped

4 chopped chili peppers

1 oz. fresh lemon juice

1 tablespoon Worcestershire sauce

1 teaspoon chopped garlic

1 teaspoon salt

¼ teaspoon cayenne pepper

4 dashes Tabasco®

Serves six

Mash avocados. Coarsely chop tomatoes and chili peppers in food processor. Add avocados and all other ingredients to processor and blend until smooth. Refrigerate in covered container. Put the avocado seed in container to prevent darkening of guacamole.

Fresh Vegetables with Dill and Garlic Dip

4 chopped hard-boiled eggs

3 tablespoons fresh dill, finely chopped

4 medium garlic cloves, minced

3 tablespoons fresh lemon juice

1 tablespoon dry mustard

1 teaspoon anchovy paste

2 cups mayonnaise (see Index)

Serves six to eight

Combine all ingredients and mix thoroughly. Refrigerate at least 12 hours. Serve with celery, green peppers, asparagus, and broccoli.

Cucumber Dill Dip

1 8 oz. package cream cheese, room temperature

1 cup sour cream

1 cup mayonnaise (see Index)

1 medium cucumber, seeded, peeled, and chopped

1 cup chopped scallions

1 tablespoon chopped fresh parsley

1 tablespoon fresh lemon juice

1 tablespoon fresh dill, finely chopped

¼ teaspoon salt

¼ teaspoon white pepper

Serves ten to twelve

Place all ingredients in a food processor until almost smooth. Pour into a bowl, cover and chill for 3 hours. Serve with celery, green peppers, asparagus, and broccoli or an acceptable cracker (see Brand Name Guide).

Fresh Dill Dip

1 cup sour cream

1 cup mayonnaise (see Index)

2 tablespoons fresh lemon juice

½ cup chopped fresh parsley

¼ cup onion, finely chopped

½ teaspoon salt

½ teaspoon pepper

½ cup chopped fresh dill

Serves six to eight

Combine all ingredients. Mix well and chill, covered, for 3 hours before serving. Serve with celery, green peppers, asparagus, and broccoli or an acceptable cracker (see Brand Name Guide).

Fresh Tomato Dip

12 oz. cream cheese, room temperature

¼ cup mayonnaise (see Index)

1 ripe tomato, quartered

1 celery stalk, cut into chunks

2 garlic cloves

2 tablespoons chopped onion

2 tablespoons fresh lemon juice

¼ teaspoon granulated Sweet 'N Low®

½ teaspoon salt

4 dashes of Tabasco®

Serves four to six

Combine all ingredients in a food processor until smooth. Place the dip in a serving bowl, cover and refrigerate for 2 hours. Serve with celery, green peppers, asparagus, and broccoli or an acceptable cracker (see Brand Name Guide).

Spinach and Artichoke Dip

1   10 oz. can artichoke hearts, drained and chopped
1   10 oz. package frozen chopped spinach, thawed and drained
1 teaspoon salt
½ teaspoon pepper
½ teaspoon celery salt
¼ teaspoon nutmeg
½ teaspoon garlic powder
½ teaspoon Tabasco®
1½ cups cream cheese, room temperature
1 cup mayonnaise plus 2 tablespoons mayonnaise (see Index)
¾ cup parsley, finely chopped
¾ cup onion, finely chopped
1 teaspoon lemon juice
2 cups shredded Mozzarela cheese
Preheat oven to 350° F.

Serves six

Sauté the spinach and 2 tablespoons mayonnaise together over medium-high heat, until spinach turns dark green. In a bowl, mix the spinach with all remaining ingredients, except Mozzarela cheese. Place mixture in a 2½ inch deep baking dish and cover with Mozzarela cheese. Place in oven for 15-20 minutes until cheese is a golden brown or the mixture is bubbling. Serve immediately with acceptable crackers (see Brand Name Guide).

Spinach Curry Dip

1	10 oz. package frozen chopped spinach, thawed and drained

1½ cups mayonnaise (see Index)

⅔ cup sour cream

½ teaspoon curry powder

½ teaspoon onion powder

½ teaspoon black pepper

salt to taste

Serves six

*I*n a medium-sized bowl, combine all ingredients. Mix well. Serve immediately with celery, green peppers, asparagus, and broccoli or an acceptable cracker (see Brand Name Guide).

Artichoke Spread

2 9 oz. packages frozen artichoke hearts, thawed and drained

1 cup mayonnaise (see Index)

2 dashes Tabasco®

1 small garlic clove, minced

1 teaspoon lemon juice

1 cup grated fresh Parmesan cheese

Preheat oven to 350° F.

Serves ten to twelve

*B*lend all ingredients in a food processor until smooth. Coat a 1½-quart baking dish with non-stick cooking spray, then pour in the mixture. Bake the mixture until lightly browned, about 30 minutes. Serve on cocktail rye bread or an acceptable cracker (see Brand Name Guide).

Stilton Cheese Ball

8 oz. extra sharp Cheddar cheese, room temperature

8 oz. cream cheese, room temperature

3 oz. Stilton cheese, room temperature

1 small clove garlic, crushed

1 tablespoon Worcestershire sauce

¾ cup pecans, finely chopped

½ cup fresh parsley, finely chopped

¼ teaspoon Tabasco®

Serves six

Break the cheese into pieces. Add the Worcestershire sauce, Tabasco®, and crushed garlic. Thoroughly mix to a creamy consistency with an electric blender. Stir in ½ cup pecans and refrigerate until firm enough to shape into a ball. Roll the cheese ball with parsley and remaining pecans until covered. Refrigerate for 24 hours before serving. Serve with an acceptable cracker (see Brand Name Guide).

Gorgonzola Spread with Walnuts

1 lb. cream cheese, room temperature

6 oz. Gorgonzola cheese, room temperature

12 walnut halves

1 bunch chives, finely chopped

Salt and pepper to taste

Serves eight

In a food processor grate the walnuts and set aside. Combine the cream cheese and Gorgonzola with a little salt and pepper. Mash until smooth and add walnuts and chives. Mix again until well blended. Serve immediately.

Marinated Mushrooms

1 lb. fresh mushrooms
⅔ cup white vinegar
⅔ cup dry white wine
1 teaspoon salt
1 teaspoon ground black pepper
2 teaspoons dried oregano
1 dried hot chili pepper, crumbled
3 whole cloves garlic
2 tablespoons parsley, finely chopped
1 small red sweet pepper, cut into ½ inch squares
1 lemon, thinly sliced, seeded and slices cut into quarters
1 clove garlic
3 tablespoons extra-virgin olive oil

Serves four to six

*T*rim off the stems of the mushrooms then wash well and pat dry with paper towel. Combine the wine and vinegar in a large stainless-steel sauce pan. Add remaining ingredients except for mushrooms. Bring to a boil and add mushrooms. Sprinkle them with the oil and boil for 6 to 7 minutes. Turn off the heat and let the mushroom mixture cool to room temperature before serving with toothpicks.

Roasted Pecans

1 lb. shelled pecans

¼ cup (½ stick) butter or margarine

1 tablespoon salt

½ teaspoon white pepper

Preheat oven to 350° F.

Serves four

*M*elt butter or margarine in a shallow baking pan in the oven. Add pecans and shake well. Bake 20 minutes, shaking every 5 minutes. Remove the pecans from the oven and add salt and pepper. Allow the pecans to cool to room temperature and serve.

Cajun Pecans

4 cups halved pecans

3 tablespoons unsalted butter or margarine, melted

¼ teaspoon cayenne pepper

½ teaspoon cinnamon

2 teaspoons salt

3 tablespoons Worcestershire sauce

4 dashes Tabasco®

Preheat oven to 300° F.

Serves eight

*M*ix all the seasonings with the melted butter or margarine. Add the pecans and toss well. Spread on a large baking sheet and bake for 10 minutes. Remove to stir and toss the pecans with a spatula so they will bake evenly. Return to the oven for 10 minutes longer until the pecans have dried slightly. Let cool to room temperature and serve.

Creole Spicy Pecans

2 tablespoons unsalted butter or margarine
1 tablespoon olive oil
1 tablespoon Worcestershire sauce
¾ teaspoon Tabasco®
¾ teaspoon ground cumin
½ teaspoon paprika
½ teaspoon garlic powder
2 cups pecan halves
2 teaspoons salt

Preheat oven to 325° F.

Serves four

In a medium-sized sauce pan heat the butter or margarine and oil over a low heat. Add the Worcestershire, Tabasco®, cumin, paprika, and garlic powder. Simmer over low heat for 3 minutes. Add pecans and toss them to coat. Spread the pecans in a single layer on a baking sheet, and bake for 15 minutes. Pour the hot pecans into a bowl and toss with salt. Serve immediately.

Tomato Bruschetta

6 fresh plum tomatoes, diced

2 teaspoons chopped garlic

3 tablespoons chopped onion

2 tablespoons chopped fresh basil

2 teaspoons balsamic vinegar

3 tablespoons extra-virgin olive oil

salt and pepper to taste

8 slices of stone ground whole wheat bread

Serves eight

In a medium bowl, toss the tomatoes, garlic, onions, basil, vinegar, olive oil, salt and pepper until mixed well and let sit at room temperature for at least 20 minutes. Brush bread with additional olive oil, cut into serving size pieces, place bread on a cookie sheet, and toast in oven until edges are lightly browned. Arrange the bread slices on a serving plate and top with the tomato mixture.

Parmesan Crackers

½ lb. grated fresh Parmesan cheese

Serves four

Place a non-stick skillet over medium heat. Place tablespoon size piles of cheese in the pan. Flatten each pile into a 2½ inch diameter. Sauté the wafers on each side for about 3 minutes, or until golden brown or crisp. Transfer to a plate and allow to cool for a few minutes.

CHAPTER SIX

Soups and Stocks

Gazpacho

2 cups cold beef broth or stock (see Index)

2 medium cucumbers, peeled, seeded, and finely chopped

1 bunch scallions, finely chopped

1 medium green pepper, finely chopped

2 tomatoes, finely chopped

2 garlic cloves, minced

1 cup tomato sauce

½ cup water

1 tablespoon red wine vinegar

½ teaspoon Tabasco®

2 teaspoons Worcestershire sauce

1 teaspoon fresh parsley, finely chopped

salt and black pepper to taste

Serves six

Pour the beef broth or stock into a large bowl, then add the cucumbers, scallions, green pepper, tomatoes, garlic, tomato sauce, water, red wine vinegar, and Tabasco®. Stir until the ingredients are well combined and season with salt and pepper. Chill in the refrigerator for at least 4 hours, then add the Worcestershire and parsley. Serve the gazpacho in chilled bowls.

Note: *For a variation of this popular soup, lump crabmeat or blanched crawfish tails may be added.*

Chilled Salmon Bisque

3 tablespoons butter or margarine
1 small onion, sliced
½ chopped green pepper
1 garlic clove, minced
1½ cups milk
1 tablespoon fresh dill, finely chopped
4 salmon fillets, about 6 oz. each
¾ cup heavy cream
2 tablespoons dry white wine
½ teaspoon cayenne pepper
salt and white pepper to taste
Dill sprigs for garnish

Serves four to six

*M*elt 2 tablespoons of the butter or margarine in a medium skillet and sauté the onion, green pepper, and garlic until tender. Remove the vegetables from the heat and set aside.

In a large saucepan, heat the milk and chopped dill to just under a boil. Season the salmon fillets on both sides with salt and pepper, then poach them in the simmering milk until flaky, about 10 minutes. Transfer the salmon along with the milk to the bowl of a food processor. Purée the salmon, then add the cream and the remaining tablespoon of butter or margarine. When the mixture is smooth, add the sautéed vegetables and purée with the salmon. Pour the soup into a stainless steel bowl, then stir in the wine and cayenne. Season with salt and white pepper, cover the bowl, and refrigerate for 1 to 2 hours until chilled.

Spoon the salmon bisque into chilled bowls and garnish with fresh dill.

Beef and Sweet Potato Pepperpot Soup

1 lb. boneless beef shank, diced
4 slices bacon, diced
2 green peppers, finely chopped
2 garlic cloves, minced
1 onion, finely chopped
2 tablespoons cooking oil
2 tablespoons stone ground whole wheat flour
6 cups hot beef broth or stock (see Index)
2 tablespoons tomato paste
½ teaspoon dried thyme
1 teaspoon Tabasco®
salt and freshly ground black pepper to taste
1 lb. sweet potatoes, peeled and diced
Chopped fresh thyme for garnish

Serves four

Heat the oil in a large pan and add onion, garlic, and green pepper. Cook for 10 minutes until softened. Add the bacon and beef, increase the heat, and cook, stirring constantly, until the beef is all browned. Pour in the flour then gradually pour in 5 cups broth or stock and bring to a boil. Lower the heat to a simmer, add the tomato paste and thyme with Tabasco® and salt and pepper. Cover, stirring occasionally for 1 hour. Add the sweet potatoes and the remaining broth or stock and bring back to a boil. Cook until the beef and sweet potatoes are tender about 30 minutes. Taste to see if more pepper sauce is necessary and sprinkle with fresh thyme for garnish.

Beef Vegetable Soup

6 lbs. beef brisket, chuck or rump roast
2 tablespoons salt
2 tablespoons black pepper
4 quarts water
2 lbs. fresh green beans, cut into 1 inch pieces
2 bunches celery, cut into 1 inch pieces
2 large onions, cut into 6 pieces each
2 green peppers, coarsely chopped
2 teaspoons fresh garlic, minced
2 29 oz. cans tomato sauce
2 tablespoons garlic powder
3 tablespoons Worcestershire sauce
1 teaspoon granulated Sweet 'N Low®
1 bag frozen peas
1 bag frozen lima beans
½ head cabbage, broken into 2 inch pieces
salt and pepper to taste

Serves ten to twelve

In a large pot of boiling water add meat, salt, and pepper. Boil for 1 hour. Skim the residue from the top of water as it cooks. Add green beans, celery, onion, green pepper, garlic, garlic powder, tomato sauce, Worcestershire sauce, and Sweet 'N Low®. Cook at a slow boil for 1 hour. Then add peas, lima beans, and cabbage. Cook for 30 minutes. Add salt and pepper. Serve meat in soup or on the side with prepared horseradish.

Squash and Zucchini Soup

2 tablespoons olive oil

1 large chopped onion

3 cups water

2 chopped yellow squash

2 chopped large ripe tomatoes

1 chopped sweet red pepper

1 chopped sweet yellow pepper

1 chopped zucchini

3 large cloves garlic, minced

1½ teaspoons salt

½ teaspoon fennel seeds

¼ teaspoon ground black pepper

½ cup grated Parmesan cheese

Serves six

In a large sauce pan, heat the oil over medium heat. Add the onion; sauté until softened for 5 minutes. Add the water, yellow squash, tomatoes, red and yellow peppers, zucchini, garlic, salt, fennel seeds, and black pepper. Bring to a boil then reduce heat and simmer until vegetables are tender about 15 minutes. In a food processor, purée 2½ cups of the soup. Then return purée to the pan with the remaining soup. Heat through, sprinkle with Parmesan cheese and serve immediately.

Zucchini Soup with Brie and Sage

2 tablespoons cooking oil
1 chopped onion
2 chopped garlic cloves
2 lbs. chopped zucchini
2½ cups chicken broth or stock (see Index)
1 cup milk
1 teaspoon dried sage
salt and pepper to taste
¼ lb. soft brie, rind removed and diced
⅔ cup heavy cream
Fresh sage leaves for garnish

Serves six

In a large pan, heat the oil and add the onion, garlic, and zucchini. Over a moderate heat cook the vegetables, stirring frequently, until the water runs from the zucchini, about ten minutes. Add the chicken broth or stock and milk and bring to a boil. Add the sage and salt and pepper. Cover and simmer for 20 minutes. Add the brie and stir until melted. In a food processor blend the soup until smooth. Strain the soup into a pan. Add the cream and reheat the soup gently stirring all the time. Season to taste and garnish with the fresh sage leaves.

Tomato and Basil Soup

4 tablespoons cooking oil

1 large chopped onion

1 teaspoon dried thyme

2 lbs. chopped ripe tomatoes

¼ cup stone ground whole wheat flour

¾ teaspoon granulated Sweet 'N Low®

2 cups chicken broth or stock (see Index)

½ cup tomato paste

salt and pepper to taste

½ cup chopped fresh basil

Serves six

In a sauce pan heat the oil. Add the onion and thyme; sauté until the onion is soft but not brown. Add the tomatoes and stir. Blend in the flour and stir for 3 minutes until the flour is fully blended into the mixture. Stir in the Sweet 'N Low®, chicken broth or stock and tomato paste. Simmer, partially covered, for 30 minutes, stirring occasionally to prevent sticking. Purée the soup mixture in a food processor and return to the pot. Season with salt and pepper. Add the basil and serve immediately.

Cream of Tomato Soup

2 tablespoons butter or margarine

1 tablespoon cooking oil

1 onion, finely chopped

1 tablespoon stone ground whole wheat flour

2 tablespoons tomato paste

2 lbs. ripe tomatoes, quartered

3 cups chicken broth or stock (see Index)

Pinch of Sweet 'N Low®

salt and pepper to taste

½ cup heavy cream

½ cup dry white wine

Serves six

In a large pan, melt the butter or margarine, add the onion, and cook until soft for 5 minutes. Add the flour and the tomato paste then stir for 2 minutes to cook the flour. Add the tomatoes and wine and bring to a boil. Add the chicken broth or stock, Sweet 'N Low®, and salt and pepper. Cover and simmer, stirring occasionally, for about 20 minutes. In a food processor, purée the soup, then strain the mixture into a pan. Stir in half of the cream and heat through. Season to taste, garnish with the remaining cream and serve immediately.

Cream of Artichoke Soup

3 cups scraped artichoke leaves and chopped hearts, using approximately
4 large steamed artichokes

1½ cups chopped onions

4 cups chicken broth or stock (see Index)

1 tablespoon butter or margarine

1 teaspoon salt

¼ teaspoon thyme

¼ teaspoon black pepper

2 tablespoons fresh lemon juice

¼ teaspoon Tabasco®

1 cup light cream

1 cup heavy cream

Serves six

Sauté chopped onions in butter or margarine 5 minutes. Add artichoke scrapings and chopped hearts, chicken broth or stock, salt, thyme, and pepper. Cover and simmer 15 minutes. Cool the mixture and purée in a food processor. Add the lemon juice and season with Tabasco® to taste. Mix in the light and heavy creams. Refrigerate overnight and reheat to serve.

Cream of Broccoli Soup

2   10 oz. packages frozen chopped broccoli, thawed and drained

2 cups chicken broth or stock (see Index)

½ cup chopped onion

½ cup (1 stick) butter or margarine

¾ teaspoon basil

1 teaspoon salt

¼ teaspoon black pepper

1 tablespoon lemon juice

1 cup light cream

Serves six

Sauté onion in butter or margarine 5 minutes. Add broccoli, chicken broth or stock, basil, salt and pepper. Cover and simmer for 15 minutes. In a food processor, purée until smooth. Reheat mixture and add lemon juice and cream. Serve immediately.

Broccoli and Cheese Soup

2   10 oz. packages frozen chopped broccoli

10 large fresh mushrooms, sliced

3½ cups chicken broth or stock (see Index)

⅔ cup celery, finely chopped

⅓ cup chopped green onions

1 tablespoon fresh parsley, finely chopped

2 teaspoons garlic salt

2 tablespoons butter or margarine

1½ cups grated sharp Cheddar cheese

½ cup sour cream

½ teaspoon Tabasco®

¾ teaspoon Worcestershire sauce

Serves six

Cook broccoli, drain and puree with 1½ cups chicken broth or stock. In a sauce pan, simmer broccoli with remaining chicken broth or stock. In a skillet, sauté vegetables in butter or margarine until tender. Season with garlic salt, add to broccoli, cover and cook for 30 minutes. Fold in cheese and sour cream. Season to taste with Tabasco® and Worcestershire sauce. Serve immediately.

Cauliflower and Cheddar Soup

3 cups milk

3 cups hot chicken broth or stock (see Index)

2 tablespoons stone ground whole wheat flour

2 tablespoons butter or margarine

1½ lbs. cauliflower, broken into florets

1 onion, finely chopped

2 cups grated sharp Cheddar cheese

2 teaspoons Dijon mustard

salt and pepper to taste

¼ teaspoon cayenne pepper for garnish

Serves four

In a large pan melt butter or margarine and add the onion. Cook for 5 minutes until softened. Add the cauliflower, sprinkle in the flour. Cook for 2 minutes, stirring constantly. Stir in the chicken broth or stock and 2 cups of milk and bring to a boil. Add salt and pepper, cover, and simmer until the cauliflower is tender about 20 minutes. Place the mixture in a food processor until smooth. Strain the mixture into another pan and add the remaining milk, ¾ of the cheese, mustard, and reheat on low heat. Season to taste. Serve hot, sprinkle with remaining cheese and cayenne pepper.

Cream of Mushroom Soup

1 lb. fresh white mushrooms

1 oz. dried Morel mushrooms

3 tablespoons virgin olive oil

2 chopped shallots

1 clove garlic, minced

1 quart hot beef broth or stock (see Index)

½ teaspoon dried thyme

salt and pepper to taste

½ cup heavy cream

Chopped fresh parsley for garnish

Serves four

Soak dried Morel mushrooms in about 1 cup warm water for about 20 minutes, then drain and reserve liquid to add extra flavor to soup. Chop the fresh white mushrooms and the Morel mushrooms. Heat the oil in a large pan and add the shallots and garlic. Cook until softened about 5 minutes. Add both types of mushrooms and stir over moderate heat for about 5 minutes. Add the beef broth or stock and Morel soaking liquid and bring to a boil, stirring. Add the thyme and salt and pepper. Cover and simmer for 30 minutes. In a food processor, blend about ¾ of the mixture until smooth. Pour back into pan, add cream and season to taste. Reheat, serve immediately, and garnish with parsley.

Cream of Onion Soup

½ cup (1 stick) butter or margarine

1 large onion, thinly sliced

½ cup stone ground whole wheat flour

2 quarts beef broth or stock (see Index)

2 tablespoons Worcestershire sauce

1 teaspoon white pepper

salt to taste

2 teaspoons egg shade or yellow food coloring (optional)

¼ cup freshly grated Parmesan cheese

Serves eight

Melt the butter or margarine in a large pot, and sauté the onion until tender, about 5 minutes. Blend in the flour and cook the mixture over medium heat another 5 minutes, stirring frequently. Add the beef broth or stock, Worcestershire sauce, and pepper. Adjust the seasoning with salt. If desired, add the food coloring. Reduce the heat and simmer until thickened, about 15 minutes. Sprinkle with Parmesan, then serve.

Chicken Noodle Soup

7 - 8 lb. hen

2 bunches parsley

2 bunches celery

2 large onions

5 quarts water

salt and pepper to taste

whole grain noodles

Serves ten to twelve

In a large pot, place all ingredients. Bring to a boil and skim residue. Lower fire to a slow boil and cook for 2 hours. Take out hen; strain vegetables. Chop parsley and cut celery into 1 inch pieces. Add parsley and celery back to soup. Add desired amount of noodles.

Note: Hen may be cut into bite-sized pieces and also added to soup or may be used for chicken salad (see Index).

French Onion Soup

2 tablespoons butter or margarine

1 tablespoon virgin olive oil

2 lbs. onions, thinly sliced

⅛ teaspoon granulated Sweet 'N Low®

salt and pepper to taste

½ cup dry red wine

2 tablespoons stone ground whole wheat flour

6 cups hot beef broth or stock (see Index)

4 slices stone ground whole wheat bread, toasted

¼ lb. Gruyere cheese, grated

Serves four

*M*elt the butter or margarine with the oil in a large heavy pan and add the onions, Sweet 'N Low®, and salt and pepper. Cover with wax paper and cook over very gentle heat, stirring frequently, for about 20 minutes until golden brown. Add the red wine and stir over moderate heat for 5 minutes or until the onions are glazed. Add the flour and stir for 2 minutes, then stir in the beef broth or stock. Bring to a boil, cover, and simmer for 30 minutes. Season to taste. Divide the soup among 4 heatproof bowls, and top with a slice of toast. Sprinkle with the cheese and place under a hot broiler until golden brown for 3 minutes. Serve immediately.

Spinach Soup

3 tablespoons butter or margarine

½ onion, sliced

1 large clove garlic, minced

1 teaspoon stone ground whole wheat flour

4 cups chicken broth or stock (see Index)

1 lb. spinach, well rinsed

salt and pepper to taste

1 cup milk

Serves four

Melt the butter or margarine in a large skillet over medium heat. Add the onion and sauté 5 minutes until golden. Add the garlic, stir and continue to cook for 5 minutes. Stir in the flour, whisk in the warm chicken broth or stock, and simmer for 40 minutes. In a separate pan, steam the spinach for 2 minutes until just wilted. Drain, squeeze out the water, and purée in a food processor. Set aside. Strain the soup. Return the broth to a large sauce pan over medium heat. Stir in the spinach purée and season with salt and pepper. Stir in the milk and warm through. Serve immediately.

Split Pea Soup

1 lb. dried green split peas

¾ lb. ham steak, cubed

2 smoked ham hocks

3 tablespoons cooking oil

2 onions, finely chopped

4 ribs celery, finely chopped

1 green pepper, finely chopped

1 tablespoon garlic, minced

1 bay leaf

2 quarts water

2 cups milk

Serves eight

Rinse peas. Sauté onions, celery, and green pepper in oil. Add ham cubes and sauté a little longer. Add all other ingredients except the milk. Cover the pot and let sit over night in the refrigerator. Put the pot on the stove over high heat. When the soup comes to a boil, lower the heat to simmer and cook for 1-1½ hours. Remove ham hocks and cut meat off of the bones and return to the pot. Discard the skin and bones. Cook an additional 1-1½ hours until tender. When peas have dissolved, add milk to the soup.

Split Pea and Barley Soup

1½ cups dried split peas

½ chopped medium-size onion

1 small chopped celery stalk

1 garlic clove

1½ quarts chicken broth or stock (see Index)

½ cup barley

Freshly ground white pepper and salt to taste

Serves six

Put the peas, onion, celery, garlic, and chicken broth or stock in a 3 quart pot and bring to a boil. Lower the heat and simmer, uncovered, for 1 hour. Pureé the soup in a food processor and return to pot. Add the barley, bring to a boil, lower the heat, and simmer until the barley is tender for 40 minutes. Add the white pepper and salt. Serve immediately.

Black Bean Soup

1 lb. dried black beans
4 tablespoons unsalted butter or margarine
2 ribs celery, finely chopped
10 cups chicken broth or stock (see Index)
2 medium onions, finely chopped
1 clove garlic, minced
1½ tablespoons stone ground whole wheat flour
1 bay leaf
Freshly ground black pepper and salt to taste
½ cup dry red wine

Serves twelve

Garnishes:

lemon slices
sour cream
chopped onion
chopped tomato
cooked brown rice (see Index)

Boil the beans in 6 to 8 cups of hot water for 2 minutes, then set aside for 1 hour. Drain the beans and place them in a large pot. Add the chicken broth or stock and bring to a boil. Reduce the heat to low, and simmer for 1½ hours, adding more water if necessary. In another pot, melt the butter or margarine over medium heat. Add the celery, onions, and garlic and sauté until softened, but not brown for about 10 minutes. Stir in the flour stirring constantly for 1 minute. Add the vegetable mixture to the beans with the bay leaf and pepper to taste. Cover and simmer over a low heat for 3 hours stirring occasionally. Add water if beans are not completely covered with liquid. Discard the bay leaf, add salt, and purée the soup in a food processor until smooth. Return the soup to the pot and add the wine. Reheat the soup, season to taste, and use desired garnish.

Southwestern Bean Soup

14 oz. can red kidney beans	
14 oz. can pinto beans	
14 oz. can black beans	
2 red bell peppers	
2 tablespoons virgin olive oil	
1 onion, finely chopped	
2 garlic cloves, minced	
2 celery stalks, diced	
1 teaspoon ground cumin	
1 teaspoon hot chili powder	
4 cups hot chicken broth or stock (see Index)	
salt and pepper	
¼ cup chopped fresh cilantro	
¼ cup sour cream	

Serves six

Broil the peppers until their skins are charred black on all sides, then place in a plastic bag. Seal the bag and let the peppers cool, then peel off the skins. Chop the peppers discarding the cores and the seeds. Rinse the beans. In a large pan, heat the oil and add the onion, garlic, and celery. Cook until the onion softens. Add the cumin and chili powder to taste and stir for 2 minutes. Add the chicken broth or stock and bring to a boil. Add the beans and salt and pepper to taste, cover, and simmer for 10 minutes. Add the chopped peppers, cilantro, and season to taste. Serve immediately garnishing with sour cream.

Lentil and Ham Soup

1 lb. lentils
6 cups beef broth or stock (see Index)
2 cups water
1 lb. ham, cut into bite-size pieces
1 cup chopped celery
1 cup chopped green onions
⅔ cup chopped onion
2 tablespoons chopped fresh parsley
1 clove garlic, minced
1 bay leaf
½ teaspoon thyme
¼ cup dry white wine
salt and pepper to taste
Tabasco®

Serves eight

In a large pot, place lentils, beef broth or stock, and water. Cover and simmer for 1 hour. In a skillet sauté ham and add to the lentils. In the ham drippings sauté vegetables until tender then add to the lentils. Add bay leaf and thyme. Cover and simmer for 1 hour. Stir occasionally and add water if necessary for desired consistency. Add wine, salt, pepper, and Tabasco® to taste. Remove bay leaf and serve immediately.

Red Bean Soup

1 cup dried red kidney beans
1 cup (2 sticks) butter or margarine
1 cup chopped onion
1 cup chopped celery
1 tablespoon garlic, minced
½ cup stone ground whole wheat flour
6 cups beef broth or stock (see Index)
½ teaspoon black pepper
salt to taste

Serves six

Rinse the kidney beans, then place them in a medium bowl and add water to cover. Soak the beans overnight; drain before preparing the soup.

Melt the butter or margarine in a large saucepan or Dutch oven and sauté the onion, celery, and garlic for 10 minutes. Blend in the flour and cook for 1 to 2 minutes, stirring constantly. Add the beef broth or stock and beans, then cook at a low boil for 1½ to 2 hours until the beans are very tender. Strain the soup in a fine sieve, mashing the beans through the strainer. Reheat the soup, adding the pepper. Season with salt and serve.

Chicken Andouille Gumbo

1 whole chicken, about 2½ to 3 lbs.

⅓ cup cooking oil

¾ cup stone ground whole wheat flour

1 cup diced green pepper

1 cup diced onion

1 cup diced celery

2 cups thinly sliced andouille or other spicy smoked sausage

4 ripe tomatoes, seeded and chopped

2 quarts chicken broth or stock (see Index)

1 teaspoon thyme leaves

4 bay leaves

1 teaspoon black pepper

1 teaspoon garlic, minced

1 tablespoon filé powder

¼ teaspoon cayenne pepper

salt to taste

3 cups sliced okra

1 cup cooked brown rice (see Index)

Preheat oven to 350° F.

Serves eight to ten

Rinse the chicken under cold water and cut it into 10 pieces; halve the breasts, for a total of 12 pieces. Place the chicken pieces, skin side down, in a large ovenproof skillet. Roast the chicken in the hot oven for 20 to 30 minutes until brown.

While the chicken is browning, combine the oil and flour in a 3-quart pot. Cook over medium heat, stirring constantly, until the mixture turns chestnut brown; watch the mixture carefully and do not allow it to burn. Add the bell pepper, onion, and celery, and cook the vegetables over medium-high heat until tender. Stir in the andouille and tomatoes; when well combined, pour in the chicken broth or stock. Add the thyme, bay leaves, black pepper, and garlic, then using a whisk, stir the filé into the gumbo. Bring the mixture to a boil, then add the cayenne. Adjust the seasoning with salt to taste.

Remove the chicken from the oven and pour off the fat. Reduce the heat under the gumbo to low, then add the chicken and okra. Simmer for 20 to 30 minutes until the okra is tender, then spoon the gumbo into bowls containing about a tablespoon of hot cooked brown rice.

Maude's Seafood Gumbo

1¼ cups cooking oil
1 large white onion, finely chopped
2 stalks celery, finely chopped
5 to 6 cloves garlic, minced
½ green pepper, finely chopped
4 sprigs fresh parsley, finely chopped
2 8 oz. cans tomato sauce
1 8 oz. can whole tomatoes, mashed
2 cups water
4 lbs. fresh raw shrimp, peeled and deveined
4 hard shell crabs, boiled and broken in half
1½ lbs. fresh chopped okra, (or 2 packages frozen chopped okra)
2 bay leaves
1½ teaspoons salt
1 teaspoon black pepper
½ lb. lump crabmeat
Cooked brown rice (see Index)

Serves six to eight

Pour the oil into a heavy 6 quart aluminum pot. Add all the chopped vegetables except the okra and simmer over medium heat until the vegetables begin to soften. Add the tomato sauce and the mashed whole tomatoes and simmer for a few minutes more. Then add the water, shrimp, crabs, okra, bay leaves, salt, and pepper. Stir gently to mix. Cover and cook over low heat until the shrimp and okra are tender. Turn off the heat and leave the gumbo in the pot covered. When you are ready to serve, turn the heat on low and add the lump crabmeat. Heat just until the gumbo and crabmeat are warmed through. Serve over cooked brown rice.

Mirliton with Shrimp Soup

3 or 4 mirlitons

2 lbs. raw shrimp

1 bunch green onions, finely chopped

3 stalks celery, finely chopped

4 cups shrimp broth

½ cup (1 stick) butter or margarine

2 cloves garlic, minced

1 bay leaf

½ pint half and half

4 tablespoons chopped parsley

Serves six to eight

*B*oil shrimp in water seasoned with onion, bay leaf, celery, lemon, salt, and pepper. Remove shrimp from water, cool and peel. Strain the broth and reserve for the soup.

Cut mirlitons in half and boil in water until tender. Let cool and scrape out the pulp, first removing the seed. In a heavy pot, sauté green onions, celery, and garlic in 1 stick of melted butter or margarine. When soft, add mirlitons and bay leaf, mashing mirlitons as it cooks. Pour in the 4 cups of strained shrimp broth. Cover and cook on low for 45 minutes. Remove bay leaf and place ½ of mixture into blender and pureé. Return pureé to pot, add shrimp and half and half. Sprinkle with parsley and serve. Because the broth is seasoned, do not add extra salt and pepper until soup is tasted.

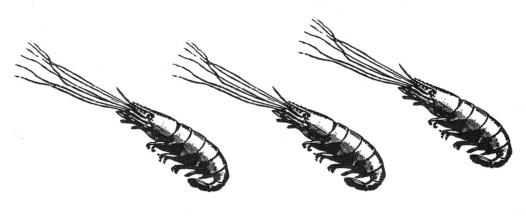

Turtle Soup

3 lbs. turtle meat
2 bay leaves
2 tablespoons plus 1 teaspoon salt
4 quarts cold water
½ cup (1 stick) butter or margarine
½ cup onion, finely chopped
½ cup celery, finely chopped
½ cup green pepper, finely chopped
½ teaspoon garlic, minced
1 cup fresh parsley, finely chopped
4 oz. (½ cup) tomato paste
¼ cup Worcestershire sauce
1 teaspoon black pepper
1 teaspoon paprika
½ cup stone ground whole wheat flour
3 large hard-boiled eggs, finely chopped
1 cup dry sherry
1 lemon, thinly sliced

Serves ten to twelve

In a stockpot, combine the turtle meat, bay leaves, and 2 tablespoons of the salt. Add 4 quarts of cold water and bring the mixture to a boil over high heat. Reduce the heat to medium and cook until the turtle meat is tender, about 2 hours; add additional water, if necessary, to maintain about 3 quarts of liquid during cooking. Strain the turtle meat, reserving the stock. Dice the turtle meat and set aside. In a large pot, melt the butter or margarine and add the onion, celery, green pepper, garlic, parsley, tomato paste, Worcestershire, pepper, paprika, and remaining teaspoon of salt. Cook the mixture over low heat until the vegetables are very tender, then stir in the flour. Increase the heat to medium and cook until the flour absorbs all of the butter or margarine. Pour the turtle stock into the pot and bring the stock to a boil. Add the turtle meat and simmer for 30 to 40 minutes. Just before serving, remove the bay leaves and add the chopped eggs, dry sherry, and lemon.

Oyster Soup

2 cups (about 48) shucked oysters
3 quarts cold water
¾ cup (1½ sticks) butter or margarine
1 cup celery, finely chopped
1½ tablespoons garlic, minced
1 cup scallions, finely chopped
4 bay leaves
1 tablespoon thyme leaves
¾ cup stone ground whole wheat flour
1½ tablespoons Worcestershire sauce
1 teaspoon salt
1 teaspoon white pepper
½ cup fresh parsley, finely chopped

Serves ten to twelve

*I*n a large saucepan, combine the oysters and 3 quarts cold water. Bring the water to a boil, then reduce the heat and simmer about 5 minutes; skim any residue from the surface. Strain the oysters, reserving the stock. Dice the oysters and set aside. Melt the butter or margarine in a large pot and sauté the celery and garlic over medium heat about 5 minutes until tender. Add the scallions, bay leaves, and thyme, then stir in the flour. Cook the mixture for 5 minutes over low heat, stirring constantly. Using a whisk, blend in the oyster stock, then add the Worcestershire, salt, and pepper. Cook the soup over medium heat about 20 minutes until thickened, then add the parsley and oysters. Simmer until the oysters are warmed through, about 5 minutes. Remove the bay leaves before serving.

Oyster Stew

4 tablespoons (½ stick) butter or margarine	
36 shucked oysters	
1 tablespoon Worcestershire sauce	
3 cups heavy cream	
1 cup milk	
¼ teaspoon white pepper	
¼ teaspoon Tabasco®	
salt to taste	

Serves six

Melt 2 tablespoons of the butter or margarine in a large saucepan, then sauté the oysters a couple of minutes until the edges begin to curl. Add the Worcestershire, cream, and milk. Reduce the heat and simmer for 15 to 20 minutes until the soup is hot; do not allow the liquid to reach a boil. Just before serving, add the white pepper, salt, Tabasco®, and remaining 2 tablespoons of butter or margarine.

Italian Clam and Pasta Soup

2 tablespoons virgin olive oil

1 large onion, finely chopped

2 garlic cloves, minced

14 oz. can crushed tomatoes with Italian herbs

3½ cups hot fish stock (see Index)

1 tablespoon tomato paste

⅛ teaspoon granulated Sweet 'N Low®

salt and pepper to taste

3 oz. whole grain pasta

2   5 oz. jars clams in natural juice

¼ cup shredded fresh basil

Serves four

Heat the oil in a large pan, add the onion, and cook until softened. Add the garlic, tomatoes, 3 cups fish stock, tomato paste, Sweet 'N Low®, and salt and pepper. Bring to a boil, cover, and simmer for 15 minutes. Add the pasta and bring back to a boil. Simmer, uncovered, for about 10 minutes until the pasta is tender. Stir to prevent the pasta from sticking. Add the clams and their juice and heat for a few minutes. Add more stock if too thick. Season to taste. Serve hot and sprinkle with fresh basil to garnish.

Chicken Stock

3 lbs. chicken bones and parts

1 small onion, diced

1 celery rib, diced

1 garlic clove

3 quarts cold water

Yields 1½ quarts

Combine all the ingredients in a stockpot and cover with 3 quarts cold water. Bring the stock to a boil over high heat, skimming away the residue that rises to the surface. Reduce the heat and cook at a low rolling boil until reduced by half, about 2 hours. Strain the stock and use immediately or cover and refrigerate. Chicken stock can be frozen in smaller quantities for use in a variety of recipes.

Beef Stock

1 lb. beef bones

1 small white onion, diced

1 celery rib, diced

1 garlic clove

½ bunch scallions, diced

4 quarts cold water

Preheat oven to 450° F.

Yields 2 quarts

Arrange the beef bones in a single layer in a roasting pan. Roast in a hot oven until brown, about 15 minutes, stirring the bones occasionally.

Transfer the bones to a stockpot and add the remaining ingredients; cover with 4 quarts cold water. Bring the stock to a boil over high heat, skimming away the residue from the surface. Lower the heat and cook at a low rolling boil until reduced by half, about 2 hours. Strain and use immediately or freeze in smaller portions for use in a variety of recipes.

Vegetable Stock

¾ lb. mixed vegetables and trimmings, chopped turnips, celery, leeks,
scallions, parsley

2½ quarts water

1 chopped onion

2 bay leaves, torn

salt and pepper to taste

Yields 2 quarts

*P*ut all ingredients in a large pot. Add water and bring to a boil.
Simmer, uncovered, for 1 hour, then drain.

Fish Stock

1½ quarts cold water

1 lb. fish bones and trimmings

½ of a lemon

½ cup dry white wine

Yields 3 cups

*B*ring 1½ quarts of cold water to a boil in a large saucepan, along with
the lemon and white wine. When the water reaches a rolling boil, add
the fish bones and trimmings. Lower the heat and simmer until reduced by
half, about 2 hours. Drain and refrigerate, covered, for several days or
freeze for future use.

CHAPTER SEVEN

Sauces and Pasta Sauces

Hollandaise Sauce

1 lb. butter or margarine
4 egg yolks
1½ teaspoons red wine vinegar
Pinch of cayenne pepper
1 teaspoon salt
1½ teaspoons water

Yields 2 cups

*M*elt the butter or margarine in a medium saucepan; skim and discard the milk solids from the top of the butter or margarine. Hold the clarified butter or margarine over very low heat while preparing the egg yolks.

Place the egg yolks, vinegar, cayenne, and salt in a large stainless steel bowl and whisk briefly. Fill a saucepan or Dutch oven large enough to accommodate the bowl with about 1 inch of water. Heat the water to just below the boiling point. Set the bowl in the pan over the water; do not let the water touch the bottom of the bowl. Whisk the egg yolk mixture until slightly thickened, then drizzle the clarified butter or margarine into the yolks, whisking constantly. If the bottom of the bowl becomes hotter than warm to the touch, remove the bowl from the pan of water for a few seconds and let cool. When all of the butter or margarine is incorporated and the sauce is thick, beat in the water.

Serve the hollandaise immediately or keep in a warm place at room temperature until use.

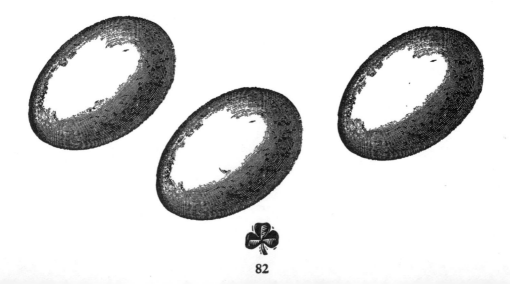

Béarnaise Sauce

1 lb. butter or margarine
4 egg yolks
1½ teaspoons red wine vinegar
Pinch of cayenne pepper
1 teaspoon salt
1½ teaspoons water
1 tablespoon tarragon vinegar
1 tablespoon dry white wine
1 tablespoon shallots, finely chopped
1 tablespoon capers, drained
1 tablespoon chopped fresh parsley

Yields 2 cups

Melt the butter or margarine in a medium saucepan; skim and discard the milk solids from the top of the butter or margarine. Hold the clarified butter or margarine over very low heat while preparing the egg yolks.

Place the egg yolks, vinegar, cayenne, and salt in a large stainless steel bowl and whisk briefly. Fill a saucepan or Dutch oven large enough to accommodate the bowl with about 1 inch of water. Heat the water to just below the boiling point. Set the bowl in the pan over the water; do not let the water touch the bottom of the bowl. Whisk the egg yolk mixture until slightly thickened, then drizzle the clarified butter or margarine into the yolks, whisking constantly. If the bottom of the bowl becomes hotter than warm to the touch, remove the bowl from the pan of water for a few seconds and let cool. When all of the butter or margarine is incorporated and the sauce is thick, beat in the water. Fold in the vinegar, wine, shallots, capers, and parsley. Serve the béarnaise immediately or keep in a warm place at room temperature until use.

Marchand De Vin Sauce

6 tablespoons butter or margarine

½ cup onion, finely chopped

1½ teaspoons garlic, minced

½ cup scallions, finely chopped

½ cup boiled ham, finely chopped

½ cup fresh mushrooms, finely chopped

⅓ cup stone ground whole wheat flour

2 tablespoons Worcestershire sauce

2 cups beef broth or stock (see Index)

½ cup red wine

1½ teaspoons thyme leaves

1 bay leaf

½ cup fresh parsley, finely chopped

salt and black pepper

Yields 3 cups

*M*elt the butter or margarine in a large saucepan or Dutch oven and sauté the onion, garlic, scallions, and ham for 5 minutes. Add the mushrooms, reduce the heat to medium and cook for 2 minutes. Blend in the flour and cook, stirring, for 4 minutes, then add the Worcestershire, beef broth or stock, wine, thyme, and bay leaf. Simmer until the sauce thickens, about 1 hour. Before serving, remove the bay leaf and add the parsley. Season with salt and pepper to taste.

Créole Sauce

½ cup (1 stick) butter or margarine

1½ cups chopped green pepper

1½ cups chopped onion

1½ cups chopped celery

1 tablespoon garlic, minced

¼ cup tomato paste

2 tablespoons paprika

1½ teaspoons Italian seasoning

1½ cups chicken broth or stock (see Index)

½ cup tomato sauce

½ cup water

1 cup peeled and chopped tomatoes

1½ teaspoons Worcestershire sauce

1½ teaspoons salt

Pinch of black pepper

Pinch of cayenne pepper

Pinch of white pepper

3 tablespoons stone ground whole wheat flour

4 to 6 tablespoons water

¼ cup chopped fresh parsley

Yields 1½ quarts

*M*elt the butter or margarine in a large saucepan and cook the green pepper, onion, celery, and garlic until tender, 5 to 8 minutes. Stir in the tomato paste, paprika, and Italian seasoning and cook an additional 3 minutes. Add 1½ cups chicken broth or stock, tomato sauce, ½ cup water, tomatoes, Worcestershire, salt, black pepper, cayenne pepper, and white pepper. Bring the mixture to a boil, then reduce the heat and simmer for 8 to 10 minutes, stirring frequently. In a small bowl, blend the flour with 4 to 6 tablespoons water until smooth. Gradually add the flour to the mixture, stirring constantly, until the sauce thickens. Sprinkle with parsley and serve. Use Créole sauce immediately or freeze indefinitely.

Lemon Butter Sauce

2 lbs. butter or margarine

juice of 3 fresh lemons

½ teaspoon lemon concentrate

¼ cup wine vinegar

Yields 4 cups

Brown butter or margarine lightly in a 12 inch pot. Add lemon juice, lemon concentrate, and vinegar. Stir over a low heat for 10 minutes.

Creamy Lemon Butter Sauce

½ cup beef broth or stock (see Index)

juice of 2 large lemons

2 cups (4 sticks) butter or margarine, room temperature

Yields 2 cups

In a medium-sized sauce pan, boil beef broth or stock, on high fire. Add the freshly squeezed lemon juice. Lower the fire and simmer until reduced by half. Add butter or margarine and whisk quickly. Remove pan from heat, whisking constantly, and return to heat, whisking constantly. Continue this process until all the butter or margarine is melted. Remove from heat and set aside. Serve immediately.

Pecan Butter Sauce

½ cup chopped pecans

3 tablespoons fresh lemon juice

Dash of Tabasco®

2 tablespoons green onions, finely chopped

½ cup (1 stick) butter or margarine, melted

½ teaspoon salt

¼ teaspoon pepper

2 teaspoons Worcestershire sauce

Yields 1 cup

In a bowl combine above ingredients; heat and serve.

Garlic Butter

1 cup (2 sticks) butter or margarine, room temperature

2 teaspoons Worcestershire sauce

6 garlic cloves, minced

2 teaspoons fresh parsley, finely chopped

2 teaspoons Tabasco®

Pinch of salt

Yields 1 cup

*C*ombine all of the ingredients in a small bowl and blend thoroughly.

Dijon Garlic Sauce

6 garlic cloves, peeled

3 tablespoons fresh lemon juice

1 tablespoon Dijon mustard

2 egg yolks

½ teaspoon salt

1 cup olive oil

½ cup fresh basil leaves

Yields 1½ cups

*P*lace garlic, egg yolks, lemon juice, mustard, and salt in a blender and blend until smooth. Continue blending and very slowly pour in olive oil. Turn off blender, add basil leaves, and blend briefly until basil leaves are coarsley chopped. Serve immediately.

Vin Blanc Sauce

1½ sticks butter or margarine, chopped

1 tablespoon heavy cream

¼ cup green onions, finely chopped

¼ cup dry white wine

¼ cup white vinegar

½ teaspoon fresh lemon juice

¼ teaspoon black pepper

⅓ teaspoon salt

⅛ teaspoon celery salt

Yields 1 cup

*I*n a small sauce pan combine white wine, white vinegar, and onions. Let simmer until it is almost a glaze. Remove the mixture from the heat and slowly add the cream. Return to a low heat, whisk in one piece of butter or margarine at a time, stir continuously. Continue to keep the sauce on a low heat adding the salt, pepper, lemon juice, and celery salt. Serve immediately.

Cream Sauce

½ cup (1 stick) butter or margarine

½ cup stone ground whole wheat flour

1 cup chicken broth or stock (see Index)

½ cup heavy cream

salt and white pepper to taste

Yields 2½ cups

*M*elt the butter in a large sauté pan, then blend in the flour. Cook over medium heat, stirring constantly, until the mixture is golden brown. Whisk in the chicken broth or stock and cream. Lower the heat and simmer the sauce for 6 to 8 minutes until thickened. Season to taste with salt and pepper.

Fresh Morel Mushroom Sauce

1 lb. fresh Morel mushrooms

4 tablespoons shallots, finely chopped

4 tablespoons unsalted butter or margarine

2 teaspoons garlic, minced

2 tablespoons chopped fresh parsley

Yields 1 cup

Do not wash the mushrooms. Cut the Morels in half lengthwise and brush out any visible dirt. In a nonstick skillet melt the butter or margarine over a low heat. Add the garlic and shallots and cook until wilted, stirring constantly about 3 minutes. Add the mushrooms and continue cooking until they are just tender about 5 minutes. Sprinkle the sauce with parsley and serve immediately.

Parmesan Cheese and Dill Sauce

2½ cups mayonnaise (see Index)

¾ cup sour cream

juice of one lemon

3 tablespoons fresh dill, finely chopped

2 teaspoons black pepper

1 garlic clove, crushed

¼ cup grated Parmesan cheese

1 teaspoon Dijon mustard

¼ cup onion, finely chopped

Yields 3 cups

In a large bowl place all ingredients and mix. Refrigerate for 2 hours before using.

Tomato Sauce

6 lbs. ripe plum tomatoes

4 cloves garlic

¼ cup extra-virgin olive oil

2 tablespoons tomato paste

½ cup dry red wine

½ cup basil leaves, coarsley torn

½ cup chopped fresh parsley

2 teaspoons dried oregano

Pinch of Sweet 'N Low®

salt and pepper to taste

Yields 8 cups

Peel and seed the tomatoes and chop them coarsley. Set them aside.
In a large heavy pot heat the oil over a medium heat. Mix in garlic
and cook, stirring, for 4 minutes. Add the tomatoes. Mix in the remaining
ingredients and simmer until the tomatoes have melted to form a sauce,
about 30 minutes. Season with salt and pepper to taste and serve
immediately.

Pepper Sauce

1 tablespoon butter or margarine

1 tablespoon stone ground whole wheat flour

1 cup beef broth or stock (see Index)

½ teaspoon tomato paste

1 cup heavy cream

1 teaspoon cracked peppercorns

2 tablespoons dry red wine

Yields 2 cups

Melt the butter or margarine in a medium sauté pan. Using a whisk,
blend in the flour, then add the beef broth or stock and tomato
paste. Cook the mixture over medium heat for 3 to 4 minutes. Add the
cream and peppercorns and simmer the sauce until thickened, about
5 minutes. Stir in red wine and serve immediately.

Horseradish Sauce

2 cups cream or milk
¼ teaspoon white pepper
¼ teaspoon salt
¼ teaspoon butter or margarine
1 tablespoon stone ground whole wheat flour
3 tablespoons horseradish

Yields 2½ cups

*I*n a saucepan, combine the cream, pepper, and salt. Cook over medium heat, but do not let the cream reach a boil. Blend the butter or margarine and flour together and form a small ball. Add the butter or margarine ball to the simmering cream. Cook until the sauce is smooth, then add the horseradish. Serve warm.

Horseradish Mustard Sauce

3 tablespoons drained prepared white horseradish
1 tablespoon fresh chives, finely chopped
1 cup heavy cream, whipped
2 tablespoons Dijon mustard
1 cup mayonnaise (see Index)

Yields 2 cups

*I*n a bowl mix the mayonnaise, mustard, horseradish, and chives together. Gently fold in the whipped cream. Refrigerate for 2 hours before use.

Barbecue Sauce

1 tablespoon cooking oil

⅓ cup onion, finely chopped

1 teaspoon garlic, minced

1 cup chicken broth or stock (see Index)

1   8 oz. can tomato sauce

1   6 oz. can tomato paste

5 tablespoons red wine vinegar with garlic

⅓ cup sugar free maple syrup

2 tablespoons Worstershire sauce

2 tablespoons parsley flakes

1 teaspoon salt

¼ teaspoon cayenne pepper

2 tablespoons liquid smoke

Yields 3 cups

Heat the cooking oil in a saucepan over moderate to high heat. Sauté the onion and garlic until golden brown. Add the remaining ingredients and cook for about 15 minutes and stir constantly. Serve immediately or refrigerate.

Eleana's Special Mustard Blend Sauce

1 cup mustard

1 cup cider vinegar

2-3 teaspoons of salt

1½ oz. regular chili powder

3 cups water

1 tablespoon paprika

Yields 5 cups

In a bowl mix above ingredients.

Note: Can be used as a Barbecue Sauce

European Steak Sauce

8 tablespoons butter or margarine

2 garlic cloves, crushed

2 tablespoons Dijon mustard

8 chopped scallions

2 tablespoons dry white wine

2 teaspoons Worcestershire sauce

Yields 1 cup

In a small pan over medium heat, sauté the scallions and garlic in butter or margarine for about 1½ minutes. Stir continuously, and slowly add the remaining ingredients. Serve immediately.

French Mustard Sauce

3 tablespoons Pommery mustard

1 egg

1 tablespoon freshly squeezed lemon juice

Dash of Tabasco®

¼ teaspoon salt

⅓ cup safflower oil

3 tablespoons extra-virgin olive oil

Yields 1 cup

In a small bowl combine the egg, Pommery mustard, lemon juice, salt, and Tabasco®. Whisk constantly and drizzle in the oils until the sauce is smooth and thickened. Refrigerate for 1 hour before using.

New Orleans Remoulade Sauce

½ cup chopped onion

2 teaspoons garlic, minced

2 teaspoons salt

¾ teaspoon cayenne pepper

2 teaspoons paprika

½ cup Creole mustard

¼ cup tarragon vinegar

¾ cup olive oil

½ cup chopped green onion

Yields 2 cups

*I*n a bowl mix all ingredients except the green onion. Place mixture in a food processor. Process for 8 seconds, turn off, stir, process for another 8 seconds. Add green onions and process for 2 seconds. Do not process any longer. Refrigerate for 12 hours before serving.

Creole Rémloulade Relish

½ cup celery, finely chopped

⅓ cup scallion tops, finely chopped

⅓ cup fresh parsley, finely chopped

¼ cup dill pickles, finely chopped

2 tablespoons garlic, minced

½ cup Créole mustard

2 teaspoons horseradish or to taste

½ cup vegetable oil

¼ cup red wine vinegar

1 tablespoon Worcestershire sauce

Pinch of salt

Pinch of white pepper

Yields 2 cups

*C*ombine all of the ingredients, through the white pepper, in a large mixing bowl. Stir until well blended, then chill in the refrigerator for 2 hours.

Southern Tartar Sauce

1 cup mayonnaise (see Index)

1 tablespoon chopped dill pickle, drained

4 teaspoons green onions, finely chopped

½ teaspoon dry mustard

1 teaspoon lemon juice

1 teaspoon capers

½ clove garlic, minced

salt to taste

Tabasco® to taste

Yields 1¼ cups

*I*n a bowl mix all ingredients. Refrigerate for 1 hour before using.

Spicy Tartar Sauce

1 cup mayonnaise (see Index)

6 dashes Tabasco®

1 tablespoon fresh lemon juice

1 teaspoon finely grated lemon zest

1 teaspoon tomato paste

1 teaspoon Dijon mustard

2 tablespoons dill pickle, very finely chopped

2 tablespoons shallots, finely chopped

2 tablespoons chopped fresh parsley

1 teaspoon jalapeno pepper, finely chopped

1 tablespoon tiny capers, drained

salt and pepper to taste

Yields 1¼ cups

*I*n a bowl combine the mayonnaise, mustard, tomato paste, lemon juice, lemon zest, Tabasco®, and pickles. Mix in parsley, jalapeno pepper, shallots, and capers. Salt and pepper to taste and refrigerate for at least 1 hour before serving.

Ketchup

1	15 oz. can tomato sauce
1	6 oz. can tomato paste
2	tablespoons red wine vinegar
1½	teaspoons onion powder
1½	teaspoons garlic powder
¼	teaspoons salt
½	teaspoon Tabasco®
½	teaspoon granulated Sweet 'N Low®

Yields 2½ cups

Cook all ingredients, except Sweet 'N Low® in a sauce pan over moderate to high heat and slowly bring to a boil. Remove from heat and allow to cool. Once at room temperature, add Sweet'N Low®. Serve immediately or refrigerate.

Alfredo Sauce

1½ sticks butter or margarine

2 cups freshly grated Parmesan cheese

1 cup heavy cream

1 cup milk

½ cup chopped fresh parsley

Freshly ground black pepper to taste

Yields 5 cups

*I*n a sauce pan melt the butter or margarine and gently stir in the cheese. Add the cream and milk and heat through; do not boil. Add the parsley and freshly ground black pepper to taste.

Lite Cheese Sauce

1 cup low fat Ricotta cheese

1 cup low fat Cottage cheese

¼ cup grated Parmesan cheese

1 garlic clove

¼ cup dry white wine

2 tablespoons fresh parsley, finely chopped

Yields 2½ cups

*I*n a food processor mince the garlic. Add the Cottage and Ricotta cheeses and process until smooth and creamy. Pour into a medium-sized sauce pan and gently heat over low-medium heat. Stir frequently for 8 minutes until the sauce is hot but not bubbly. Add the Parmesan cheese, wine, and parsley, stirring until the sauce is well blended and hot. Serve immediately.

Basil Pesto Sauce

2 tablespoons freshly grated Romano cheese

½ cup freshly grated Parmesan cheese

2 large garlic cloves

2 cups fresh basil leaves

¼ cup pine nuts

½ cup extra-virgin olive oil

2 tablespoons heavy cream

salt and pepper to taste

Yields 2 cups

*I*n a food processor combine the basil leaves, garlic, cheeses and pine nuts. Slowly add the olive oil. Salt and pepper to taste. Let stand for 5 minutes and add a few tablespoons of cream before serving.

Garlic Pasta Sauce

3 garlic cloves, minced

¾ cup olive oil

1 teaspoon crushed dried red pepper flakes

½ cup grated Parmesan cheese

½ cup chopped fresh parsley

Freshly ground black pepper to taste

Yields 1½ cups

*I*n a skillet heat the oil. Add the garlic and red pepper and sauté over medium heat for 3 minutes until the garlic is pale gold. Remove from the heat and add the parsley, cheese, and fresh ground pepper.

Bolognese Sauce

3 lbs. ground beef

¼ cup olive oil

2 cups chopped onions

1 stalk celery with leaves, finely chopped

8 garlic cloves, crushed

2   28 oz. cans tomatoes, chopped (reserve and use the juice)

1 cup beef broth or stock (see Index)

1 cup dry red wine

16 chopped fresh basil leaves

2 teaspoons dried oregano

½ cup chopped parsley

1 teaspoon dried red pepper flakes

salt and pepper to taste

Yields 2 quarts

*I*n a large, heavy pot put the ground meat and cook over a medium high heat for about 10 minutes until well cooked. Remove from the heat and drain off all the fat. Stir in the olive oil and continue to heat. Add the onions, celery, garlic, and sauté for 5 minutes. Stir well and add the remaining ingredients. Bring slowly to a boil, and reduce the heat to a simmer. Partially cover and simmer for 2 hours.

Marinara Sauce

3½ lbs. fresh tomatoes, peeled, seeded, and chopped

3 medium-sized garlic cloves, minced

1½ cups chopped onion

¼ cup olive oil

6 basil leaves, finely chopped

1 teaspoon dried oregano

½ teaspoon crushed red pepper flakes

salt and pepper to taste

Yields 4 cups

*I*n a heavy sauce pan heat the olive oil over medium heat for 3 minutes. Add the garlic and onions and cook for 3 minutes. Add the remaining ingredients and cook at a slow boil until the sauce has reduced some and thickened for about 15 minutes. Serve immediately.

Quick Tomato Sauce

4 tablespoons butter or margarine

1 small garlic clove, minced

½ cup chopped onion

2 cups canned crushed tomatoes

1 teaspoon dried marjoram

1¼ cups whipping cream

Yields 3½ cups

In a sauce pan over medium heat, melt the butter or margarine. Add the onion and garlic and sauté for 5 minutes until the onion is pale gold. Add the tomatoes and marjoram. Continue to stir, add the cream, and heat until hot. Serve immediately.

Tomato Butter Sauce

3 cups peeled, seeded, chopped fresh tomatoes

3 tablespoons butter or margarine

6 basil leaves, chopped

salt and pepper to taste

Yields 3 cups

In a skillet melt the butter or margarine over medium heat. Add the tomatoes, basil, and salt and pepper to taste. Increase the heat and cook until the sauce begins to boil. Reduce the heat to a simmer and cook for about 20 minutes, or until the juice has cooked away a bit. Serve immediately.

Tomato Spinach Sauce

1½ cups crushed canned tomatoes

2 cups chopped fresh spinach leaves

1 cup chopped parsley leaves

½ cup fresh basil leaves

2 garlic cloves

½ cup grated Parmesan cheese

juice of one lemon

¼ cup walnuts

Yields 4 cups

*I*n a food processor combine all ingredients and blend until you have a coarsely textured sauce. Pour into a sauce pan and heat over medium heat, stirring constantly until hot. Serve immediately.

Tomatoes and Wine Sauce

1½ lbs. fresh plum tomatoes

6 tablespoons extra-virgin olive oil

4 cloves garlic, minced

½ cup dry white wine

salt

Freshly ground white pepper

Yields 2 cups

*W*arm the olive oil over medium heat. Add the garlic, reduce the heat to very low and cook very slowly for about 5 minutes. Add the white wine, raise the heat to high, and cook 3 minutes until the wine evaporates. Add the tomatoes, salt to taste, and plenty of white pepper. Cook uncovered, stirring often, until light and slightly thickened about 5 minutes. Serve immediately.

Broccoli Bleu Cheese Sauce

1¼ cups crumbled Gorgonzola cheese

1 cup chicken broth or stock (see Index)

6 cups chopped broccoli stems and florets

3 cups chopped zucchini

Freshly ground black pepper to taste

Yields 4 cups

*I*n a sauce pan heat the chicken broth or stock to a boil. Add the zucchini and broccoli. Cover, reduce the heat, and simmer for 5 minutes until tender. Pour the mixture into a bowl, sprinkle in the cheese, and add black pepper.

Pistachio Parmesan Sauce

2 large garlic cloves

2 cups fresh basil leaves

½ cup olive oil

⅓ cup shelled unsalted pistachio nuts

¼ cup freshly grated Parmesan cheese

salt and freshly ground black pepper to taste

Yields 1½ cups

*I*n a food processor combine the garlic, basil, cheese, and pistachio nuts. With the machine running slowly add the olive oil. Season with salt and pepper to taste and process to desired consistency adding additional olive oil or water. Let stand for 5 minutes then serve.

Clam Sauce

¼ cup olive oil

2 tablespoons butter or margarine

2 garlic cloves, minced

¼ cup chopped shallots

1½ cups bottled clam juice

2 cups fresh clams, finely chopped

½ cup chopped fresh parsley

Yields 4 cups

*I*n a sauce pan heat the olive oil and butter or margarine over medium heat. Add the garlic and shallots and sauté for 5 minutes. Add the clam juice and simmer for 5 minutes. Stir in the clams and parsley. Bring the sauce to a boil, then remove from the heat. Serve immediately.

Smoked Salmon and Mushroom Sauce

1 lb. smoked salmon, cut into bite-sized pieces
3 tablespoons butter or margarine
3 scallions, thinly sliced
¼ cup chopped shallots
1 cup fresh mushrooms, finely chopped
1 cup dry white wine
1½ cups half and half
2 tablespoons stone ground whole wheat flour
2 tablespoons chopped fresh dill
salt and pepper to taste

Yields 4 cups

In a medium-sized skillet melt the butter or margarine over medium heat. Add mushrooms, shallots, scallions, and sauté for 3 minutes. Add ¾ cup of dry white wine. Reduce the heat and slowly cook until the liquid has reduced by half. Add the half and half and increase the heat to medium, stirring the sauce until it is hot and not bubbling. Make a thin paste by combining the flour with the remaining ¼ cup dry white wine. Slowly add the paste to the sauce, stirring constantly, and cook until the sauce has thickened for about 5 minutes. Add the dill, salmon, salt, and pepper. Stir to blend and cook for 3 minutes. Serve immediately.

CHAPTER EIGHT

Salads and Salad Dressings

Beef Salad Vinaigrette

1½ lbs. boneless sirloin steak, 1 inch thick

3 tablespoons chopped fresh oregano

3 tablespoons chopped fresh thyme

¾ lb. string beans

½ lb. fresh mushrooms, sliced

3 medium tomatoes, wedged

½ red onion, thinly sliced

¾ cup canned hearts of palm, thinly sliced, cut into 2 inch lengths

1 bunch of watercress, bottom stem removed

Serves six

Dressing:

4 teaspoons capers, drained

3 teaspoons lemon juice

½ cup red wine vinegar

4 teaspoons Dijon mustard

1 cup cooking oil

½ cup extra-virgin olive oil

¾ teaspoon salt

¼ teaspoon freshly ground black pepper

Yields 2 cups

B roil the steak for 5 minutes on each side, until medium rare. Cut into thin slices. Combine the vinaigrette ingredients, in a glass jar. Shake well. Use about ⅓ of dressing to marinate the beef slices for 2 hours before serving. In a pot of boiling water, blanch the green beans until tender, about 4 minutes. Rinse under cold water and drain well. Set aside. Blanch the red onion in boiling water for 20 seconds. Rinse under cold water and drain well. Set aside. Remove the meat from the marinade and combine with other salad ingredients in a bowl. Toss with enough vinaigrette to coat. Garnish with chopped oregano and thyme. Serve immediately.

Chicken Salad Théodore

6 whole boneless, skinless chicken breasts
2 teaspoons white pepper
1 cup celery, finely chopped
½ cup scallions, finely chopped
⅓ cup shallots, finely chopped
¾ cup mayonnaise (see Index)
¼ cup Dijon mustard
¼ cup chopped fresh parsley
½ cup chopped pecans
1 head iceberg lettuce, shredded

Preheat a grill or broiler.

Serves six to eight

Season the chicken breasts with 1 teaspoon of the white pepper, then grill or broil until fully cooked, about 5 to 7 minutes per side. Refrigerate the cooked breasts until cold, then chop them into a large dice. Place the diced chicken in a large bowl and combine with the celery, scallions, shallots, mayonnaise, mustard, remaining white pepper, and parsley. Mix well and chill completely before serving.

Spread the pecans on a pie pan and toast about 5 minutes in an oven preheated to 300° F. Let cool.

Arrange a bed of shredded lettuce on 6 chilled serving plates. For each serving, pack salad into a 1 cup mold, then invert onto the lettuce beds. Sprinkle each salad with toasted pecans and serve.

107

Southwestern Chicken Salad

4 cups cooked skinned chicken breast, cut into bite-size pieces
½ cup shredded sharp Cheddar cheese
1 15 oz. can black beans, rinsed
½ cup chopped green onion
½ cup chopped green pepper
¼ cup mayonnaise (see Index)
⅔ cup sour cream
1 teaspoon chili powder
½ teaspoon ground cumin
¼ teaspoon dried basil
salt and pepper to taste
2 chopped medium tomatoes
1 head lettuce, shredded
Tabasco® to taste

Serves six

*B*lend the mayonnaise, sour cream, chili powder, cumin, basil, salt, pepper, Tabasco®. Set aside. Mix the chicken, cheddar cheese, black beans, onion, and green pepper, and toss with dressing until well coated. Refrigerate for 2 hours. Serve on a bed of shredded lettuce topped with chopped tomatoes.

Sliced Turkey and Endive

24 endive leaves
1 lb. sliced baked turkey breast
¼ cup walnuts
¼ cup chopped pecans
¼ cup extra-virgin olive oil
¼ cup freshly squeezed lemon juice
salt and pepper to taste

Serves four

*A*rrange the endive leaves, 6 to a plate. Place the sliced turkey on top of the leaves. In a food processor, blend the nuts, oil, lemon juice, salt and pepper to taste until smooth. Pour the dressing over the salad. Serve immediately.

Chicken Salad with Curry

2 cups diced cooked chicken, skinned

½ cup toasted slivered almonds

½ cup celery, coarsely chopped

¼ cup sliced water chestnuts

½ cup chopped pecans

Serves six

Dressing:

1 cup mayonnaise (see Index)

1½ teaspoons curry powder

2 teaspoons soy sauce

2 teaspoons fresh lemon juice

In a bowl mix chicken with water chestnuts, pecans, celery, and almonds. Combine dressing ingredients and add to the chicken mixture. Refrigerate for 2 hours. Serve immediately.

Chef Salad

1 cup shredded lettuce

1 hard-boiled egg, sliced

2 oz. roasted, sliced, skinless turkey or chicken breast

2 oz. boiled, sliced ham

¼ cup cucumber, sliced

4-6 cherry tomatoes

½ cup French dressing (see Index)

Serves two

In a large bowl, add all ingredients. Toss with French dressing. Serve immediately.

Duck Breast Salad

3 cups balsamic vinegar
¾ cup olive oil
5 teaspoons green peppercorns
1 cup sliced red onion
5 teaspoons chopped garlic
¾ teaspoon salt
6 skinless duck breasts, about 6 to 8 oz. each
3 heads romaine lettuce, chopped into bite-size pieces
Preheat a grill or broiler

Serves six

In a large bowl, combine the balsamic vinegar, olive oil, green peppercorns, onion, garlic, and salt.

Place the duck breasts in a single layer in a shallow dish and cover with the vinegar mixture. Marinate in the refrigerator for 2 hours, turning the breasts once.

Remove the duck from the marinade and grill or broil about 10 minutes until medium rare. Let the breasts cool for 10 minutes, then cut them on the diagonal into thin slices. While the duck is cooling, place the marinade, along with any juices from the duck, in a saucepan and reduce by a third.

Mound a bed of chopped romaine on six plates and fan slices of duck on top of the lettuce. Spoon the reduced marinade over each salad and serve.

Cobb Salad

4 whole boneless, skinless chicken breasts
2 tablespoons butter or margarine
1½ cups chicken broth or stock (see Index)
1 head iceberg lettuce
2 tomatoes, diced
¼ cup crumbled cooked bacon
¼ cup crumbled bleu cheese
2 avocados, diced
1⅓ cups Classical French dressing (see Index)
1 teaspoon garlic, minced
salt and black pepper

Serves four

Season the chicken breasts with salt and pepper. Combine the butter or margarine and chicken broth or stock in a large sauté pan and heat the broth or stock to just below the boiling point. Place the chicken breasts in the hot broth or stock and poach for 15 to 20 minutes until the chicken is cooked through. Remove the chicken breasts from the broth or stock and cut into a large dice.

Wash the lettuce and set aside 4 large leaves. Chop the remaining lettuce into bite-size pieces.

In a large bowl combine the chicken with the chopped lettuce, tomatoes, bacon, bleu cheese, and avocado. Toss the ingredients together, then add the Classical French dressing and garlic and toss again.

Serve the salad on chilled plates lined with lettuce leaves.

Louis Milian's Caesar Salad

1 medium clove garlic
1 tablespoon olive oil, plus ½ cup
4 flat anchovy fillets, drained
⅛ teaspoon dry mustard
1 teaspoon Worcestershire sauce
2½ tablespoons red wine vinegar
juice of ½ lemon
¼ teaspoon salt
½ teaspoon freshly ground black pepper
1 head romaine lettuce, cut into chunks
1 coddled egg (see note below)
1 heaping tablespoon grated Parmesan cheese
Optional: grilled chicken or shrimp as a topping

Serves four

*C*ut up the garlic and put it in a large wooden salad bowl. Mash with a fork. Add the tablespoon of olive oil and the anchovies, and mash the anchovies into the oil until a paste is formed. Add the mustard, Worcestershire, the remaining olive oil, vinegar, and lemon juice. Mix well. Sprinkle in the salt and pepper. Add the chunks of romaine and toss lightly, then break the coddled egg into the bowl. Toss quite thoroughly this time to mix the ingredients well. Add the cheese and toss one more time. Serve on chilled salad plates.

Note: Coddled egg–place the egg in very hot water for 5 minutes.

Jackson Salad

2 heads iceberg lettuce

4 chopped hard-boiled eggs

1 cup chopped chives

1 cup crumbled cooked bacon

1 cup crumbled bleu cheese

¾ cup French dressing (see Index)

1¼ cups Gorgonzola dressing (see Index)

Serves eight

*W*ash and core the lettuce. Reserve 4 large leaves for presentation; chop the remaining lettuce into bite-size pieces.

Place the chopped lettuce into a large bowl with the eggs, chives, bacon, and bleu cheese. Toss the ingredients, then add the French and Gorgonzola dressings. Toss the salad until well coated with dressing, then mound on chilled plates lined with lettuce leaves.

Hearts of Palm with Pepper Vinaigrette

1 small head iceberg lettuce

15 ½ oz. can (about 8) hearts of palm, chilled

1⅓ cups chilled Pepper Vinaigrette dressing (see Index)

8 black olives

8 cherry tomatoes

Serves four

*W*ash and core the lettuce. Reserve 4 large leaves for presentation; shred the remaining lettuce. Slice the hearts of palm in half lengthwise.

Line 4 chilled plates with large leaves, then top with shredded lettuce and sliced hearts of palm. Spoon Pepper Vinaigrette over each salad and garnish with black olives and cherry tomatoes.

Spinach Salad

10 oz. fresh spinach leaves, stemmed and washed

2 cups sliced fresh mushrooms

4 strips of bacon, cooked crisp and crumbled

1 cup Créole Vinaigrette dressing (see Index)

4 large lettuce leaves

8 thin slices onion

2 tablespoons chopped hard-boiled eggs

Serves four

*I*n a large bowl, toss the spinach, mushrooms, bacon, and salad dressing. Line four chilled plates with lettuce leaves, then mound some of the dressed spinach on each leaf. Garnish the salads with onion slices and chopped egg.

Green Salad with Stilton Cheese and Walnuts

1 lb. fresh salad greens, cleaned, dried, and chilled

4 tablespoons extra virgin olive oil

¼ teaspoon salt

¼ cup crumbled Stilton cheese

¼ cup minced walnuts, lightly toasted

salt and pepper to taste

juice of 2 lemons

Serves four

*I*n a large bowl place the salad greens, Stilton cheese, and walnuts. Toss with olive oil, lemon juice, salt and pepper. Serve immediately.

Garden District Salad

6 large leaves Romaine lettuce

6 cups chopped Iceberg lettuce

2 cups sliced ripe avocado

3 medium ripe tomatoes, sliced

2 cups red onion, sliced into rings

1 small head cauliflower (to yield 24 florets) blanched in boiling water

1 medium cucumber, sliced

Serves six

Dressing:

¾ cup olive oil

½ cup plus 1 tablespoon vegetable oil

3 tablespoons red wine vinegar

Pinch of Sweet 'N Low®

1 teaspoon salt

2 teaspoons basil

2 teaspoons oregano

½ teaspoon lemon juice

¼ teaspoon black pepper

½ tablespoon chopped parsley

Pinch of garlic powder

¼ teaspoon grated Romano cheese

A few dashes of Worcestershire sauce

½ hard-boiled egg

Place all the ingredients for the dressing in a food processor, and process for 1 minute. Refrigerate the dressing before using it. Line 6 salad bowls with the Romaine lettuce. Top with the chopped Iceberg lettuce. Prepare the other vegetables, and arrange them in an attractive manner over the lettuce. Top each salad with ¼ cup of the dressing. Serve immediately.

Tomatoes and Onions

2 large tomatoes

1 small onion

2 tablespoons fresh parsley, finely chopped

Serves four

Dressing:

¼ cup olive oil

1 tablespoon red wine vinegar

½ teaspoon dried basil

½ teaspoon dried oregano

¼ teaspoon granulated Sweet 'N Low®

salt and pepper to taste

⅛ teaspoon mustard powder

½ teaspoon garlic powder

In a blender, combine all dressing ingredients and set aside. Cut the tomatoes into ¼ inch slices. Arrange the tomato slices in a dish and sprinkle the onion and parsley over the tomatoes. Pour the dressing on top of the salad and marinate for 2 hours. Serve immediately.

Italian Pasta Salad

1½ cups uncooked whole grain pasta

1 cup mayonnaise (see Index)

2 tablespoons red wine vinegar

1 garlic clove, minced

1 tablespoon chopped fresh basil

½ cup chopped red onion

salt and black pepper to taste

1 cup quartered cherry tomatoes

½ cup chopped green pepper

½ cup chopped ripe olives

Serves four

*C*ook pasta until tender, rinse in a collander with cold water. In another bowl, combine mayonnaise, vinegar, garlic, basil, salt, and black pepper. Add pasta, red onions, cherry tomatoes, green pepper, and olives; toss to coat well. Refrigerate for 2 hours. Serve immediately.

Tomato and Mozzarela Cheese

¾ lb. Mozzarela cheese, thinly sliced

4 tomatoes, thinly sliced

1 tablespoon capers, rinsed

8 black olives, pitted

4 anchovy fillets, finely chopped

¼ cup extra-virgin olive oil

salt and pepper to taste

Serves four

*A*rrange the tomato and Mozzarela slices on a serving dish, alternating the slices. Decorate the plate with capers, olives, and anchovy pieces. Sprinkle to taste with salt and pepper, drizzle the oil in a thin stream over the top and serve.

Wild Rice Stuffed Tomatoes

6 oz. cooked wild rice

1   10oz. package frozen peas, room temperature

1   15 oz. can black beans, rinsed

1 green pepper, finely chopped

1 bunch scallions, finely chopped

⅓ cup balsamic vinegar

¼ teaspoon granulated Sweet 'N Low®

2 tablespoons freshly squeezed lemon juice

¼ teaspoon paprika

½ teaspoon dry mustard

½ teaspoon garlic, finely chopped

10 large tomatoes

salt and pepper to taste

Serves eight

*C*ombine the cooked wild rice, peas, beans, scallions, and green pepper. In another bowl, blend together the vinegar, Sweet 'N Low®, lemon juice, paprika, dry mustard, and garlic. Pour over the wild rice mixture and toss well. Halve the tomatoes and scoop out the pulp and seeds. Salt and pepper the inside of each tomato shell. Fill each tomato with the wild rice mixture and serve immediately.

Egg Stuffed Tomatoes

4 ripe tomatoes
1 teaspoon Dijon mustard
salt and pepper to taste
¼ cup extra-virgin olive oil
1 teaspoon fresh parsley, finely chopped
1 teaspoon fresh mint, finely chopped
1 teaspoon fresh basil, finely chopped
4 chopped anchovy fillets
3 hard-boiled eggs, coarsely chopped
12 capers

Serves four

Slice each tomato in half. Scoop out the pulp and seeds. Salt and pepper the insides of the tomatoes. Mix the mustard with the salt and pepper to taste. Add the oil and mix with the parsley, mint, basil, anchovies, capers, and eggs. Fill each tomato with ¼ of the mixture. Serve immediately.

Egg Salad

8 hard-boiled eggs
1 teaspoon Dijon mustard
¾ cup mayonnaise (see Index)
2 tablespoons chopped fresh dill
salt to taste
white pepper to taste
Tabasco® to taste

Serves six

Coarsely chop the eggs. Gently fold together the eggs with the remaining ingredients. Refrigerate for 2 hours. Serve immediately.

Asparagus in Mustard Vinaigrette

1 lb. asparagus, par-boiled and drained

Serves four

Mustard Vinaigrette:

¼ cup olive oil

2 tablespoons red wine vinegar

2 tablespoons chopped pimentos

½ tablespoon chopped garlic

1 tablespoon dried parsley flakes

salt and pepper to taste

½ teaspoon mustard powder

In a blender, combine all of the dressing ingredients, toss the asparagus with the dressing. Refrigerate for 4 to 6 hours. Serve immediately.

Broccoli Vinaigrette

3 lbs. broccoli, cut into florets

6 tablespoons white wine vinegar

1½ teaspoons Dijon mustard

¾ cup fresh parsley, finely chopped

¾ cup olive oil

½ cup chopped fresh chives

3 tablespoons shallots, finely chopped

1 teaspoon salt

Freshly ground black pepper to taste

Serves eight

In boiling salted water, cook the broccoli until the stems are tender, about 10 minutes. Drain well. In a bowl, combine the mustard and the vinegar. Whisk in the oil and continue until the vinaigrette is blended. Add the parsley, chives, shallots, salt and pepper. Toss well. Pour enough dressing over the hot, well-drained broccoli to coat. Serve immediately.

Broccoli and Avocado Salad

1½ lbs. young, tender broccoli
1 avocado
2 tablespoons fresh lemon Iuice
½ cup chopped pecans
1 tablespoon Dijon mustard
salt to taste
¼ cup extra-virgin olive oil
1 tablespoon fresh parsley, finely chopped

Serves four

Remove the broccoli florets from the large stems. In a sauce pan with boiling salted water add the florets and boil about 3 minutes until almost tender. Drain, cool under running water, drain again. Set aside. Peel, pit and cut avocado into cubes. In a small bowl, coat the avocado with 1 tablespoon of lemon juice to prevent darkening. Place the avocado and broccoli in a salad bowl and add the pecans. In a small bowl stir together the remaining lemon juice, the mustard and salt to taste until well combined. Stir in the oil and parsley until blended. Pour the dressing over the salad. Toss and serve immediately.

Broccoli and Cauliflower Salad

1 bunch broccoli, cut into florets
1 head cauliflower, cut into florets
1 bunch chopped scallions
1½ cups mayonnaise (see Index)
½ cup grated Parmesan cheese
salt and pepper to taste

Serves four

In a large bowl, mix together all ingredients and stir to coat broccoli and cauliflower florets. Refrigerate for 2 hours. Serve immediately.

Cucumber with Onion Salad

8 cups thinly sliced cucumbers, about 5 cucumbers
1 large onion, thinly sliced
1½ cups white vinegar
3 garlic cloves, minced
1 tablespoon olive oil
4 teaspoons salt
1 cup water
½ teaspoon white pepper
3 tablespoons chopped fresh dill

Serves six

*I*n a large bowl, combine cucumber and onion; set aside. Over a high heat bring the vinegar, garlic, oil, salt, and water; to a boil, stirring continuously. Pour the mixture over the cucumber and onions; add the pepper and dill and mix well. Refrigerate for 2 hours. Serve immediately.

Cucumber Dill Salad

4 cucumbers, peeled and thinly sliced
3 tablespoons extra-virgin olive oil
3 cloves garlic
⅔ cup plain yogurt
1 tablespoon fresh lemon juice
2 tablespoons fresh dill, finely chopped
salt
white pepper

Serves four

*P*lace cucumber slices on a plate. Lightly salt the cucumbers and drain off any excess water. Let stand for 1 hour. Using a garlic press, press the garlic cloves into a small bowl. Add the yogurt, lemon juice, dill, salt and white pepper to taste. Stir well. Add the oil and stir vigorously until blended. Place the cucumber slices in a salad bowl, pour the dressing over the top and toss gently. Refrigerate for 2 hours. Serve immediately.

Bean Salad

1	16 oz. can kidney beans, undrained

1   16 oz. can kidney beans, undrained
1   16 oz. can garbanzo beans (chick peas), undrained
⅓ cup olive oil
¼ cup lemon juice
3 chopped scallions
1 tablespoon chopped red bell pepper
½ teaspoon dried basil
¾ teaspoon salt
¼ teaspoon black pepper

Serves eight

*I*n a medium-sized sauce pan place the beans. Boil the beans, then drain. Add remaining ingredients. Refrigerate for 2 hours. Serve immediately.

Green Bean Salad

1 lb. fresh green beans, cut in halves and par-boiled
½ small onion, thinly sliced
½ cup garbanzo beans, rinsed and drained
1 cup halved cherry tomatoes
1 tablespoon red wine vinegar
2 tablespoons water
2 teaspoons olive oil
1 teaspoon basil leaves, finely chopped
¼ teaspoon dry mustard powder
salt and pepper to taste

Serves six

*I*n a bowl, toss the green beans, onion, garbanzo beans, and cherry tomatoes. In another bowl, blend the remaining ingredients. Toss the vegetables with the blended dressing. Refrigerate for 2 hours. Serve immediately.

123

German Cole Slaw

1 large or 2 small heads of cabbage

2 teaspoons salt

1 teaspoon black pepper

1 medium-sized white onion, finely chopped

2 stalks celery, finely chopped

¼ cup olive oil

3 tablespoons red wine vinegar with garlic

Serves eight

Slice the cabbage quite thin, about ¼ inch, on a chopping board. Place in a colander and rinse under cold running water. Drain well, and put into a large serving bowl. Sprinkle with salt and pepper, then add the chopped vegetables. Toss together to mix thoroughly. Add the olive oil and vinegar and mix well. Taste, and adjust seasonings, if desired. Cover the bowl with plastic wrap and refrigerate until served. Toss again thoroughly just before serving.

Prepare this several hours in advance. It tastes best when it marinates.

Louisiana Cole Slaw

2 heads cabbage, shredded

1 green pepper, thinly sliced

2 medium-sized onions, thinly sliced

2 oz. capers, drained

Serves four

Dressing:

3 cups mayonnaise (see Index)

2 tablespoons Dijon mustard

1 tablespoon dill seed

1 tablespoon celery seed

6 tablespoons lemon juice

¾ teaspoon granulated Sweet 'N Low®

salt to taste

Freshly ground black pepper to taste

Combine mayonnaise, mustard, celery seed, dill seed, lemon juice, and Sweet 'N Low®. Mix well. To prepare slaw: toss cabbage, peppers, onions, and capers together. Toss dressing with slaw, salt, and pepper. Refrigerate for 2 hours and serve immediately.

Sea Slaw

1 lb. shrimp, boiled and peeled (see Index)

1 lb. cabbage
(for color use green and purple cabbage)

8 green onions, thinly sliced

salt and pepper to taste

Serves six

Dressing:

¼ cup lemon juice

¼ teaspoon granulated Sweet 'N Low®

1 teaspoon salt

1 teaspoon dry mustard

½ teaspoon Worcestershire sauce

½ teaspoon Tabasco®

¾ cup mayonnaise (see Index)

B lend all dressing ingredients together and pour over slaw. Toss and chill for 2 hours before serving.

Egg Salad with Smoked Salmon

6 hard-boiled eggs

3 oz. smoked salmon, coarsely chopped

2 teaspoons fresh dill, finely chopped

2 teaspoons capers, finely chopped

2 teaspoons shallots, finely chopped

¼ cup sour cream

2 tablespoons mayonnaise (see Index)

1 teaspoon fresh lemon juice

black pepper to taste

Serves four

*C*oarsely chop the eggs. Chop the salmon. Mix the salmon into the eggs. Stir in the shallots, capers, fresh dill, and black pepper. In another bowl, combine the remaining ingredients and fold gently into the salad. Refrigerate for 2 hours. Serve immediately.

Homemade Tuna Salad

2 6 oz. cans of Tuna fish, drained

2 tablespoons mayonnaise (see Index)

3 tablespoons chopped dill pickle or dill pickle relish

Serves four

*M*ix all ingredients well. Serve immediately or refrigerate.

Salmon Salad

1 tablespoon salt
¼ teaspoon black pepper
¼ teaspoon white pepper
½ teaspoon cayenne pepper
6 Salmon fillets, about 6 to 8 oz. each
6 cups chopped (1 large head) romaine lettuce
12 strips bacon, fried crisp and crumbled
1½ cups sliced hearts of palm
1½ cups warm Pepper Vinaigrette dressing (see Index)
6 oz. goat cheese, crumbled
Preheat a grill or broiler

Serves six

*I*n a small bowl, combine the salt, black pepper, white pepper, and cayenne pepper. Sprinkle the Salmon fillets on both sides with the seasoning mixture. Grill or broil the Salmon until the meat is firm and flaky, about 4 to 7 minutes per side.

Place the Salmon in a large bowl, and add the romaine, bacon, and hearts of palm. Toss the ingredients together, breaking the Salmon into bite-size pieces.

Mound salad on 6 chilled plates, then spoon ¼ cup warm Pepper Vinaigrette dressing over the greens. Top each salad with about 2 tablespoons crumbled goat cheese. If desired, garnish with fresh or pickled vegetables.

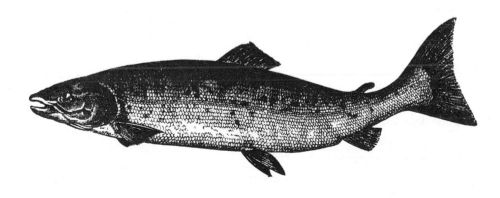

Crabmeat and Asparagus

24 fresh asparagus spears

4 large lettuce leaves

2 cups shredded lettuce

4 thin slices ripe tomato

12 oz. lump crabmeat,

picked over to remove any shell and cartilage

¼ cup onion, finely chopped

½ cup French dressing (see Index)

Chopped chives for garnish

Serves four

Trim the lower part of the asparagus spears, then remove the woody skin with a peeler. Steam the asparagus about 12 minutes until tender. Refrigerate the spears until cold.

Place the lettuce leaves on 4 chilled plates. Mound ½ cup shredded lettuce on the leaves, then arrange 6 asparagus spears radiating out from the center of each plate, with the tips toward the edge of the plate. Set a tomato slice in the center, then top with crabmeat and onion. Spoon 2 tablespoons of French dressing over the crabmeat and garnish with chives.

Cocodrie Crabmeat Salad

1 lb. fresh lump crabmeat, picked over to remove any shell and cartilage

Serves six

Dressing:

4 tablespoons mayonnaise (see Index)

2 tablespoons chopped fresh parsley

2 green onions, finely chopped

1 tablespoon lemon juice

½ teaspoon dry mustard

1 teaspoon Worcestershire sauce

½ teaspoon Tabasco®

⅛ teaspoon garlic salt

1½ cups celery, coarsely chopped

Mix all dressing ingredients well and pour over crabmeat. Refrigerate for 2 hours. Serve immediately.

Seafood Salad

1 head romaine lettuce
8 oz. lump crabmeat, picked over to remove any shell and cartilage
8 oz. boiled shrimp, peeled and deveined (see Index)
1 cup freshly grated Parmesan cheese
1 cup Créole Vinaigrette dressing (see Index)

Serves four

*W*ash the romaine and set aside 4 large leaves. Chop the remaining leaves into bite-size pieces and place in a large bowl with the crabmeat, shrimp, and Parmesan. Toss the ingredients, then pour the dressing over the salad and toss again.

Line 4 plates with lettuce leaves, then top with salad. If desired, garnish with cherry tomatoes and slices of hard-boiled eggs.

Tomato, Crabmeat and Onion

4 large lettuce leaves
2 cups shredded lettuce
4 thin slices ripe tomato
¼ cup onion, finely chopped
12 oz. lump crabmeat, picked over to remove any shell and cartilage
½ cup French dressing (see Index)
½ teaspoon chopped chives

Serves four

*P*lace the lettuce leaves on 4 chilled plates, then mound ½ cup shredded lettuce in the center of each leaf. Set a slice of tomato on the shredded lettuce and top with crabmeat and onion. Spoon 2 tablespoons of French dressing over the crabmeat and garnish with chopped chives.

Shrimp Stuffed Artichoke Vinaigrette

| 4 medium artichokes |
| 2 lemons, halved |
| ¼ cup chopped celery |
| 4 garlic cloves |
| 1 teaspoon white pepper |
| 3 tablespoons butter or margarine |
| 2 lbs. medium raw shrimp, peeled and deveined |
| 1 tablespoon chopped fresh parsley |
| salt and black pepper |
| 2 cups warm Pepper Vinaigrette dressing (see Index) |

Serves four

*W*ash the artichokes, then remove the stems and trim the sharp points from the leaves. Fill a large pot ¾ full with cold water. To the water, add the lemon, celery, garlic, white pepper, and a pinch each of salt and black pepper. Bring the water to a boil, then stand the artichokes upright in the pan; place a plate or other weight on top of the artichokes to keep them in position during cooking. Cook the artichokes at a rolling boil until tender, about 50 minutes. Remove the artichokes from the water, drain them, and let cool. When cool enough to handle, spread open the artichokes from the top and remove the furry choke, exposing the heart.

Melt the butter or margarine in a skillet and add the shrimp. Season the shrimp with a pinch of salt and pepper, and sprinkle with parsley. Sauté the shrimp a few minutes, until they turn pink, then remove them from the heat. Fill the centers of the artichokes with the shrimp. Spoon warm vinaigrette over the artichokes and serve immediately.

Avocado and Shrimp Salad

4 avocados, peeled and halved

1½ cups boiled shrimp (see Index)

1 14 oz. can hearts of palm

1 tablespoon lemon juice

⅓ cup olive oil

¼ cup onion, finely chopped

1 teaspoon Dijon mustard

1½ teaspoons salt

¼ teaspoon pepper

½ teaspoon garlic salt

3 tablespoons red wine vinegar

Serves four

Cut the hearts of palm in ⅛ inch rounds. In a bowl combine vinegar, mustard, salt, pepper, garlic salt, onion, olive oil, and lemon juice. To the mixture, add the shrimp and hearts of palm. Fill each avocado shell with mixture. Refrigerate for 1 hour. Serve immediately.

Créole Shrimp Salad

1 small head iceberg lettuce

64 fresh asparagus spears, steamed or blanched

64 boiled shrimp, peeled and deveined (see Index)

3 cups Créole mayonnaise (see Index)

Serves eight

Core and wash the lettuce. Reserve 8 large leaves; shred the remaining lettuce.

Place lettuce leaves on 8 chilled plates, then top with shredded lettuce. Arrange 8 asparagus spears and 8 shrimp on each plate. Spoon about ⅓ cup Créole mayonnaise over the salads and serve.

Fresh Berry Salad

3 pints fresh strawberries

1 pint fresh blueberries

1 pint fresh blackberries

1 pint fresh raspberries

2 tablespoons unsweetened apple juice concentrate

2 tablespoons fresh orange juice

2 tablespoons finely grated orange zest

¼ cup chopped fresh mint leaves

Serves twelve

*W*ash all berries and drain on paper towels. Cut stems off the strawberries and cut into halves or quarters. In a large bowl, place strawberries with blueberries, blackberries, and raspberries. In another bowl, mix the apple juice concentrate, orange juice, orange zest, and the chopped mint leaves. Add to the berries, wait 1 hour. Serve at room temperature.

*Note: Fruit Salads must be eaten 30 minutes before a meal or at least
2 hours after a meal.*

Fresh Fruit Salad

1 cantaloupe

2 peaches, pitted and sliced

6 apricots, pitted and sliced

1 small bunch seedless grapes (about 6 oz.)

⅔ teaspoon granulated Sweet 'N Low®

juice of one orange

juice of one lemon

Serves four

*F*rom the cantaloupe scoop out the flesh into small balls and place into a bowl. Add the peaches and apricots to the bowl holding the melon balls along with the grapes. Sprinkle the Sweet 'N Low® over the top and then add the orange and lemon juices. Stir well. Refrigerate for 1 hour. Serve immediately.

*Note: Fruit Salads must be eaten 30 minutes before a meal or at least 2
hours after a meal.*

Bleu Cheese Dressing

4 oz. Danish Bleu cheese, crumbled

¾ cup sour cream

½ teaspoon dry mustard

½ teaspoon black pepper

½ teaspoon salt

½ teaspoon garlic powder

1 teaspoon Worcestershire sauce

1½ cups mayonnaise (see Index)

Yields 2½ cups

*I*n a food processor blend all ingredients except bleu cheese for 3 minutes. Stir in the bleu cheese and blend for another 3 minutes. Refrigerate for 12 hours and serve.

Gorgonzola Dressing

1 cup Gorgonzola cheese, room temperature

2 cups mayonnaise (see Index)

1 cup heavy cream

1 cup sour cream

2 teaspoons lemon pepper seasoning

Yields 4 cups

*C*ombine all of the ingredients in a medium bowl and mix thoroughly. Refrigerate the dressing for 2 hours before serving.

Roquefort Dressing

¼ lb. crumbled Roquefort cheese, room temperature

½ cup mayonnaise (see Index)

½ cup cream

½ cup sour cream

2 tablespoons fresh parsley, finely chopped

2 teaspoons Worcestershire sauce

2 tablespoons freshly squeezed lemon juice

2 teaspoons onion, finely chopped

½ teaspoon garlic powder

salt and pepper to taste

Yields 2 cups

In a food processor combine all ingredients until well blended. Refrigerate for 1 hour. Serve immediately.

Caesar Dressing

1 can flat anchovies, drained

2 eggs

1 cup olive oil

2 teaspoons garlic, finely chopped

2 tablespoons lemon pepper marinade

¼ cup milk

2 tablespoons Parmesan cheese

juice of 2 lemons

2 tablespoons sour cream

Yields 1 cup

In a small bowl cover anchovies with milk. Let the anchovies sit in the milk for at least 10 minutes. Drain again, then chop the anchovies in the food processor. Add eggs and beat well. Add all remaining ingredients except olive oil and blend well. Then add olive oil to blended mixture until smooth and creamy.

134

Classical French Dressing

2½ cups olive oil

1 cup red wine vinegar

1½ oz. Worcestershire sauce

1 teaspoon Tabasco®

1¼ tablespoons black pepper

¾ tablespoon salt

¾ teaspoon Dijon mustard

4 large garlic pods, crushed

juice of one medium lemon

Yields 4 cups

Blend all ingredients in a food processor. Shake well before each use.

French Dressing

8 egg yolks

½ teaspoon dry mustard

3 cups olive oil

¾ cup red wine vinegar

½ teaspoon Worcestershire sauce

salt and black pepper

Yields 5 cups

Beat the egg yolks in a stainless steel bowl until foamy and slightly thickened. Mix in the dry mustard. Add 1 cup of the oil, whisking constantly, then whisk in ¼ cup of the vinegar. Add the remaining oil and vinegar ⅓ at a time, alternating the 2 ingredients. Stir in the Worcestershire and season to taste with salt and pepper. Refrigerate the dressing for 2 hours before serving.

Italian Dressing

½ cup grated Romano or Parmesan cheese

½ cup olive oil

¼ cup tarragon vinegar

½ cup mayonnaise (see Index)

salt and pepper to taste

Yields 1½ cups

*I*n a food processor combine all ingredients until well blended. Serve immediately.

Lemon-Soy Dressing

4 oz. freshly squeezed lemon juice

4 oz. soy sauce

4 oz. olive oil

Yields 1½ cups

*S*queeze approximately 4-6 lemons to get 4 oz. lemon juice. Add soy sauce and olive oil. Blend together well.

Green Goddess Dressing

2 cups mayonnaise (see Index)

8 anchovy fillets, finely chopped

2 scallions, cut into 2 inch pieces

¼ cup fresh chives, finely chopped

¼ cup fresh parsley, finely chopped

2 tablespoons fresh tarragon, finely chopped

¼ cup red wine vinegar

Yields 3 cups

*I*n a food processor blend all of the ingredients except anchovies and scallions. When mixture is blended well add anchovies and scallions and blend for not longer than 2 minutes. Serve immediately.

Ranch Dressing

⅓ cup plain yogurt

⅓ cup mayonnaise (see Index)

½ cup buttermilk

2 teaspoons onion, finely chopped

1 tablespoon garlic, minced

1 tablespoon fresh chives, finely chopped

salt and pepper to taste

Yields 1¼ cups

*W*hisk together all of the ingredients and refrigerate. Serve when chilled.

137

Vinaigrette

¾ cup olive oil

¼ cup red wine vinegar

½ teaspoon Worcestershire sauce

1 teaspoon garlic, minced

¼ teaspoon granulated Sweet 'N Low®

salt and pepper to taste

¼ teaspoon dry mustard

⅛ teaspoon thyme

Yields 1½ cups

*I*n a food processor combine all ingredients until well blended. Serve immediately.

Vinaigrette and Crumbled Bleu Cheese Dressing

¼ lb. crumbled Bleu cheese, room temperature

1 tablespoon water

2 whole eggs

1 teaspoon dried mustard

2 garlic cloves

1 teaspoon black pepper

1 teaspoon paprika

1 teaspoon salt

1 cup red wine vinegar

3 cups olive oil

Yields 3½ cups

*W*hisk together water, eggs, mustard, garlic, pepper, paprika, and salt. Boil vinegar and blend in with mixture. Blend in the oil. Add Bleu cheese to mixture and stir vigorously. Refrigerate for 2 hours. Serve immediately.

Creole Vinaigrette

| 1 medium onion, finely chopped |
| 1 cup Créole mustard |
| 2 tablespoons garlic, minced |
| ¼ cup olive oil |
| ½ cup red wine vinegar |
| salt and black pepper |

Yields 2½ cups

*C*ombine the onion, mustard, and garlic in a stainless steel bowl. Whisk in the oil and vinegar, then season the dressing to taste with salt and pepper.

Green Onion and Mustard Vinaigrette

| 1 tablespoon Dijon mustard |
| ¼ teaspoon granulated Sweet 'N Low® |
| salt and pepper to taste |
| ¼ cup red wine vinegar |
| ½ cup olive oil |
| 3 tablespoons green onions, finely chopped |

Yields 1 cup

*W*hisk together all of the ingredients except the green onions. Stir in the green onions and salt and pepper to taste. Serve immediately.

Hazelnut Vinaigrette

½ cup hazelnut oil

¾ cup olive oil

½ cup hazelnuts, roasted and skinned

¼ cup red wine vinegar

1 teaspoon soy sauce

1 teaspoon thyme leaves, finely chopped

1 egg white

salt and pepper to taste

Yields 2 cups

*I*n a food processor combine all ingredients until well blended. Serve immediately.

Pepper Vinaigrette Dressing

1½ cups diced green pepper

1½ cups diced red bell pepper

1½ cups scallions, finely chopped

½ cup red wine vinegar

1 cup olive oil

1½ cups chopped hard-boiled egg whites

salt and black pepper

Yields 4 cups

*I*n a large stainless steel bowl, combine the green pepper, red bell pepper, and scallions. Alternate the vinegar and oil, adding about ¼ cup vinegar at a time, followed by ½ cup oil. Blend in enough vinegar and oil to cover the chopped ingredients.

Fold the egg whites into the pepper mixture, then season with salt and black pepper to taste. The vinaigrette is delicious cold or hot; chill it in the refrigerator or warm it slightly over low heat before serving.

Sherry Vinaigrette

1 egg

2 tablespoons freshly squeezed lemon juice

2 tablespoons red wine vinegar

1 tablespoon dry sherry

1½ cups olive oil

1 teaspoon garlic, finely chopped

½ teaspoon tarragon

½ teaspoon anchovy paste

salt and pepper to taste

Yields 2 cups

*I*n a food processor combine all ingredients until well blended. Serve immediately.

Tomato Vinaigrette

1 large ripe tomato peeled, finely chopped

1 tablespoon green onions, finely chopped

1 teaspoon garlic, minced

½ cup tomato sauce

¼ cup water

¼ cup balsamic vinegar

¼ cup olive oil

salt and pepper to taste

Yields 1½ cups

*I*n a sauce pan, cook the chopped tomato over low heat for 5 minutes, until all liquid has evaporated. Place the tomatoes in a bowl and allow to cool. Mix all remaining ingredients with the tomatoes. Wait 3 hours before serving.

Yogurt Dill Dressing

1 cup plain yogurt

1 tablespoon freshly squeezed lemon juice

¼ cup extra-virgin olive oil

salt and pepper to taste

2 teaspoons fresh dill, finely chopped

Yields 1⅓ cups

*I*n a food processor combine all ingredients until well blended. Refrigerate for 1 hour. Serve immediately.

Spinach Salad Dressing

2 teaspoons salt

1 teaspoon white pepper

½ teaspoon freshly ground black pepper

½ teaspoon dry mustard

1 teaspoon Dijon mustard

1 teaspoon fresh lemon juice

2 teaspoons chopped fresh garlic

5 tablespoons red wine vinegar

4 tablespoons olive oil

1 cup cooking oil

3 eggs

Yields 2 cups

*B*eat eggs very slowly, add olive oil. In a seperate bowl, mix in the other ingredients beginning with the dry mustard. Make sure all the lumps are out of the mixture. Slowly add other ingredients in the bowl with the olive oil and eggs. Finally, add the vegetable oil to the dressing.

Homemade Mayonnaise

2 egg yolks

½ teaspoon salt

1 teaspoon lemon juice

½ teaspoon dry mustard

Pinch of cayenne

2 cups cooking or olive oil

2 tablespoons boiling water

Yields 2¼ cups

*C*ombine the egg yolks, salt, lemon juice, dry mustard, and cayenne in a mixing bowl; beat with an electric mixer or whisk until slightly thickened, about 5 minutes. Add 1 cup of the oil a teaspoon at a time, beating constantly, until the mixture becomes a thick emulsion. Add the remaining 1 cup of oil, 1 to 2 tablespoons at a time. When all of the oil is incorporated, beat in 2 tablespoons boiling water. Cover and refrigerate until ready to use.

Créole Mayonnaise

2 tablespoons scallions, finely chopped

2 tablespoons parsley, finely chopped

½ teaspoon garlic, minced

juice of 1 small lime

(Lemon can be substituted.)

1 teaspoon Tabasco®

¼ cup Créole mustard

¾ cup mayonnaise (see Index)

2 egg whites

Yields 1½ cups

*I*n a stainless steel bowl, combine all of the ingredients, except the egg whites; blend thoroughly with a whisk.

In another bowl, whip the egg whites until thick. Using a whisk, gently fold the egg whites into the mayonnaise. Cover and chill the dressing before serving.

Bleu Cheese Mayonnaise

¼ cup mayonnaise (see Index)

¼ cup sour cream

¼ cup Bleu cheese, crumbled

1 teaspoon fresh chives, finely chopped

Freshly ground black pepper to taste

Yields ¾ cup

*I*n a bowl combine the mayonnaise and sour cream. With a fork mash the Bleu cheese into the mixture. Add the chives and pepper. Serve immediately or set aside.

Note: Use with crudite, cold meats, and sandwiches.

Garlic Mayonnaise

3 garlic cloves, peeled

1 cup olive oil

1 egg

1 tablespoon lemon juice

½ teaspoon salt

Yields 1 cup

*I*n a blender place the garlic, egg, lemon juice, and salt and blend until smooth. Slowly add the oil into the blender, blend until the mixture is thick. Refrigerate until ready to use.

Note: Use with crudite, cold meats, and sandwiches.

144

CHAPTER NINE

Breakfast at Brennan's®

Basic Omelette

4 large eggs
⅛ teaspoon salt
⅛ teaspoon black pepper
3 tablespoons butter or margarine

Serves two

In a small bowl, beat the eggs, salt, and pepper with a fork until blended. Melt the butter or margarine in an 8 inch skillet or omelette pan. Pour in the egg mixture and stir briskly. Cook the eggs over low heat; lift the edges of the omelette and shake the pan several times during cooking to keep the eggs from sticking. When the eggs are firm and the bottom is light brown, fold the omelette over and transfer it to a heated plate.

Cheddar and Ham Omelette

4 large eggs
⅛ teaspoon salt
⅛ teaspoon black pepper
3 tablespoons butter or margarine
¾ cup diced ham
¾ cup grated sharp Cheddar cheese

Serves two

In a small bowl, beat the eggs, salt, and pepper with a fork until blended. Melt the butter or margarine in an 8 inch skillet or omelette pan, then add the egg mixture and ham, stirring briskly. Cook the eggs over low heat; lift the edges of the omelette and shake the pan several times during cooking to keep the eggs from sticking. When the eggs are almost set, fold in the cheese. Cook until the bottom forms a golden crust, then fold the omelette over and transfer it to a heated plate.

Crabmeat Omelette

4 large eggs
⅛ teaspoon salt
⅛ teaspoon black pepper
3 tablespoons butter or margarine
¾ cup lump crabmeat, picked over to remove any shell or cartilage
½ cup hollandaise sauce (see Index)

Serves two

*I*n a small bowl, beat the eggs, salt, and pepper with a fork until blended. Melt the butter or margarine in an 8 inch skillet or omelette pan, then add the egg mixture and crabmeat, stirring briskly. Cook the eggs over low heat; lift the edges of the omelette and shake the pan several times during cooking to keep the eggs from sticking.

Cook until the bottom forms a golden crust, then fold the omelette over and transfer it to a heated plate. Top the omelette with hollandaise and serve.

Florentine Omelette

4 large eggs
⅛ teaspoon salt
⅛ teaspoon black pepper
3 tablespoons butter or margarine
¾ cup stemmed and washed spinach leaves
¾ cup creamed spinach (see Index)

Serves two

*I*n a small bowl, beat the eggs, salt, and pepper with a fork until blended. Melt the butter or margarine in an 8 inch skillet or omelette pan, then add the egg mixture and spinach leaves, stirring briskly. Cook the eggs over low heat; lift the edges of the omelette and shake the pan several times during cooking to keep the eggs from sticking.

Cook until the bottom forms a golden crust, then fold the omelette over and transfer it to a heated plate. Top the omelette with creamed spinach and serve.

Russian Omelette

4 large eggs

⅛ teaspoon salt

⅛ teaspoon black pepper

3 tablespoons butter or margarine

6 tablespoons salmon caviar

½ cup heavy sour cream

Serves two

*I*n a small bowl, beat the eggs, salt, and pepper with a fork until blended. Melt the butter or margarine in an 8 inch skillet or omelette pan, then add the egg mixture, stirring briskly. Cook the eggs over low heat; lift the edges of the omelette and shake the pan several times during cooking to keep the eggs from sticking. When the eggs are almost set, add 4 tablespoons salmon caviar. Cook until the bottom forms a golden crust, then fold the omelette over and transfer it to a heated plate. Spoon the sour cream over the top, and garnish with the 2 remaining tablespoons of caviar.

Egg Casserole

6 slices stone ground whole wheat toast, cut into small pieces

6 large eggs

2 cups milk

1 lb. ham, bacon or sausage, or a combination of all 3

4 oz. butter or margarine

½ lb. sliced fresh mushrooms

8 green onions, finely chopped

¼ teaspoon dry mustard

1 cup Colby and Monterey Jack cheeses

Serves ten

*S*pray a 9x13 inch casserole pan with cooking spray. Sauté meats and drain. Melt butter or margarine. Add garlic, mushrooms, and green onions, and sauté; then add to meat and mix thoroughly. Beat eggs with milk, mustard, and salt. Add toast and ¾ cup of cheese. Add meat and blend together. Fill pan with mixture and sprinkle with remaining cheese. Cover and refrigerate over night. Preheat oven to 350°F. and bake 40-45 minutes.

Poached Eggs

1½ quarts water
2 cups vinegar
8 large eggs

Serves four

*B*ring the water and vinegar to a boil in a large saucepan. Crack the eggs one at a time and drop them gently into the boiling water, being careful not to break the yolks. Simmer for 3 to 4 minutes, moving the eggs several times with a spoon to cook them evenly.

When firm, remove the eggs from the water with a slotted spoon and place in a pan filled with cold water until serving.

Eggs Benedict

2 tablespoons butter or margarine
8 slices Canadian bacon (Smoked ham can be substituted)
8 slices stone ground whole wheat toast
8 poached eggs (see Index)
2 cups hollandaise sauce (see Index)

Serves four

*M*elt the butter in a large sauté pan and warm the Canadian bacon over low heat. Place 2 slices stone ground whole wheat toast on each plate and cover with slices of warm Canadian bacon. Set a poached egg on the bacon, then top each egg with hollandaise sauce. Serve immediately.

Eggs Hussarde

2 tablespoons butter or margarine

8 slices Canadian bacon

(Smoked ham can be substituted)

8 slices stone ground whole wheat toast

2 cups marchand de vin sauce (see Index)

8 poached eggs (see Index)

2 cups hollandaise sauce (see Index)

Grilled Tomatoes for garnish (see Index)

Serves four

*M*elt the butter in a large sauté pan and warm the Canadian bacon over low heat.

Place two slices stone ground whole wheat toast on each plate and cover with slices of warm Canadian bacon. Spoon marchand de vin sauce over the meat, then set a poached egg on each slice. Ladle hollandaise sauce over the eggs; garnish the plates with grilled tomatoes and serve.

Eggs Sardou

8 artichokes

3 cups creamed spinach (see Index)

8 poached eggs (see Index)

2 cups hollandaise sauce (see Index)

Serves four

*R*emove the stems of the artichokes and cut off the tops, removing all of the leaves. Steam or blanch the artichoke bottoms until tender, then scoop out the furry choke.

Mound creamed spinach on 4 plates and top with 2 warm artichoke bottoms. Set a poached egg in each artichoke bottom, spoon hollandaise sauce over the eggs and serve.

Eggs St. Charles

8 fried trout fillets (see Index), about 3 oz. each (Red snapper, Drum or Redfish can be substituted)

8 poached eggs (see Index)

2 cups hollandaise sauce (see Index)

Serves four

*D*ivide the fried trout between 4 serving plates and top each fillet with a poached egg. Spoon hollandaise over the eggs and serve.

Eggs Ellen

8 Salmon fillets, about 3 oz. each

8 poached eggs (see Index)

2 cups hollandaise sauce (see Index)

salt and black pepper

Preheat a grill or broiler

Serves four

*S*eason the Salmon with salt and pepper, then grill or broil the fish until flaky and cooked through, about 4 minutes per side.

Divide the Salmon between 4 warm plates and top each fillet with a poached egg. Spoon hollandaise sauce over the eggs and serve.

Quiche Lorraine

1 lb. sliced bacon
4 tablespoons butter or margarine
3 large onions, finely chopped
3 cloves garlic, minced
1¼ cup half and half
6 eggs, beaten
2 egg yolks, beaten
1 cup whipping cream
¾ pound Swiss cheese, grated
2 - 3 tablespoons fresh parsley, finely chopped
½ teaspoon nutmeg
1½ teaspoons salt
1¼ teaspoons black pepper
Quiche Pie Crust (see Index)

Preheat oven to 350° F.

Serves six to eight

Sauté bacon in a pan until crisp, place bacon on paper towels to cool and drain. Melt butter or margarine in pan with the bacon grease. Sauté garlic and onion, until a golden brown. Drain excess grease and let cool. In a mixing bowl, beat the eggs, egg yolks, half and half and whipping cream. Once the bacon has cooled, crumble finely and fold into the batter with the onion and garlic mixture. Add nutmeg, pepper, and salt to batter. Pour batter into the partially cooked pie shell and bake for 30 minutes or until a toothpick comes out clean.

Quiche Pie Crust

2 cups stone ground whole wheat pastry flour

½ teaspoon salt

Dash of Sweet 'N Low®

½ cup cold butter or margarine

2 - 3 tablespoons shortening

5 tablespoons cold water

Yields one pie shell

*P*lace all ingredients, except water, in a mixing bowl. Combine mixture with your hands, until mixture has formed into a smooth ball. Place ball into bowl and put into refrigerator for several hours or into the freezer for 45 minutes. Place on a wooden counter or cutting board, and using a rolling pin, flatten the dough, to about ⅛ inch thick. Place the flattened dough into a 10 inch baking dish and cover with wax paper. Use dried beans to hold the paper down. Bake pie crust in a 400°F. oven for 8 to 10 minutes.

French Toast

4 large eggs, beaten

4 slices stone ground whole wheat bread

¾ cup milk

½ teaspoon cinnamon, optional

1¼ teaspoons vanilla extract

Serves two

*I*n a bowl, beat eggs. Add milk, vanilla and cinnamon, whisk until mixture is fully combined. Take each piece of bread and dip into egg batter, soaking each side until saturated. In a frying pan, coat with desired cooking oil and add bread. Cook each side on a medium heat until golden brown. Serve with margarine or butter and sugar-free syrup.

Mame's Pancakes

2 cups stone ground whole wheat flour
4 teaspoons baking soda
1 teaspoon salt
1½ cups milk
⅓ cup cooking oil
1 large egg

Serves four

Beat egg well. Add milk and oil. Mix flour, salt, and baking soda. Add to egg and beat mixture vigorously. Heat a skillet, coat with cooking oil of your choice. Drop the mixture by tablespoons into the hot oil. Brown pancakes on both sides, then drain on paper towels. Serve with butter or margarine and sugar-free syrup.

Pecan Oatmeal Waffle

4 tablespoons oatmeal
2 tablespoons stone ground whole wheat flour
½ teaspoon granulated Sweet 'N Low®
1 teaspoon baking soda
2 dashes salt
2 large eggs, separated
½ cup milk
½ oz. shelled pecans, finely chopped

Serves two

In a small bowl combine oatmeal, flour, Sweet 'N Low®, baking soda, and salt. In another small bowl whisk together egg yolk, milk, and pecans. Stir into oatmeal mixture until just combined. Set aside. In a separate small bowl, with electric mixer on high speed, beat egg whites until stiff; fold into oatmeal mixture. Pour batter into preheated waffle iron. Close and bake on high, about 4 minutes, until golden brown. Serve immediately.

Italian Pancakes

2 large eggs
1 cup Ricotta cheese
½ cup stone ground whole wheat flour
zest of ½ lime
zest of ½ orange
2 tablespoons butter or margarine, melted
⅛ teaspoon salt
¼ teaspoon vanilla extract
½ teaspoon granulated Sweet 'N Low®
cooking oil

Serves four

*I*n a large bowl, beat the eggs. Gradually stir in the Ricotta cheese and the flour. Combine the orange and lime zest, blend them into the mixture with the remaining ingredients except for the oil. In a large skillet, heat the oil. Drop the mixture by tablespoons into the pan. Cook until both sides are golden brown. Drain on paper towels. Serve with butter or margarine and sugar-free syrup.

Italian Cheese Frittata

8 large eggs, beaten
¾ cup chopped onion
¾ cup chopped green pepper
¼ cup grated sharp Cheddar cheese
¼ teaspoon salt
¼ teaspoon black pepper
¼ teaspoon dried oregano
¼ teaspoon dried basil
2 tablespoons butter or margarine
grated Parmesan cheese

Serves eight

*I*n a large bowl, mix together all the ingredients except butter or margarine and Parmesan cheese. In a large non-stick skillet, melt butter or margarine. Pour mixture into hot skillet. Turn heat to medium-low, cover, and cook 30 minutes until mixture is solid. Invert onto platter and cut into serving size portions. Sprinkle with Parmesan cheese and serve immediately.

Calves' Liver With Sautéed Onions

1 cup (2 sticks) butter or margarine

2 large onions, thinly sliced

2 lbs. calves' liver, cut into 8 slices

salt and black pepper

Serves four

*M*elt ½ cup of the butter or margarine in a large skillet and cook the onions over medium heat until lightly browned; transfer the onions to a platter and place in a warm oven.

In the same pan, melt the remaining ½ cup butter. Season the calves' liver on both sides with salt and pepper, then cook the slices over medium heat, about 8 to 10 minutes per side. Just before serving, place the onions on top of the liver and braise for 2 minutes.

Arrange slices of liver topped with sautéed onions on plates.

Note: May be served with cooked brown rice.

Texas Breakfast Rice

2 large eggs, lightly beaten

5 large egg whites, lightly beaten

1 cup chopped onion

1 green pepper, seeded and chopped

1 cup sliced fresh mushrooms

¾ cup chopped tomato

½ cup milk

½ cup butter or margarine

salt and pepper to taste

4 cups cooked brown rice

¾ cup shredded sharp Cheddar cheese

Serves six

*I*n a skillet coated with butter or margarine cook the onion, green pepper, mushrooms, and tomato over medium-high heat about 5 minutes until tender. In a large bowl combine the eggs, egg whites, milk, and salt and pepper. Reduce to medium heat and pour the egg mixture into the pan. Continue cooking, while stirring, for 4 minutes. Mix in the brown rice and cheese. Cook for an additional 2 to 4 minutes, until the eggs are done and the cheese is melted. Serve immediately.

Grillades

8 thinly pounded veal escalopes, about 3 oz. each
½ cup butter or margarine
½ cup olive oil
½ cup chopped onion
½ cup chopped scallions
3 garlic cloves, minced
1½ cups chopped green pepper
½ cup chopped celery
1 bay leaf
1½ teaspoons Italian seasoning
4 ripe tomatoes, diced
1 tablespoon Worcestershire sauce
2 tablespoons tomato paste
1 quart beef broth or stock (see Index)
4 tablespoons stone ground whole wheat flour
¼ cup water
2 tablespoons chopped fresh parsley
salt and black pepper

Preheat oven to 175° F.

Serves eight

Season the veal escalopes on both sides with salt and pepper. Heat the butter or margarine in a large skillet and sauté the veal until lightly browned, about 3 minutes per side. Transfer the cooked meat to a platter and place in the warm oven while preparing the sauce.

Heat the olive oil in a large saucepan, then sauté the onions, scallions, garlic, green pepper, and celery in the hot oil until tender. Stir in the bay leaf, Italian seasoning, tomatoes, Worcestershire, and tomato paste. When the mixture is well blended, add the beef broth or stock and cook for 5 minutes, stirring frequently. In a small bowl, blend the flour with ¼ cup water. Stir the liquid flour into the sauce, then add the parsley. Season with salt and pepper to taste and cook over medium high heat until the sauce is reduced by about one-fourth. Before serving, remove the bay leaf.

Spoon grillade sauce onto 8 plates and center a veal escalope on each. Ladle additional sauce over the veal and serve.

Note: May be served with cooked brown rice.

CHAPTER TEN

Entrées

Crab Cakes with Créole Mayonnaise

1 lb. lump crabmeat, picked over to remove any shell and cartilage

¼ cup celery, finely chopped

¼ cup green pepper, finely chopped

¼ cup scallions, finely chopped

1 teaspoon thyme leaves

¼ teaspoon cayenne pepper

2 large eggs, lightly beaten

¼ cup heavy cream

¾ cup bread crumbs (see Index)

2 tablespoons butter or margarine

salt and black pepper

Créole mayonnaise (see Index)

Serves four to six

Combine the ingredients, through the heavy cream, in a large bowl and stir until well mixed. Fold in the bread crumbs and season to taste with salt and pepper. Form the crab mixture by hand into 12 balls. Flatten the balls into cakes and place on wax or parchment paper.

Melt the butter or margarine in a large skillet and cook the crab cakes over medium heat until golden brown and heated through, about 6 minutes per side.

Serve immediately with Créole mayonnaise.

Note: One pound finely chopped blanched crawfish tails can be substituted.

Crabmeat Imperial

1 lb. lump crabmeat, picked over to remove any shell and cartilage

½ cup scallions, finely chopped

½ cup green pepper, finely chopped

¼ cup chopped pimentos

1 egg yolk

1 teaspoon dry mustard

2 tablespoons paprika

1 cup mayonnaise (see Index)

¼ cup freshly grated Parmesan cheese

¼ cup bread crumbs (see Index)

salt and black pepper

Preheat oven to 375° F.

Serves four

*I*n a large bowl, combine the crabmeat, scallions, green pepper, pimento, egg yolk, dry mustard, paprika, and ½ cup of the mayonnaise. Stir until well mixed, then season with salt and pepper to taste.

Spoon the crabmeat mixture into 4 one cup baking dishes, then cover with the remaining mayonnaise. Sprinkle Parmesan and bread crumbs on top and bake in the hot oven for 15 to 20 minutes until heated through. Serve immediately.

Note: One pound of blanched crawfish tails can be substituted for the crabmeat.

Stuffed Crab

1 lb. claw crabmeat

½ cup (1 stick) butter or margarine

1 onion, finely chopped

4 chopped green onions

2 stalks celery, finely chopped

1 bay leaf

⅛ teaspoon thyme

4 or 5 slices stone ground whole wheat toast

1 cup milk

1 clove garlic, minced

1 hard-boiled egg, finely chopped

1 raw egg

bread crumbs (see Index)

salt and pepper to taste

Preheat oven to 350° F.

Serves six

Melt 1 stick butter or margarine and sauté green onions, celery, and garlic until soft. Soak toasted bread in milk. Squeeze as dry as possible and add to sautéed greens. Cook for about 15 minutes. Beat egg and add to mixture in pan and stir well. Add chopped hard-boiled egg, crabmeat, salt and pepper to taste, and thyme. Stir well. Place in buttered shells or ramekins. Sprinkle with bread crumbs. Dot with butter or margarine and bake in oven for about 20 minutes.

Crabmeat au Gratin

2 lbs. fresh lump crabmeat

10 oz. sharp Cheddar cheese, grated

1   12 oz. can evaporated milk

1   5 oz. can evaporated milk

2 egg yolks

1 large onion, finely chopped

4 green onions, finely chopped

3 chopped stalks celery

½ lb. butter or margarine

4 tablespoons stone ground whole wheat flour

3 dashes Tabasco®

Preheat oven to 350° F.

Serves six

*I*n a medium-size sauce pan sauté onions, celery, and butter or margarine until soft. Add flour and blend. Add milk and blend. Remove from heat and add all remaining ingredients. Put in small individual casserole dishes. Sprinkle tops with cheese and bake until golden brown.

Oysters En Brochette

2 large eggs

½ cup milk

48 shucked oysters

12 strips of bacon, quartered

stone ground whole wheat flour for dredging

salt and black pepper

oil for deep frying

1½ cups lemon butter sauce (see Index)

Serves four

*I*n a shallow bowl or pan, beat the eggs with the milk. Set the egg wash aside. Wrap the oysters in the bacon pieces and thread 12 oysters onto a skewer, spearing them through the bacon. Repeat the process, assembling 4 skewers in all. Season the wrapped oysters with salt and pepper, then dredge them in flour. Dip the skewers in egg wash, then recoat with flour.

Heat oil in a deep fryer or large saucepan to 375° F.

Fry the oysters for 3 to 5 minutes until golden brown and crisp. Drain on paper towels.

Slide the oysters off the skewers onto 4 plates. Top the Oysters en Brochette with lemon butter sauce. Serve immediately.

Oysters Pan Roast

1 cup (2 sticks) butter or margarine

⅔ cup chopped shallots

½ cup stone ground whole wheat flour

2 cups oyster water, if necessary, add water to yield this volume

¼ teaspoon cayenne pepper

24 shucked oysters

2 tablespoons freshly grated Parmesan cheese

Preheat a broiler.

Serves four

Melt the butter or margarine in a large skillet and sauté the shallots for 2 to 3 minutes until tender. Blend in the flour and cook over medium heat for 3 to 5 minutes, stirring, then whisk in the oyster water and cayenne. When the sauce begins to thicken, fold in the oysters and cook until heated through.

Pour the mixture into 4 one cup baking dishes and sprinkle Parmesan over the top, then broil about 2 minutes until the cheese begins to brown.

Fried Oysters

4 dozen oysters, drained

3 cups pulverized Triscuit® crumbs (see note below)

Serves four

Coat oysters with crumbs thoroughly and deep fry in oil until the oysters float to the top of the oil.

Note: Instead of Triscuit® crumbs, stone ground whole wheat flour or bread crumbs (see Index) can be used.

Scallops Créole

20 oz. bay scallops
4 teaspoons olive oil
1 cup onion, finely chopped
1 cup green pepper, finely chopped
4 teaspoons garlic, minced
4 cups tomatoes, coarsely chopped
½ cup tomato paste
1 teaspoon dried basil
½ teaspoon dried thyme
½ teaspoon crushed red pepper flakes
¼ teaspoon dried oregano
4 cups cooked brown rice

Serves four

*I*n a large skillet heat oil. Add onion, green pepper, and garlic. Cook over medium-high heat for 3 minutes until soft. Stir in remaining ingredients except scallops and rice. Reduce heat to medium-low and cook for 5 minutes. Add scallops and cook for 4 minutes until scallops are done. Spoon brown rice onto heated platter; top with scallop mixture.

Sautéed Scallops

20 oz. bay scallops
4 teaspoons butter or margarine
4 cups sliced fresh mushrooms
2 cups onion, finely chopped
2 teaspoons garlic, minced
2 tablespoons freshly squeezed lime juice
1 teaspoon dried thyme
1 teaspoon lemon pepper marinade
2 cups cooked brown rice

Serves four

*I*n a large skillet, melt butter or margarine and sauté the mushrooms, onions, and garlic. Cook over medium-high heat, for about 3 minutes, until soft. Stir in remaining ingredients, except for the rice, and cook, stirring occasionally for about 4 minutes until scallops are done. Spoon brown rice onto heated platter; top with scallop mixture.

Bay Scallops with Lemon Butter

1 lb. bay scallops
1 tablespoon unsalted butter or margarine
3 tablespoons cooking oil
¼ cup chopped fresh parsley
creamy lemon butter sauce (see Index)
salt and pepper to taste

Serves four

*P*lace scallops in a large sauté pan, without over crowding the scallops. Heat the cooking oil and 1 tablespoon of butter or margarine until nearly smoking. Add the scallops to the pan and salt and pepper to taste. Allow the scallops to brown well on one side. Gently turn them and allow to brown on the other side. Serve with creamy lemon butter sauce. Sprinkle with fresh parsley.

Stuffed Mirliton with Shrimp

3 mirlitons
½ cup green onions, finely chopped with tops
1 onion, finely chopped
2 cloves garlic, minced
½ cup parsley, finely chopped
1 chopped tomato
1½ dozen shrimp, half or quartered depending on size
¾ cup bread crumbs (see Index)
½ cup (1 stick) butter or margarine, melted
salt and pepper to taste

Preheat oven to 350° F.

Serves six

*C*ut mirlitons in half and place in boiling, salted water. Boil until tender, remove and cool. Scoop out the tender pulp, remove seeds, and mash. Be careful not to break the shells. Brown garlic and onions in butter or margarine, add tomato, parsley, salt and pepper. Fry the pulp of the mirlitons for about 5 minutes. Soak bread crumbs and squeeze out excess water and add pulp to mixture. Add shrimp to the mixture and mix well. Fill the shells with the stuffing, placing additional bread crumbs over the top and drizzle butter or margarine over the shells. Bake in oven for about 15 minutes until golden brown.

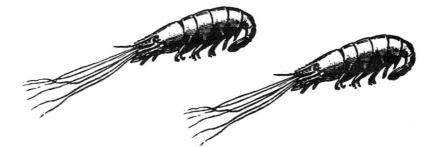

Barbecued Shrimp

5 lbs. jumbo raw whole shrimp, washed

4 teaspoons garlic, minced

1 tablespoon Tabasco®

2 cups (4 sticks) butter or margarine

1½ tablespoons black pepper

2 tablespoons Worcestershire sauce

1 tablespoon cayenne pepper

juice of four lemons

1 tablespoon lemon zest

Preheat oven at 350° F.

Serves four to six

*I*n a large pan, melt butter or margarine and add all ingredients, except shrimp. Cook over low fire until well blended. Place the shrimp in a baking pan, pour the mixture over the shrimp and place in oven for 20 minutes. Turn shrimp and bake another 15 minutes. Serve immediately.

Marinated Shrimp

4 lbs. boiled shrimp, peeled (see Index)

1½ cups olive oil

½ cup red wine vinegar

4 tablespoons capers with brine

2 bay leaves

3 teaspoons celery seed

1 teaspoon dried dill

salt and pepper to taste

¾ teaspoon Tabasco®

1 tablespoon freshly squeezed lemon juice

2 tablespoons lemon zest

1 onion, thinly sliced

Serves four

*I*n a large bowl, combine all ingredients adding the shrimp last. Cover and refrigerate for 24 hours before serving.

Spicy Shrimp

2 lbs. raw jumbo shrimp, peeled

3 tablespoons cooking oil

¼ cup garlic, minced

2 cups red onions, thinly sliced

2 cups white onions, thinly sliced

½ cup seeded fresh red chili peppers, diced

8 tomatoes, each cut into 6 wedges

salt and freshly ground black pepper to taste

½ cup tomato sauce

½ cup water

½ cup chopped green onions

¼ cup chopped parsley

¼ cup chopped cilantro

Serves six

In a large pot, warm the oil over moderately high heat. Add the garlic and onions and sauté for 5 minutes. Stir in the chilis, tomatoes, salt and pepper, and shrimp. Cook, stirring and tossing for 5 minutes. Add the tomato sauce, water, and green onions and bring the mixture to a simmer. Stir in the parsley and cilantro and cook for 1 minute. Serve immediately.

Singing Shrimp

½ cup (1 stick) butter or margarine

½ cup chopped white onion

1 cup sliced fresh mushrooms

¼ cup garlic, minced

1 lb. andouille or other spicy smoked sausage, sliced

2 lbs. peeled, deveined raw shrimp

½ cup chopped scallions

1 tablespoon chopped parsley

½ cup white wine

2 cups brown rice (see Index)

Serves four

*M*elt the butter or margarine in a large skillet and sauté the onion for several minutes until tender. Add the mushrooms and garlic, and cook the mixture for 3 to 4 minutes. Stir in the andouille, shrimp, and scallions, sauté an additional 4 minutes, then add the parsley and white wine. Reduce the heat and simmer briefly. Season with salt and pepper to taste.

Mound ½ cup brown rice on 4 plates and top with a generous serving of the shrimp mixture.

Shrimp or Crawfish Étouffée

¾ cup (1½ sticks) plus 2 tablespoons butter or margarine

¾ cup onion, finely chopped

½ cup celery, finely chopped

1 tablespoon garlic, minced

1 cup chopped fresh or canned tomatoes

¼ teaspoon salt

½ teaspoon black pepper

1 lb. raw shrimp or blanched crawfish tails

1 tablespoon paprika

1 teaspoon thyme leaves

2 bay leaves

2 tablespoons stone ground whole wheat flour

2 cups chicken broth or stock (see Index)

¾ cup chopped scallions

Pinch of cayenne pepper

1 tablespoon Worcestershire sauce

1 tablespoon chopped fresh parsley plus extra for garnish

2 cups cooked brown rice (see Index)

Serves four

*M*elt ¾ cup butter or margarine in a large saucepan and sauté the onion and celery until tender. Add the garlic and cook another minute, then stir in the tomatoes, salt, pepper, shrimp or crawfish, paprika, thyme, and bay leaves. Blend the flour into the mixture, then whisk in the chicken stock or broth. Add the scallions, cayenne, and Worcestershire; cook over medium heat for 15 to 20 minutes, stirring occasionally. When the sauce has thickened, remove the bay leaves and fold in the parsley. Add the remaining 2 tablespoons butter or margarine to finish the sauce. Serve the Étouffée over hot brown rice and garnish with chopped parsley.

Shrimp Créole

½ cup (1 stick) butter or margarine
1½ cups chopped green pepper
1½ cups chopped onion
1½ cups chopped celery
1 tablespoon garlic, minced
¼ cup tomato paste
2 tablespoons paprika
1½ teaspoons Italian seasoning
1½ cups chicken broth or stock (see Index)
½ cup tomato sauce
½ cup water
1 cup peeled and chopped tomatoes
1½ teaspoons Worcestershire sauce
1½ teaspoons salt
Pinch of black pepper
Pinch of cayenne pepper
Pinch of white pepper
2 tablespoons stone ground whole wheat flour
4 tablespoons water
3 lbs. medium raw shrimp, peeled and deveined
¼ cup chopped fresh parsley
4 cups cooked brown rice (see Index)

Serves eight

*M*elt the butter or margarine in a large saucepan and cook the green pepper, onion, celery, and garlic until tender, 5 to 8 minutes. Stir in the tomato paste, paprika, and Italian seasoning and cook an additional 3 minutes. Add 1½ cups chicken stock or broth, tomato sauce, ½ cup water, tomatoes, Worcestershire, salt, cayenne, black, and white peppers. Bring the mixture to a boil, then reduce the heat and simmer for 8 to 10 minutes, stirring frequently. In a small bowl, blend the flour with 4 tablespoons water until smooth. Gradually add the flour to the shrimp sauce, stirring constantly, until the sauce thickens. Add the shrimp and parsley to the sauce and bring the mixture to a boil. Lower the heat and simmer for 5 to 8 minutes until the shrimp are cooked through; do not overcook. Serve the Shrimp Créole over the cooked brown rice.

Note: Whole grain pasta can be substitued for brown rice.

Shrimp & Pasta Bordelaise

1 lb. whole grain pasta
1 cup (2 sticks) butter or margarine
5 chopped shallots
3 tablespoons garlic, minced
2 lbs. peeled and deveined medium raw shrimp
½ cup dry white wine
1 teaspoon white pepper
1 bunch chopped scallions
3 tablespoons chopped fresh parsley

Serves six to eight

Cook the pasta in boiling water according to the package directions and drain. Melt ½ cup of the butter or margarine in a large sauté pan and sauté the shallots for 30 seconds. Add the garlic, cook another 30 seconds, then stir in the shrimp. Cook over moderately high heat until the tails of the shrimp curl, then reduce the heat to medium and add the wine. Cook the mixture for 5 minutes, then add the pepper, scallions, and parsley. Lower the heat and simmer the sauce for a few minutes.

Just before serving, toss the drained pasta in the sauce, then remove the pan from the heat and fold in the remaining ½ cup of butter or margarine.

Lemon Baked Fish

4 fresh fish fillets

½ cup (1 stick) butter or margarine

1 oz. lemon juice

2 teaspoons garlic, minced

blackened fish seasoning to taste

lemon pepper marinade to taste

Preheat oven to 350° F.

Serves four

*I*n a small pan, melt and combine butter or margarine, lemon juice and garlic. Sprinkle fish fillets with blackened fish seasoning and lemon pepper marinade on both sides of the fillets. Place fillets in a baking pan and pour butter or margarine sauce over the fillets. Bake 30–40 minutes depending on the size of the fillets. Baste periodically by spooning butter or margarine sauce over the top of the fillets.

Fried Fish

1 large egg

¼ cup milk

8 fish fillets, about 3 oz. each

½ cup stone ground whole wheat flour

½ cup Triscuit® crumbs

¼ cup cooking oil

salt and black pepper

Serves four

*P*ulverize one box of Triscuit® to use for breading. In a shallow bowl, beat the egg with milk. Season the fish with salt and pepper, then dredge the fillets in flour. Dip the fish in the egg wash and coat with Triscuit® crumbs.

Heat oil in a large skillet, then fry the fish over moderately high heat until crisp, about 4 to 5 minutes per side; blot on paper towels. Serve immediately.

Note: This recipe can be used for frying shrimp.

Baked Catfish With Créole Sauce

Creole Sauce (see below)

4 Catfish fillets

cooking spray

Garnish: 4 tablespoons parsley, finely chopped

Preheat oven to 375° F.

Serves four

Place the Catfish in a baking dish sprayed with cooking spray. Add the Créole Sauce and bake uncovered about 20 minutes or until fish is tender. When ready to serve, remove fish to a warm platter and pour Créole Sauce over fish and garnish with chopped parsley.

Créole Sauce

½ tablespoon olive oil

½ cup peeled and diced tomatoes

¼ cup onions, finely chopped

¼ cup green pepper, finely chopped

¼ cup celery, finely chopped

1 teaspoon garlic, minced

Seasonings:

¾ teaspoon fresh oregano, finely chopped

½ teaspoon fresh basil, finely chopped

½ teaspoon fresh thyme, finely chopped

Pinch white pepper

Pinch black pepper

Pinch paprika

¾ cup chicken broth or stock (see Index)

Heat the oil in a large skillet over medium heat. Add tomatoes, onions, celery, green pepper, garlic, and seasonings, stirring thoroughly to combine. Cook until the onions are translucent, about 5 minutes. Stir in the stock or broth and bring to a boil. Reduce heat and simmer, stirring occasionally until the vegetables are tender about 20 minutes.

Redfish Pontchartrain

2 medium filleted Redfish

1 lb. well picked lump crabmeat

4 oz. butter or margarine

1 oz. dry vermouth

½ cup parsley, finely chopped

½ cup chopped green onions

1 quart hot fish stock (see Index) or clam juice

2 cups hollandaise sauce (see Index)

salt and pepper to taste

Serves four

*M*elt butter or margarine in pan and sauté crabmeat and green onions until heated through. Add vermouth and sauté 3 minutes more. Set aside and keep warm. Poach Redfish in fish stock or clam juice until they flake when touched. Remove and drain. Place fish on heated platters and top each fillet with ¼ of crabmeat mixture. Top each fillet with ½ cup of hollandaise sauce and sprinkle with parsley.

Broiled Flounder

4   8 oz. Flounder fillets

4 tablespoons mayonnaise (see Index)

2½ tablespoons grated Parmesan cheese

2 tablespoons chopped onion

2 tablespoons chopped fresh parsley

3 teaspoons garlic, minced

Preheat broiler.

Serves four

*I*n a bowl combine all ingredients except Flounder. Place Flounder on broiler pan; spread the mixture evenly over each fillet. Broil the Flounder for 8 to 10 minutes. Serve immediately.

Red Snapper Provencale

8 small, Red Snapper fillets, about 3 oz. each

6 large tomatoes, coarsely chopped, with juices reserved

1 cup chopped onions, coarsely chopped

¼ cup fennel, finely chopped

1   10 oz. package frozen spinach

½ cup fish stock (see Index)

2 tablespoons unsalted butter or margarine

1   10oz. can lima beans, drained

salt and pepper to taste

Preheat the oven to 350° F.

Serves four

*I*n a large saucepan or skillet, combine ⅔ of the tomatoes, the tomato juice, the onions, and fennel. Cook, stirring frequently, for 7 minutes, until the onions are soft and the juices have almost evaporated. Cook the spinach, drain, and keep warm. Pour the fish stock into a large oven-proof skillet and place the fish fillets side by side. Cover and bake until the fish is cooked, about 15 minutes. Remove the fish and set aside. Place the skillet over medium-high heat and add butter or margarine, lima beans, salt and pepper. Heat and stir for about 3 minutes. Place 4 of the fish fillets on a serving plate, and top each one with ¼ of the spinach and ⅛ of the tomato sauce. Place the remaining fillets on top and cover with the remaining tomato sauce. Pour the lima bean sauce over the fillets, sprinkle with the remaining chopped tomatoes. Serve immediately.

Lemon Broiled Red Snapper

4 Red Snapper fillets, about 8 oz. each

¼ cup olive oil

salt and freshly ground black pepper to taste

⅓ cup freshly squeezed lemon juice

1 clove garlic, crushed

½ tablespoon tiny capers, drained

½ teaspoon finely grated lemon zest

1 tablespoon chopped fresh basil

Preheat the broiler

Serves four

*L*ine a baking sheet with aluminum foil. Brush the Red Snapper lightly with 1 tablespoon olive oil, and sprinkle them with salt and pepper. Place the fish on a baking sheet and broil 8 to 10 minutes. Combine the remaining olive oil, lemon juice, garlic, capers, and lemon zest in a sauce pan. Cook over low heat, for 3 minutes, salt and pepper to taste. Add the chopped basil, serve the fish on a platter, and spoon the sauce over it. Serve immediately.

Red Snapper Au Gratin

6 Red Snapper fillets, about 8 oz. each

juice of one lemon

salt and pepper to taste

2 tablespoons chopped fresh parsley

1   14 oz. can artichoke hearts, drained and crushed

1 pint mayonnaise (see Index)

2   4 oz. packages grated Mozzarela cheese

3 tablespoons grated Parmesan cheese

Preheat oven to 350° F.

Serves six

*W*ash and dry fillets. Place fillets in a baking dish. Squeeze lemon juice over fish. Add salt and pepper to taste and parsley. Top the fish with artichokes, mayonnaise, Mozzarela, and Parmesan cheese. Bake 30-45 minutes. Serve immediately.

Broiled Salmon with Red Pepper Salsa

Red Pepper Salsa (see below)

4 Salmon fillets, 4 oz. each

cooking spray

Garnish: zest of 1 lemon, sprigs of fresh cilantro

Preheat the broiler

Serves four

*P*repare the Red Pepper Salsa as directed. Place the fish in a shallow heat resistant dish or pan. Spray the rack of the pan with cooking spray and broil the fish for about 7 to 10 minutes, turning once. The fish should spring back when touched. When ready to serve, place the fish on a heated platter or dinner plate and spoon 2 tablespoons of salsa across the top of each fish steak. Garnish with lemon zest and sprigs of fresh cilantro.

Red Pepper Salsa

1 medium red bell pepper, roasted

2 teaspoons fresh oregano, finely chopped

2 tablespoons red wine vinegar

½ cup tomato concasse (see Index)

½ jalapeno pepper, seeded and minced

¼ cup red onion, finely chopped

1 clove garlic, minced

*P*repare the peppers as directed. Soak oregano in red wine vinegar in a small nonreactive bowl for about 10 minutes. Dice ½ inch red bell pepper strips and mix thoroughly with jalapeno pepper, tomato concasse, red onion, garlic, oregano, and red wine vinegar in nonreactive container and set aside.

Marinated Salmon Steaks

4 8 oz. Salmon steaks
1 tablespoon red wine vinegar
¼ cup water
¼ cup freshly squeezed lime juice
¼ cup freshly squeezed lemon juice
1 tablespoon Worcestershire sauce
4 cloves sliced garlic
½ cup olive oil
¼ cup cilantro, finely chopped
salt and freshly ground black pepper to taste

Preheat the broiler

Serves four

*I*n a bowl, combine all ingredients except the olive oil, cilantro, salt and pepper. Gradually, whisk in the olive oil, stir in the cilantro with the salt and pepper. Place the Salmon steaks in a glass baking dish. Pour the mixture over the Salmon and marinate for 60 minutes. Broil the Salmon for 6 minutes on each side until cooked through. Serve with 1 tablespoon of marinade over each Salmon steak. Serve immediately.

Grilled Salmon Pacifica

4 Salmon fillets, 4 to 6 oz. each

3 tablespoons chopped fresh dill

4 tablespoons capers, finely chopped

2 cups hollandaise sauce (see Index)

salt and black pepper

steamed or sautéed mixed fresh vegetables for garnish

Preheat a grill or broiler

Serves four

Season the Salmon fillets on both sides with salt and pepper. Grill or broil the Salmon until flaky and cooked through, about 6 minutes per side. Transfer the Salmon to heated serving plates.

Fold the dill and capers into the hollandaise sauce, then spoon about ½ cup of the mixture over the Salmon fillets. Garnish the plates with cooked fresh vegetables and serve.

Trout Amandine

4 Trout fillets, 6 to 8 oz. each (Red Snapper, Halibut, Drum or Redfish can be substituted)
1 large egg
¼ cup milk
stone ground whole wheat flour for dredging
1 cup almonds, finely chopped
½ cup (1 stick) plus 2 tablespoons butter or margarine
juice of 2 lemons
3 tablespoons Worcestershire sauce
1 tablespoon chopped fresh parsley
salt and black pepper
Grilled Tomatoes (see Index)

Serves four

Season the trout fillets on both sides with salt and pepper. In a shallow bowl or pan, beat the egg with the milk. Dredge the fish in the flour, then dip in the egg wash. Coat each fillet with chopped almonds.

Melt ½ cup butter or margarine in a large skillet and cook the fish about 4 minutes per side over medium heat until golden brown. Transfer the fillets to a platter and place in a warm oven while preparing the sauce.

To the skillet, add the lemon juice, Worcestershire, parsley, and remaining 2 tablespoons butter or margarine. Warm the sauce over low heat and pour over the trout. Serve with a grilled tomato.

Trout Nancy

8 Trout fillets, 6 to 8 oz. each (Red Snapper, Halibut, Drum or Redfish can be substituted)

stone ground whole wheat flour for dredging

¼ cup (½ stick) butter or margarine

1½ lbs. lump crabmeat, picked over to remove any shell or cartilage

½ cup capers

1½ cups creamy lemon butter sauce (see Index)

salt and black pepper

Serves eight

Season the Trout fillets on both sides with salt and pepper, then dredge in flour. Melt the butter or margarine in a large sauté pan and cook the fish over medium heat until flaky, about 4 minutes per side. Remove the fish from the pan and place in a warm oven until serving.

Cook the crabmeat and capers briefly in the pan drippings until hot.

Place a Trout fillet on 8 plates and top with the crabmeat and capers. Spoon creamy lemon butter sauce over the fish and serve.

Trout Meunière

4 Trout fillets, 6 to 8 oz. each (Red Snapper, Halibut, Drum or Redfish can be substituted.)

stone ground whole wheat flour for dredging

6 tablespoons butter or margarine

1 cup creamy lemon butter sauce (see Index)

salt and black pepper

Grilled Tomatoes (see Index)

Serves four

Season the Trout fillets on both sides with salt and pepper, then dredge in flour.

Melt the butter or margarine in a large skillet and sauté the fish until flaky, about 4 minutes per side.

Place a Trout fillet on each plate and top with creamy lemon butter sauce.

Serve with a grilled tomato.

Créole Seafood Jambalaya

⅓ cup butter or margarine

½ cup chopped scallions

⅓ cup chopped green pepper

½ cup chopped celery

1 tablespoon garlic, minced

8 oz. medium raw shrimp, peeled and deveined

24 shucked oysters

2 cups fresh or canned tomatoes

1 cup water

1 bay leaf

½ teaspoon salt

¼ teaspoon cayenne pepper

1 cup raw brown rice, rinsed

Serves four

Melt the butter or margarine in a large saucepan or Dutch oven, and add the scallions, pepper, celery, and garlic. Sauté the vegetables until tender, then add the shrimp and oysters. Cook the mixture another 5 minutes, then add the remaining ingredients, except the rice. Reduce the heat and simmer for 10 to 15 minutes. Stir in the rice and cover the pan. Cook the jambalaya for 45 minutes to an hour until rice is tender.

Stuffed Eggplant Dauphine

2 eggplants, about 1 lb. each
2 tablespoons olive oil
1 shallot, finely chopped
4 small tomatoes, peeled, seeded and diced
1 teaspoon fresh oregano leaves, finely chopped
1¼ teaspoons fresh basil leaves, finely chopped
1¼ teaspoons fresh thyme leaves, finely chopped
1½ cups chicken stock or broth (see Index)
1 bay leaf
1 lb. lump crabmeat, picked over to remove any shell and cartilage
1 teaspoon garlic, minced
4 oz. (½ cup) peeled and deveined raw medium shrimp, diced
2 tablespoons chopped fresh parsley
1¼ cups seasoned bread crumbs (see Index)
½ cup freshly grated Parmesan cheese

Serves four

Split the eggplants in half lengthwise and scoop out the pulp, being careful not to tear the skin. Chop the eggplant pulp and set it aside. Heat the olive oil in a large saucepan or Dutch oven and sauté the shallot until tender. Add the tomatoes, oregano, basil, thyme, and eggplant pulp and stir until well combined. Place the remaining ingredients, through the parsley, in the pan, and mix well. Fold in 1 cup of the bread crumbs and cook the stuffing for 3 to 5 minutes over medium heat; remove the bay leaf. Preheat oven to 375° F. Fill the eggplant shells with the stuffing and sprinkle with the remaining bread crumbs and the Parmesan cheese. Place the eggplants on a lightly oiled baking sheet and bake in the hot oven for 20 to 25 minutes until hot.

Bertha's Red Beans and Rice

2 lbs. dried Red or Kidney beans (may use Butter, Lima, Navy, or White beans)

5 quarts water

⅓ cup olive oil

6 stalks celery, finely chopped

2 large onions, finely chopped

2 medium green peppers, finely chopped

2 tablespoons garlic, minced

4 tablespoons margarine or butter

1 tablespoon salt

2 tablespoons garlic powder

black or crushed red pepper to taste

sausage or ham, cut into 1 inch pieces

Serves eight to ten

Rinse beans in a colander 3 or 4 times. Sauté chopped seasoning in olive oil until soft. Add rinsed beans to water. Bring to a boil and cook for 15 to 20 minutes. Reduce to low-medium heat and cook until beans are soft, about 3 hours. Add the margarine or butter and cook until the beans reach a creamy consistency, about 30 to 45 minutes. Brown ham or sausage, in a skillet and add to beans. Pepper to taste. Serve immediately over cooked brown rice.

Chicken and Artichoke Rice Casserole

2 whole or 4 split chicken breasts

2 oz. lemon juice

salt and pepper to taste

4 oz. olive oil

Rice

1 cup cooked brown rice (see Index)

2 boxes frozen artichoke hearts, defrosted and drained

4 oz. olive oil

1 medium chopped onion

2 teaspoons garlic, minced

1 oz. fresh lemon juice

salt and pepper to taste

Serves eight

Pound chicken breasts until flat and marinate for 1 hour in lemon juice. Drain off lemon juice, cut into bite size pieces and season with salt and pepper. Sauté chicken pieces in olive oil until cooked through. Defrost, drain, and quarter artichoke hearts. Discard olive oil used for frying the chicken. Add fresh olive oil to pan, add onions, and cook until limp. Add garlic and sauté in oil. Add artichokes and lemon juice and sauté until artichokes are heated through. Stir in cooked rice and chicken. This recipe can be prepared without the chicken as a delicious side dish.

Chicken & Sausage Jambalaya

⅓ cup butter or margarine
½ cup chopped onion
½ cup chopped green pepper
½ cup chopped celery
1 tablespoon garlic, minced
½ cup chopped scallions
1½ cups diced uncooked chicken
1½ cups sliced andouille or other spicy smoked sausage
2 cups fresh or canned whole tomatoes
½ cup tomato paste
1 cup chicken broth or stock (see Index)
1 bay leaf
½ teaspoon salt
¼ teaspoon cayenne pepper
1 cup raw brown rice, rinsed

Preheat oven to 350° F.

Serves four

*M*elt the butter or margarine in a large ovenproof saucepan or Dutch oven. Add the onion, pepper, celery, and garlic and cook over moderately high heat until tender. Stir in the scallions, chicken, and sausage. Sauté the mixture an additional 5 minutes, then add the remaining ingredients, except the rice. Reduce the heat to low and simmer for 10 to 15 minutes. Stir in the rice, cover the pan, then place in the hot oven until the rice is tender, about 1 hour; stir the mixture occasionally during cooking. Alternatively, the jambalaya may be simmered on the stove top, covered, for 30 to 40 minutes. Fluff the cooked jambalaya with a fork, remove the bay leaf, then serve.

Chicken and Bean Chili

1 lb. dried great Northern beans

1   10 oz. can diced tomatoes and green chilies, drained

1 large chopped onion

1 teaspoon garlic, minced

1 tablespoon jalapeno pepper, finely chopped

1 tablespoon dried oregano

Dash of cayenne pepper

2 teaspoons ground cumin

 2 chopped green peppers

5 cups chicken broth or stock (see Index)

1 tablespoon chili powder

⅛ cup lime juice

3 cups cooked chicken breast, skinned and diced

½ cup fresh cilantro, finely chopped

⅓ cup grated sharp Cheddar cheese

Serves eight

Soak beans over night. Place beans in a large pot and cover in water. Add the onion, garlic, jalapeno pepper, oregano, cayenne, cumin, green pepper, chili powder, and chicken broth or stock. Bring to a boil. Reduce the heat and simmer, covered, for 1½ hours. Add the tomatoes and chilies, lime juice, and chicken. Continue cooking, covered, over low heat for about 30 minutes. Serve with chopped cilantro and Cheddar cheese.

Chicken Kalamata

1 fryer cut up

salt and pepper

2 tablespoons cooking oil

2 cups red or green bell peppers, diced

2 cups onion, coarsely chopped

2 cloves garlic, minced

¼ lb. smoked ham, cubed

3½ cups tomatoes and liquid

¾ cup Parmesan cheese

¼ cup stone ground whole wheat flour

4 tablespoons butter or margarine

20 sliced black olives

¾ cup red wine

Serves four

Season chicken with salt and pepper, brown in oil in 10 inch skillet, and remove. Add onions, garlic, pepper, and ham, cook until tender. Add tomatoes, ½ cup cheese, and chicken. Cover and simmer 25 to 30 minutes or until tender, adding water as needed. Remove chicken to serving dish. Keep warm. Add combined flour and butter or margarine, cook, stirring constantly, until thickened. Add olives and red wine, simmer for a few minutes, and pour sauce over chicken. Season to taste with salt and pepper. Sprinkle with remaining cheese. Serve with brown rice or whole grain pasta.

Baked Chicken Supreme

1	3 lb. chicken, cut into 8 pieces

1 teaspoon salt

1 teaspoon black pepper

1 cup chicken broth or stock (see Index)

2 tablespoons olive oil

1 tablespoon lemon juice

1 tablespoon soy sauce

1 tablespoon Italian seasoning

1 teaspoon paprika

1 teaspoon garlic powder

½ teaspoon onion powder

½ teaspoon dry mustard

¼ teaspoon ground ginger

Preheat the oven to 350° F.

Serves four

*P*lace the chicken in a baking dish and season with salt and pepper. In a bowl, combine the remaining ingredients; pour over the chicken, coating well. Bake for 1¼ hours, and baste occasionally. Serve immediately.

Rosemary Chicken

1   4lb. chicken, quartered

6 teaspoons garlic, minced

2 tablespoons fresh rosemary

½ cup freshly squeezed lime juice

½ cup olive oil

½ teaspoon salt

¼ teaspoon freshly ground black pepper

Serves four

*I*n a bowl, combine all the ingredients. Place the chicken in the bowl and coat with the marinade. Refrigerate for 3–4 hours. Heat a large skillet and fry the chicken pieces, covered, for 15 minutes on each side until crispy. Serve immediately.

Chicken with Fresh Mint

4 skinless, boneless, chicken breast halves

2 tablespoons cooking oil

1 tablespoon freshly ground black pepper

2 tablespoons salt

4 cloves garlic, crushed

2 teaspoons dried oregano

2 tablespoons olive oil

3 tablespoons fresh mint leaves, coarsely chopped

4 tablespoons fresh lime juice

Serves four

*I*n a bowl, mash together the pepper, salt, garlic, oregano, olive oil, mint leaves and 1 tablespoon lime juice until it forms a paste. Rub ¼ of the paste over both sides of each chicken breast. Heat the cooking oil in a large pan over medium-high heat. Add the chicken breasts to the pan, turning the chicken alternately, until cooked through. Baste the chicken with the paste continuously until done. Serve immediately.

Southern Fried Chicken

1 whole chicken, cut into pieces

¾ cup stone ground whole wheat flour

1 teaspoon salt

¼ teaspoon black pepper

cooking oil

Serves six

*S*prinkle chicken pieces with salt and pepper on both sides. Combine the flour, salt, and pepper in a plastic bag or container. Shake each piece 1 at a time inside the bag or container. Be sure to coat all of the chicken with the flour mixture. Fill ¾ of a heavy skillet with cooking oil over moderate to high heat. Fry in the cooking oil for about 20 minutes, total cooking time, turning pieces occasionally. Drain on paper towel. Serve immediately.

Poulet Brennan

2 chickens, 2¼ to 2½ lbs. each
3 cups Oyster Dressing (see Index)
Melted butter or margarine for brushing
salt and black pepper
2 cups marchand de vin sauce (see Index)
Sweet Potatoes (see Index)
Preheat oven to 375° F.

Serves four

*P*lace the chickens, breast side down, on a cutting board. Make an incision along the spine and split the chickens open. Using a small, sharp knife, bone the breasts and lower portion of the leg, being careful not to pierce the skin as you cut flesh from bone. Rinse the partially boned chickens and pat them dry.

Season the meat inside and out with salt and pepper. Spoon oyster dressing into the cavity of both chickens, then close the birds and truss with string. Brush the chickens with butter or margarine and place on a rack in a large roasting pan. Roast in the hot oven for 45 minutes.

Remove the string from the roasted chickens and slice them in half lengthwise. Place one half of a chicken on each plate, top with marchand de vin sauce and serve with sweet potatoes on the side.

Chicken Au Poivre

8 pieces chicken breast

½ cup cracked black peppercorns

2 cups (4 sticks) butter or margarine

1 teaspoon salt

1 tablespoon lemon juice

3 tablespoons parsley, finely chopped

Prepare the broiler

Serves eight

*P*ound the cracked peppercorns into both sides of the pieces of chicken. Melt the butter or margarine in a saucepan, then add the salt, lemon juice, and parsley. Brush a broiling rack or baking sheet with some of the butter sauce. Place the chicken breasts bottom side up on the rack. Baste with some of the butter or margarine sauce and set to broil, about 5 inches from the heat, for 15 minutes. Remove the pan from the broiler, turn the chicken breasts over, and baste with a bit more butter sauce. Return the pan to the broiler and broil for about 12 minutes. To serve, place the chicken on preheated plates, then spoon the pan drippings from the broiling pan over them. Top with the remaining butter or margarine sauce.

Chicken with Fresh Mushrooms

1 lb. chicken breasts, skinned and boned

1 tablespoon stone ground whole wheat flour

⅛ teaspoon salt

Pinch of black pepper

1 tablespoon cooking oil

1 tablespoon butter or margarine

½ lb. sliced fresh mushrooms

¼ cup dry white wine

¼ cup chicken broth or stock (see Index)

¼ teaspoon dry rosemary

¼ teaspoon dry thyme

¼ teaspoon dry tarragon

¼ teaspoon marjoram

½ teaspoon garlic powder

Serves four

Pound the chicken to a ½ inch thickness. In a shallow dish, combine the flour, salt, and pepper. Coat the chicken with the flour mixture. Heat the oil and butter or margarine in a large skillet on medium heat. Add the chicken and cook for 4 minutes on each side. Remove the chicken and keep warm. In the same skillet, add the remaining ingredients and cook for 4 minutes. Pour the sauce on top of the chicken and serve.

Chicken Cacciatore

1	3lb. chicken, cut into 8 pieces
1	28 oz. can whole tomatoes
1 medium sliced onion	
¼ cup cooking oil	
½ cup fresh parsley, finely chopped	
1 teaspoon dried basil	
1 teaspoon salt	
1 teaspoon dried rosemary	
1 teaspoon dried oregano	
1 garlic clove, minced	
¼ teaspoon black pepper	
⅛ teaspoon crushed red pepper	
1 cup sliced fresh mushrooms	

Serves four

Heat the oil in a large skillet; add the chicken and brown. Remove the chicken and set aside. Add the onion to the drippings and cook until tender. Drain the excess oil and add remaining ingredients. Put the chicken back in the skillet. Do not cover skillet. Simmer the chicken for 40–45 minutes, turn the chicken every so often. Serve immediately.

Chicken Lazone

1 teaspoon salt

1½ teaspoons chili powder

1½ teaspoons onion powder

2 teaspoons garlic powder

4 whole boneless, skinless chicken breasts

¼ cup (½ stick) butter or margarine

½ cup heavy cream

Serves four

*I*n a small bowl, combine the salt, chili powder, onion powder, and garlic powder. Coat the chicken breasts with the seasoning mixture.

Melt 2 tablespoons of the butter or margarine in a large sauté pan, then cook the chicken breasts over medium heat about 7 to 8 minutes, turning them once. Pour the cream into the pan and lower the heat. Simmer for several minutes, stirring, until the sauce thickens, then fold in the remaining 2 tablespoons butter or margarine. When the butter or margarine is melted, transfer the chicken breasts to 4 plates and top with the sauce.

Buttermilk Chicken

1 cup buttermilk

½ cup onion, finely chopped

1 tablespoon paprika

1 teaspoon dried tarrragon

1½ teaspoons garlic powder

1 teaspoon celery powder

½ teaspoon freshly ground black pepper

1 lb. chicken parts

Preheat oven to 350° F.

Serves six

*C*ombine all ingredients, except chicken, until well blended. Place the chicken in a baking pan and coat both sides with the seasoned mixture. Bake for 1 hour, turning twice. Serve immediately.

Citrus Chicken

4 whole chicken breasts, skinned and boned

Preheat a broiler

Serves four

Sauce:

¼ cup butter or margarine

juice of one lemon

¾ teaspoon salt

½ teaspoon paprika

½ teaspoon dried oregano

¼ teaspoon garlic powder

¼ teaspoon black pepper

*I*n a large skillet, mix together sauce ingredients; cook over low heat until butter or margarine has melted. Place chicken breasts in a baking dish. Pour sauce over chicken. Broil until done, about 45 minutes, turning chicken occasionally to coat well with sauce. Serve over brown rice or whole grain pasta.

Chicken with Dijon Mustard

16 pieces of chicken, boned

2 cups of milk, with one teaspoon salt added

2 tablespoons Worcestershire sauce

1½ cups sour cream

1 cup Dijon mustard

3 teaspoons paprika

2 teaspoons celery salt

3 teaspoons lemon juice

3 cloves garlic, minced

black pepper

1 cup bread crumbs (see Index)

Preheat oven to 400° F.

Serves six

In a bowl, mix the 2 cups milk with 1 teaspoon of salt. Put the chicken breasts in the milk solution, marinate for about 45 minutes to an hour. In another bowl add all remaining ingredients except the bread crumbs and pepper. Pat dry the chicken with paper towels and sprinkle with pepper. Smother the chicken pieces with the mixture and sprinkle with bread crumbs. Place the chicken on a greased rack in a 1½ inch baking pan. Bake for 15 minutes. Then lower oven temperature to 350° F. Continue baking for 30 minutes and serve immediately.

Chicken with Fresh Chives

8 skinless, boneless chicken breast halves, cut into bite-size pieces

3 large tomatoes, roughly chopped, with seeds and juices reserved

3 tablespoons cooking oil

1 chopped medium onion

4 cloves garlic, minced

2 tablespoons chopped fresh rosemary

1 lb. sliced fresh mushrooms

1 cup dry white wine

⅔ cup heavy cream

6 tablespoons chopped fresh chives

salt and pepper to taste

Serves eight

*W*arm the oil in a large pan over medium heat. Add the onion and garlic and sauté for 1 minute. Add the chicken and rosemary and stir fry for 3 minutes until the chicken is brown on all sides. Remove the chicken and set aside. To the sauté pan add the mushrooms, tomatoes, and white wine and cook 5 minutes until slightly tender. Add the cream and chives and stir. Return the chicken to the pan and bring the mixture almost to a boil. Simmer for 10 minutes until the chicken is cooked through. Add salt and pepper to taste. Serve immediately.

Stewed Chicken

1 3½ lb. chicken, cut into 12 pieces
2 cups fresh mushrooms
¼ cup cooking oil
1 cup heavy cream
1 tablespoon fresh thyme
2 cups pearl onions
2 tablespoons unsalted butter or margarine
salt and freshly ground black pepper to taste

Serves four

Season the chicken with the salt and pepper. Warm the oil in a large sauté pan over medium-high heat. Add half the chicken pieces, skin side down, and reduce the heat to medium. Cook the chicken, turning frequently, until almost cooked through to a golden brown, about 15 minutes. Drain the chicken on paper towels. Cook the remaining chicken in the remaining oil. Remove and drain the chicken. Add the mushrooms to the remaining oil in the pan and cook, stirring frequently for 5 minutes. Add the cream and thyme and stir well. Return the chicken to the pan, cover, and simmer until cooked through. In another small sauce pan over medium-high heat add the onions and the butter or margarine, with just enough water to cover them. Cover and cook until the onions are tender. Add the onions to the chicken and mushroom cream mixture. Serve immediately.

Chicken Florentine

¼ cup (½ stick) butter or margarine

4 whole boneless, skinless chicken breasts

2 tablespoons stone ground whole wheat flour

1 cup scalded milk

2 tablespoons freshly grated Parmesan cheese

4 cups Creamed Spinach (see Index)

1 teaspoon paprika

salt and white pepper

Serves four

Melt the butter or margarine in a large skillet, and cook the chicken breasts over moderately high heat until cooked through, about 4 to 5 minutes per side. Remove the chicken from the pan and slice the breast in half. Set the chicken aside while preparing the sauce.

Over medium heat, whisk the flour into the pan drippings. Gradually, incorporate the milk into the flour, stirring constantly until smooth and thick enough to coat the back of a wooden spoon. Add the Parmesan cheese and season to taste with salt and pepper. Reduce the heat and simmer the sauce another 2 minutes. Adjust the consistency with additional milk if the sauce seems too thick.

Cover the bottoms of 4 ovenproof serving plates with creamed spinach. Top the spinach with the chicken, then pour cream sauce over the breasts.

Chicken and Pasta Casserole

3 whole or 6 split skinless boneless chicken breasts

salt, pepper, and garlic powder to taste

12 oz. whole grain pasta

2 cups chicken broth or stock (see Index)

¼ cup plus ¼ cup olive oil

1 medium chopped onion

¾ lb. fresh sliced mushrooms

1 tablespoon chopped garlic

2 cups shredded Colby and Monterey Jack cheese

Preheat oven to 350° F.

Serves six

*P*repare pasta according to package directions. While pasta is boiling, pound chicken breasts flat. Season chicken breasts to taste. Drain pasta and place in a large greased casserole pan. Sauté onions, mushrooms, and garlic in ¼ cup oil. Remove with slotted spoon and mix with pasta. Add chicken broth or stock and 1½ cups cheese to pasta and stir. Add additional ¼ cup olive oil to pan and brown chicken breasts on both sides. Place chicken breasts on top of pasta mixture and top each breast with rest of cheese. Cover and bake in oven for 30 minutes.

Roast Pork

1 boneless 2½ lb. pork loin roast
½ teaspoon salt
¾ teaspoon dried oregano
¾ teaspoon dried thyme
¼ teaspoon freshly ground black pepper
3 dashes Tabasco®
3 cloves garlic, cut into slivers
3 tablespoons Dijon mustard
1 tablespoon olive oil
Preheat the oven to 375° F.

Serves four

*C*ut small slits in the roast. In a small bowl mix together the salt, oregano, thyme, and pepper. Coat the garlic slivers with the spice mixture. Insert the garlic slivers into the slits in the roast and rub the remaining mixture over the top of the meat. Combine the mustard, Tabasco®, and oil and baste the meat with half of the mixture. Place the meat in a roasting pan on a rack. Roast, uncovered for 1 hour. Baste roast with the remaining mustard mixture. Roast 1 hour more. Serve immediately.

Breaded Pork Chops

4 center cut pork chops
2 cups bread crumbs (see Index)
2 eggs, beaten
salt, pepper, and garlic powder to taste
3 tablespoons cooking oil

Serves four

*S*eason pork chops with salt, pepper, and garlic powder. Place in bread crumbs and coat well on both sides; dip in eggs and place back in bread crumbs, coating well on both sides once again. Heat oil in frying pan and cook pork chops over medium heat until brown on the outside and cooked internally.

Pork Chop and Rice Casserole

4 center cut pork chops

1 cup brown rice

4 sliced green onions

½ lb. sliced fresh mushrooms

1 tablespoon garlic, minced

4 oz. butter or margarine

1 sliced tomato

1 sliced onion

1 green pepper, sliced in rings

1½ cups beef broth or stock (see Index)

Preheat oven to 375° F.

Serves four

Spray a 9" x 13" casserole pan with cooking spray. Put raw rice in casserole pan. Melt butter or margarine and sauté mushrooms, green onions, and garlic in a frying pan. Mix with the rice. Brown pork chops on both sides and place on top of rice mixture. Place a slice of tomato, onion and green pepper on each pork chop. Pour beef broth or stock over the casserole. Cover with foil and bake in the oven for 1 hour.

Sautéed Lamb Chops

8 loin lamp chops, ½ inch thick, well trimmed
1 egg, slightly beatened
1 teaspoon salt
2 teaspoons garlic, minced
¾ teaspoon black pepper
2 teaspoons fresh parsley, finely chopped
½ teaspoon dried rosemary
½ teaspoon dried thyme
4 tablespoons butter or margarine
1 tablespoon Worcestershire sauce
¾ cup heavy cream
¼ teaspoon sage

Serves four

*I*n a bowl, mix all ingredients except for the lamb, cream, and sage. Mix well. Coat both sides of lamb chops. Cover and let sit for 1 hour. Melt the butter or margarine in a large skillet and cook the lamb chops for 8 minutes on each side. Place chops on a warmed plate. Add cream and sage to the skillet and cook until the sauce thickens, stirring constantly. Pour over lamp chops and serve immediately.

Broiled Lamp Chops

8 rib lamp chops, cut 1 inch thick

Serves four

Marinade:

¼ cup olive oil

3 tablespoons Dijon mustard

2 tablespoons freshly squeezed lemon juice

2 tablespoons Worcestershire sauce

1 tablespoon garlic, minced

2 teaspoons Tabasco®

½ teaspoon paprika

salt to taste

Preheat a broiler

*C*ombine all marinade ingredients. Coat the lamb chops well with the marinade. Refrigerate for at least 6 hours, and turn the chops every couple of hours. Broil the lamb chops and baste with the marinade. Broil 6 to 7 minutes per side for medium doneness. Serve immediately.

Lamb Chops Mirabeau

8 lamb chops

4 oz. (½ cup) tomato sauce

1 cup béarnaise sauce (see Index)

8 strips of crisp cooked bacon

salt and black pepper

Preheat a grill or broiler.

Serves four

*S*prinkle the lamb with salt and pepper, then grill or broil the chops until done to preference.

Heat the tomato sauce gently and spoon 2 tablespoons of warm tomato sauce onto 4 plates. Crisscross 2 lamb chops in the center of each plate, then cover the eye of the chops with béarnaise sauce. Surround the lamb chops with the bacon strips and serve.

Baby Rack of Lamb Bouquetière

4 racks of lamb, about 1 lb. each

½ teaspoon salt

½ teaspoon black pepper

½ cup garlic butter (see Index)

½ cup bread crumbs (see Index)

1 cup béarnaise or marchand de vin sauce (see Index)

Any combination of steamed cauliflower, broccoli,
asparagus or grilled tomatoes for garnish

Preheat a broiler.

Serves four

Season the racks with salt and pepper and place on a baking sheet. Broil the lamb for 5 to 7 minutes until browned.

Preheat oven to 375° F.

Spread garlic butter on the racks and sprinkle with bread crumbs. Roast the lamb in the hot oven about 45 minutes until done to preference. Remove the racks from the oven and cut between the bones into chops.

Place the chops on a serving platter and top with either béarnaise or marchand de vin sauce. Arrange the cooked vegetables around the lamb and serve.

Tenderloin of Lamb

1	5lb. loin of lamb

salt and freshly ground black pepper to taste

2 tablespoons cooking oil

2 tablespoons fresh rosemary

1 tablespoon chopped parsley

1 clove garlic, minced

zest of one lemon

¼ cup of butter or margarine

Preheat the oven to 375° F.

Serves six

Sprinkle the lamb with salt and pepper. Warm the cooking oil in a frying pan over medium heat. Place the lamb in the pan and brown each side for 1 minute. Season with rosemary and put in oven for 45 minutes–1 hour. In a small bowl, mix together the parlsey, garlic, and lemon zest. Remove the lamb from the oven, place it on a serving plate and coat the lamb with the parsley mixture. Place the pan that the lamb was roasted in on top of the range at a medium heat. Put the butter or margarine in the pan and scrape the pan drippings into the melting butter or margarine to make a sauce. Pour the sauce over the lamb and serve immediately.

Veal Escalopes With Lemon

1½ lbs. veal escalopes, pounded

freshly ground black pepper

Salt

3 tablespoons olive oil

2 tablespoons butter or margarine

¾ cup beef broth or stock (see Index)

1 tablespoon butter or margarine

¼ cup lemon juice

2 tablespoons stone ground whole wheat flour

Serves four

Season veal escalopes with salt and pepper, lightly coat with flour and shake off excess flour. In a heavy skillet heat 2 tablespoons butter or margarine and 3 tablespoons olive oil and add veal, 4 to 5 at a time and sauté them for about 2 minutes on each side or until golden brown. Transfer the veal to a plate. Add ½ cup beef broth or stock to skillet and boil it briskly for 1 or 2 minutes, stirring constantly and scraping in any brown bits clinging to the bottom of pan. Add veal; cover the skillet and simmer over low heat for 10 to 15 minutes, or until veal is tender.

To serve, transfer escalopes to a heated platter. Add ¼ cup of remaining beef broth or stock to juices in skillet, heat and add a small amount of flour to thicken, if desired. Add lemon juice and cook, stirring for 1 minute. Remove pan from heat, swirl in 2 tablespoons soft butter or margarine and pour sauce over escalopes. Decorate with lemon slices.

Veal with Morel Mushrooms

1 cup red wine
2 cups water
24 Morel mushrooms
¾ cup (1½ sticks) butter or margarine
1 cup onion, finely chopped
½ cup stone ground whole wheat flour, plus extra for dusting
1 quart chicken broth or stock (see Index)
½ cup heavy cream
8 veal escalopes, 4 to 6 oz. each, lightly pounded (see note below)
salt and white pepper

Serves four

*I*n a stainless steel or glass bowl, combine ½ cup of the red wine with 2 cups water. Place the mushrooms in the liquid and marinate at room temperature for 15 minutes. Strain off the marinade. Drain the mushrooms, then quarter or halve each cap, depending on its size. Melt ¼ cup of the butter or margarine in a medium skillet and sauté the onion until tender, about 5 minutes. Reduce the heat to medium and blend in the flour. Cook for 2 to 3 minutes, then pour in the chicken broth or stock. Whisk the mixture until smooth and cook for 15 minutes over low heat, stirring frequently. Stir in the cream, the remaining ½ cup of red wine and the mushrooms. Reduce the sauce until thickened, then adjust the seasoning with salt and white pepper.

While the sauce is reducing, season the veal escalopes on both sides with salt and pepper, then dust with flour. Melt the remaining ½ cup butter or margarine in a large sauté pan and cook the veal over moderately high heat about 3 minutes per side. Serve the veal on warm plates topped with red wine mushroom cream sauce.

Note: Chicken breasts can be substituted for the veal.

Veal Kottwitz

6 veal escalopes, 4 to 6 oz. each, lightly pounded (see note below)

6 tablespoons butter or margarine

28 oz. sliced artichoke bottoms

1 lb. sliced fresh mushrooms

2 tablespoons dry white wine

1 cup creamy lemon butter sauce (see Index)

salt and black pepper

Serves six

Season the veal with salt and pepper. Melt the butter or margarine in a large sauté pan and cook the escalopes over moderately high heat about 3 minutes per side. Remove the veal from the pan and place in a warm oven until serving.

Combine the sliced artichoke bottoms and mushrooms in the sauté pan. Add the wine, then cook the mixture for 5 minutes over medium heat. Blend in the creamy lemon butter sauce and warm gently.

Serve the veal topped with the artichoke-mushroom mixture.

Note: Four Trout fillets, Halibut, Red Snapper, Drum or Redfish, 4 to 6 ounces each, can be substituted for the veal escalopes.

Oven Baked Veal Chops

4 white veal chops, about 16 oz. each

2 medium tomatoes, peeled, seeded, and chopped

½ cup dry white wine

¼ cup green pepper, finely chopped

¼ cup onion, finely chopped

1 tablespoon garlic, minced

1 tablespoon parsley, finely chopped

1 tablespoon dried tarragon

3 dashes Tabasco®

salt and pepper to taste

Preheat broiler

Serves four

Salt and pepper the veal chops. Broil under high heat on both sides until brown. In a pan, sauté tomatoes, wine, Tabasco®, green pepper, onion, garlic, parsley, and tarragon and simmer for 5 minutes. Preheat oven to 350° F. Cover veal chops with tomato mixture and bake in a casserole until the chops are cooked through. Serve immediately.

Breaded Veal

4 veal cutlets

2 cups bread crumbs (see Index)

2 eggs, beaten

salt, pepper, and garlic powder to taste

3 tablespoons cooking oil

Serves four

Pound veal cutlets and season veal with salt, pepper, and garlic powder. Cut into serving size pieces. Place in bread crumbs and coat well on both sides; dip in eggs and place back in bread crumbs, coating well on both sides once again. Heat oil in a frying pan and cook the veal cutlets over medium heat until brown on the outside and cooked internally.

Osso Bucco

4 thick veal shanks, 6 to 8 oz. each

stone ground whole wheat flour for dusting

1 cup cooking oil

1 cup chopped onion

3 garlic cloves, minced

1½ cups diced tomato

1 cup dry white wine

1 cup beef broth or stock (see Index)

¼ cup fresh parsley, finely chopped

Salt and black pepper

Preheat oven to 350° F.

Serves four

Sprinkle the veal shanks on both sides with salt and pepper, then dust with flour. Heat the oil until almost smoking in a Dutch oven or roasting pan. Sear the veal shanks on both sides until brown, then remove them from the pan and set aside.

Drain all but ¼ cup of the oil from the pan, then return the pan to medium heat. Add the onion, garlic, and tomato, and cook the mixture for 3 to 4 minutes; do not let the onions brown. Stir in the wine, broth or stock, and parsley, then season with salt and pepper to taste. Place the veal shanks on top of the vegetable mixture. Cover and roast in the hot oven for 1 hour, until the meat is tender.

Serve the veal shanks over whole grain pasta or brown rice, topped with the tomato mixture.

Veal Stew

3 lbs. boneless veal, cut into 1½ inch pieces

24 small peeled onions

4 tablespoons cooking oil

2 tablespoons stone ground whole wheat flour

3 cups beef broth or stock (see Index)

salt and pepper to taste

Serves four

D redge the meat lightly in stone ground whole wheat flour. Heat oil in a heavy skillet and add the meat and onions. Stir the ingredients and brown the meat on all sides. Set aside. Pour off all but 2 tablespoons of oil and stir in 2 tablespoons stone ground whole wheat flour until well blended. Stir in beef broth or stock until smooth. Add the meat and onions. Simmer covered 1½-2 hours until the meat is very tender. Season to taste.

Venison Chops

8 chops farm raised venison

3 tablespoons olive oil

1 clove garlic, minced

1 teaspoon ground cumin

1 tablespoon chili powder

salt and freshly ground black pepper to taste

Serves four

I n a bowl, combine 2 tablespoons of the olive oil with the garlic, cumin and chili powder. Coat the venison chops with the mixture. In a large skillet, heat the remaining olive oil over medium heat until hot. Salt and pepper the venison chops and lay them in the skillet. Cook 3 minutes on each side. Serve immediately

Hamburger Brennan

2 lbs. ground chuck

⅓ cup scallions, finely chopped

¼ cup onion, finely chopped

2 tablespoons Worcestershire sauce

1 tablespoon chopped fresh parsley

2 large eggs

Pinch of nutmeg

1½ teaspoons salt

½ teaspoon black pepper

1½ cups Sauce Maison (below)

Preheat a grill or broiler.

Serves six

*C*ombine all of the ingredients in a large bowl. When the mixture is well combined, shape into 6 oval patties. Grill or broil the patties until cooked according to your preference; reserve 1 cup cooking juices for preparation of the accompanying sauce. Drizzle Sauce Maison on each patty and serve.

Sauce Maison:

¾ cups (1½ sticks) butter or margarine

2 tablespoons Worcestershire sauce

1 cup meat juices (beef broth or stock, see Index, can be substituted)

1 teaspoon chopped fresh parsley

Yields 1½ cups

*I*n a small skillet, cook the butter or margarine over medium heat until golden brown. Stir in the Worcestershire and meat juices and cook for 1 minute. Add the parsley and keep the sauce warm until serving.

Louisiana Hamburgers

2 lbs. ground beef

3 teaspoons garlic, minced

1 green pepper, finely chopped

½ cup green onions, finely chopped

2 teaspoons ground cumin

2 teaspoons dried oregano

1 teaspoon dried thyme

2 teaspoons paprika

1 tablespoon Tabasco®

salt and black pepper to taste

Serves six

Combine all ingredients with the beef. Shape into 6 hamburger patties. Broil or fry the meat to desired doneness. Serve immediately.

Hamburgers Stuffed with Sharp Cheddar Cheese

4 lbs. ground beef

2 tablespoons Worcesterhsire sauce

6 tablespoons fresh chives, finely chopped

1 tablespoon fresh basil, finely chopped

2 teaspoons dried oregano

⅔ teaspoon chili powder

½ teaspoon salt

¾ teaspoon freshly ground black pepper

1 lb. sharp Cheddar cheese, crumbled

Serves eight

Mix all ingredients, except the Cheddar cheese and shape into 8 thick patties. Make a pocket in the center of each patty, fill with the Cheddar cheese, and cover the cheese with meat. Broil or fry the meat to desired doneness. Serve immediately.

Meat Loaf

2 lbs. ground beef

1 small chopped green pepper

1 medium chopped onion

2 chopped ribs celery

2 tablespoons garlic, minced

¼ cup parsley, finely chopped

1 large tomato, peeled, seeded, and chopped

1 cup bread crumbs (see Index)

salt, pepper, and Tabasco® to taste

Preheat oven to 500° F.

Serves eight

Sauce:

2 tablespoons butter or margarine

¼ lb. sliced fresh mushrooms

2 tablespoons onions, finely chopped

1 teaspoon garlic, minced

2 tablespoons stone ground whole wheat flour

1 cup beef broth or stock (see Index)

salt and pepper to taste

*M*ix all ingredients together blending well and form into the shape of a loaf. Spray a roasting pan with cooking spray. Place the meat loaf in a pan and bake for 1 hour and 15 minutes, adjusting the oven temperature to 350°F. Remove meat loaf from oven and sauté butter, mushrooms, onions, and garlic in a sauce pan until soft. Add flour gradually while stirring mixture and add broth or stock until sauce reaches a smooth consistency. Season to taste.

Maude's Spaghetti and Meatballs

2 lbs. ground veal round (Ground beef can be substituted)
2 medium onions, finely chopped
4 celery ribs, finely chopped
1 small green pepper, finely chopped
10 garlic cloves, minced
3 tablespoons freshly grated Parmesan cheese
3 large eggs, well beaten
1 cup Italian bread crumbs (see Index)
cooking oil for frying
4 sprigs fresh parsley, finely chopped
1 scallion, finely chopped
6 oz. (¾ cup) tomato paste
½ teaspoon granulated Sweet 'N Low®
16 oz. (2 cups) tomato sauce
2⅓ cups water
2 bay leaves
salt and black pepper
2 lbs. whole grain pasta
Freshly grated Romano cheese for garnish

Serves eight

*I*n a large bowl, combine the veal, ½ the onion, ½ the celery, ½ the green pepper, and 4 of the minced garlic cloves. Sprinkle in the Parmesan cheese, then add the eggs. Season with 2 teaspoons salt and at least ¾ teaspoon black pepper, then gently knead the mixture with your fingers, blending the ingredients thoroughly.

Spread the bread crumbs on a plate. Form about ¼ cup of the meat mixture into a ball, roll the ball in the bread crumbs, then set it on a clean tray or platter. Follow the same procedure with the remainder of the meat mixture.

Pour vegetable oil to a depth of ½ inch into a large, deep skillet. Heat the oil over moderately high heat to a temperature of about 340° F. Fry the meatballs, in batches, in the hot oil until brown on all sides. Remove the cooked meatballs from the pan with a slotted spoon and set aside. Reserve the pan drippings.

To make the tomato sauce, sauté the remaining onion, celery, green pepper, parsley, and scallions in the meatball pan drippings. Cook the vegetables a few minutes, then stir in the tomato paste. Simmer another 2 minutes, then add the Sweet 'N Low®, tomato sauce, 2⅓ cups water, and the bay leaves. Season the sauce with at least 1½ teaspoons salt and ¾ teaspoon pepper. When the ingredients are well combined, place the meatballs in the sauce and cook over low heat for about 1 hour; stir gently several times during cooking, being careful not to break apart the meatballs. Remove the bay leaves before serving.

Cook the pasta in boiling salted water until al dente. Drain the pasta and place a portion on each plate. Top the pasta with about ⅔ cup sauce and 2 meatballs. Garnish with freshly grated Romano cheese.

Lasagne

1 box whole grain lasagne noodles	
1 cup shredded Mozzarella cheese	
2 lbs. ground meat	
4 tomatoes skinned, cored, and chopped	
½ lb. fresh sliced mushrooms	
1 tablespoon garlic, minced	
2 chopped onions	
1 chopped rib celery	
½ chopped green pepper	
¼ cup chopped parsley	
1 teaspoon sweet basil	
1 bay leaf	
1 teaspoon oregano	
1 teaspoon rosemary	
1 teaspoon thyme	
3 tablespoons olive oil	
salt and pepper to taste	
1 cup water	

Prepare the broiler

Serves eight

To skin tomatoes, place tomatoes in a pot of boiling water for 30 seconds, or until skin starts to peel. Take out of pot and skin. Place meat in a roasting pan and run under broiler to brown. Continually turn meat with a spoon until the meat is no longer pink. While the meat is browning, chop onions, celery, and green pepper. Sauté vegetables in oil until translucent. Core tomatoes and chop in food processor. Put tomatoes in the pot with cooked vegetables; add garlic, and seasonings. Cook until bubbling. Add meat and water to the pot and bring to a boil. Turn down heat and simmer sauce for about 2 hours. Add salt and pepper. While sauce is simmering, make Bechamel Sauce.

Bechamel Sauce

Preheat oven to 350° F.

2 tablespoons butter or margarine

2 tablespoons stone ground whole wheat flour

1 cup milk

1 cup grated Mozzarella cheese

¼ teaspoon grated nutmeg

salt and pepper to taste

*M*elt butter or margarine. Add flour. Stir for a few minutes. Add milk and stir constantly over high heat. Sauce will thicken when it comes to a boil. Add Mozzarella cheese. Reduce heat and simmer for 2 more minutes. Add nutmeg, salt, and pepper.

Layer noodles alternately with meat sauce, Bechamel sauce, and mozzarella cheese. Sprinkle additional Mozzarella cheese over the top; cover and bake in oven 30–45 minutes.

Beef and Bean Chili

4 lbs. ground beef
4 green peppers, cut into 1 inch pieces
4 medium onions, cut into 1 inch pieces
6 teaspoons garlic, minced
½ cup cooking oil
2 teaspoons garlic powder
2 tablespoons chili powder
1½ teaspoons granulated Sweet 'N Low®
2 29 oz. cans tomato sauce
2 tablespoons salt
1 tablespoon pepper
2 15 oz. cans red kidney beans

Serves eight to ten

Sauté seasoning in cooking oil until slightly softened. Add meat and brown. Add remaining ingredients except for the kidney beans, and cook on a medium-low heat for 1 hour. Add kidney beans. Serve immediately.

Beef Stew

2 lbs. beef shoulder round, cut into bite-size pieces
¼ cup butter or margarine
1 medium onion, wedged
1 cup sliced fresh mushrooms
2 chopped celery stalks
1 garlic clove, minced
¼ teapoon salt
¼ teaspoon black pepper
½ cup dry red wine
2 10½ oz. cans beef broth or stock (see Index)

Serves four

Melt the butter or margarine in a large skillet. Add the beef and brown. Add the onion, celery, mushrooms, garlic, salt, and pepper. Reduce the heat to medium-low and let mixture simmer for 20 minutes. Add the red wine and beef broth or stock; cover and simmer until the meat is tender about 1 hour. Serve with whole grain pasta or brown rice.

San Antonio Beef

2 lbs. boneless beef chuck roast

3 cloves garlic, minced

3 tablespoons Worcestershire sauce

¾ cup tomato paste

3 tablespoons cooking oil

2½ cups water

2 cups onions, finely chopped

1½ cups celery, finely chopped

¾ cup green pepper, finely chopped

3 tablespoons red wine vinegar

1 tablespoon Tabasco®

2 teaspoons salt

2 teaspoons finely ground black pepper

Serves eight

Pat the roast dry with paper towels. In a large pot heat oil and brown beef on all sides. Add remaining ingredients. Cover and cook for 4 hours, stirring until the beef is easily shredded. Serve immediately.

Baby Back Ribs

4 slabs baby back ribs

6 lemons, juiced

2 tomatoes, coarsely chopped

2 tablespoons garlic, minced

1½ cups barbecue sauce (see Index)

Preheat oven to 325°F.

Serves eight

Cut through ribs vertically and horizontally. Combine lemon juice, tomatoes, and garlic. Pour over ribs to marinate for at least 2 hours. Place ribs in a large cooking pan, meat side up, cover with foil, and roast for 3½ hours. Uncover the ribs and baste with barbecue sauce. Roast for an additional 30 minutes uncovered. Serve immediately.

Roasted Brisket of Beef

1   4½ lbs. fresh brisket of beef
1 lb. fresh mushrooms, cleaned and cut into halves
3 small onions, quartered
10 garlic cloves
1   6 oz. can tomato paste
2 cups water
2½ teaspoons salt
¾ teaspoon pepper
1 bay leaf
Preheat oven to 350° F.

Serves ten

Place the brisket in a large roasting pan and set aside. In a food processor, purée the remaining ingredients except bay leaf. Pour the mixture over the brisket and add bay leaf. Cover with foil, place in oven and roast for 3½ hours. Slice brisket and return it to the pan and cook for 5 more minutes. Remove bay leaf. Serve immediately.

Barbecue Oven Smoked Brisket

4-6 lbs. beef brisket
celery salt
garlic powder
onion powder
2 tablespoons liquid smoke
1 cup beef broth or stock (see Index)
1½ cups barbecue sauce (see Index)

Serves eight

Place brisket in roasting pan. Drizzle liquid smoke and beef broth or stock over the brisket. Sprinkle with celery salt, garlic powder, and onion powder all over the brisket. Cover tightly with foil and marinate overnight. Uncover the pan, pour off the marinade and discard. Liberally cover the brisket with beef broth or stock and sprinkle with salt and pepper. Lightly cover the pan again and place in a 275° F. oven for 4 hours. Uncover the pan and pour off all but 1 cup of liquid. Spread barbecue sauce over the top of the brisket. Bake uncovered for 1 hour. Slice thinly across the grain to serve.

New Orleans Roast Beef

1   3½ lb. beef eye of round roast
1 tablespoon plus 2 teaspoons cooking oil, divided
10 whole garlic cloves, peeled
1 teaspoon paprika
½ teaspoon onion powder
2 tablespoons Worcestershire sauce
¾ teaspoon salt
½ teaspoon black pepper

Preheat oven to 350° F.

Serves six

*U*sing a long, thin knife, carefully make a horizonal slit through the roast. Twist the knife gently to make a ½ inch hole. In a small sauce pan, heat the 2 teaspoons of oil on medium-high heat. Sauté the garlic cloves for 4 minutes, stirring often. Allow the garlic cloves to cool. In a small bowl, combine the remaining ingredients, except the roast; mix well and set aside. When the garlic is room temperature, push the cloves into the hole in the center of the roast until they fill the hole. Rub the oil mixture over the entire roast. Place the roast in a baking dish. Roast for 75 minutes or until desired doneness. Serve immediately.

Glazed Tenderloin

2½ lbs. beef tenderloin, trimmed
1 tablespoon spicy Dijon mustard
2 tablespoons mayonnaise (see Index)
¼ teaspoon salt
½ teaspoon garlic powder
¼ teaspoon dried ground thyme
½ teaspoon freshly ground black pepper

Preheat oven to 350° F.

Serves six

*P*lace the tenderloin in a baking dish. In a small bowl combine the remaining ingredients. Rub all over the tenderloin. Bake for 45 minutes for medium-rare or for desired doneness. Slice the tenderloin and serve.

Roast Tenderloin of Beef

4 lbs. trimmed beef tenderloin, center cut

½ cup cooking oil

Freshly ground black pepper and salt to taste

Preheat oven to 400° F.

Serves eight

*H*eat the oil in a large skillet. Place the tenderloin in the skillet and rub the beef with pepper. Sear the meat on all sides for about 7 minutes. Remove the tenderloin from the skillet and place on a well-oiled rack in a roasting pan. Roast in the oven for 40 minutes for medium rare. Sprinkle the beef with salt and slice. Serve with horseradish, remoulade or mustard sauce (see Index). Serve immediately.

Beef Tenderloin with Garlic and Tarragon

1   2lb. beef tenderloin, cut into ½ inch medallions

13¾ oz. beef broth or stock (see Index)

2 tablespoons cooking oil

2 tablespoons unsalted butter or margarine

1 cup onion, finely chopped

1 tablespoon garlic, minced

1 cup dry red wine

2 tablespoons Dijon mustard

2 tablespoons chopped fresh tarragon

⅔ cup plain yogurt

salt and pepper to taste

Serves four

*W*arm the oil and the butter or margarine over medium-high heat in a large pan. Add the beef and sauté for 1½ minutes on each side. Remove the beef and add the onions and garlic to the pan. Cook until tender. Add the wine, mustard, tarragon, beef broth or stock, and stir. Reduce the heat to medium, add the yogurt and simmer the sauce until slightly thickened about 7 minutes. Season to taste. Ladle the sauce over the beef and serve immediately.

Filet Brennan

2 tablespoons butter or margarine

½ cup sliced fresh mushrooms

1 tablespoon stone ground whole wheat flour

¼ cup red wine

½ cup beef broth or stock (see Index)

¼ teaspoon Worcestershire sauce

4 filets mignons, 9 oz. each

salt and black pepper

Grilled Tomatoes (see Index)

Preheat a grill or broiler

Serves four

*M*elt the butter or margarine in a small sauté pan and cook the mushrooms over low heat until tender. Blend in the flour and cook, stirring, until lightly browned. Stir in the wine, stock or broth, and Worcestershire. Season the sauce with salt and pepper to taste and simmer until slightly thickened.

Sprinkle the steaks with salt and pepper on both sides, then grill or broil until done to preference.

Place the filets on 4 warm plates and spoon mushroom sauce over the meat. Garnish with the grilled tomatoes and serve.

Steak Au Poivre

4 beef filets, 9 oz. each

4 tablespoons cracked black peppercorns

2 cups pepper sauce (see Index)

Preheat a grill or broiler

Serves four

*W*ith the knife parallel to the work surface, butterfly the beef filets; do not cut all the way through the filets. Open the filets and press peppercorns onto both sides of the meat. Grill or broil until done to preference.

Place the filets on warm plates and top with pepper sauce.

Medallions of Beef with Stilton Cheese

6	6 oz. beef tenderloin medallions

¼ cup butter or margarine

1 cup onion, finely sliced

¾ cup heavy cream

2 tablespoons parsley, finely chopped

1 tablespoon chives, finely chopped

¾ cup crumbled Stilton cheese

6 teaspoons crumbled Stilton cheese, for garnish

1 teaspoon freshly ground black pepper

Serves six

*I*n a large pan, sauté the beef medallions approximately 6 minutes a side until browned on each side. Remove from pan and add the sliced onions. Sauté the onions until soft. Add the cream and cook over medium-high heat until reduced by half. Add the parsley, chives, pepper, and crumbled Stilton cheese. Stir until combined well. Pour the mixture over the medallions, and garnish with 1 teaspoon crumbled Stilton cheese for each serving.

Châteaubriand Bouquetière

2 lbs. beef tenderloin

¼ cup (½ stick) melted butter or margarine

salt and black pepper

1 cup béarnaise sauce (see Index)

Preheat a grill or broiler

Serves four

*S*prinkle the beef on both sides with salt and pepper. Place the filet on the hot grill or under the broiler and baste with melted butter or margarine. Cook for 15 to 30 minutes until done according to your preference; when the internal temperature reaches 120° F., the meat is cooked rare. Slice the beef and serve topped with béarnaise. Garnish with sautéed fresh seasonal vegetables.

Stuffed Sirloin Steak

1   3lb. sirloin steak, 2 inches thick

2 tablespoons Worcestershire sauce

salt and pepper to taste

1 dozen raw oysters

Preheat the broiler

Serves six

*S*plit the steak in half, through its thickness to make a pocket. Leave it attached at one end. Mix the Worcestershire sauce, salt, and pepper. Rub all over the steak, inside and out. Cover and refrigerate for 1 hour. Stuff the pocket of the steak with raw oysters, then sew shut with thick thread. Broil for desired doneness. Slice the steak and serve immediately.

Maude's Steak Diane

4 small tournedos or filets, about 1¼ inch thick,
each sliced across, to make 8 slices

4 tablespoons (½ stick) butter or margarine

3 cloves garlic, minced

1 small white onion, finely chopped

2 stalks celery, finely chopped

3 sprigs fresh parsley, finely chopped

1½ teaspoons salt

¾ teaspoon black pepper

¾ cup Worcestershire sauce

juice of ½ lemon

3 dashes Tabasco®

Serves four

*M*elt the butter or margarine in a large skillet over low heat. When the butter or margarine is melted, place the slices of meat in the skillet and simmer until medium done. Turn the slices over and cook on the other side. When the meat is cooked, remove it to a large serving platter and set aside. Add the chopped vegetables, salt, and pepper to the melted butter or margarine remaining in the pan. Simmer for a few minutes, then add the Worcestershire, lemon juice, and Tabasco®. Cook a few minutes longer, just until the sauce is slightly thickened. Put the slices of meat back in the skillet and cook about 30 seconds on each side. Place the slices on the serving platter again, then pour the sauce from the pan evenly over them. Serve from the platter with sauce spooned over each portion.

Stuffed Bell Peppers

4 large green bell peppers

2 quarts water

½ cup (1 stick) butter or margarine

½ cup onion, finely chopped

1 lb. ground beef

3 garlic cloves, minced

½ cup chopped scallions

1 teaspoon Italian seasoning

¼ cup beef broth or stock (see Index)

3 chopped ripe tomatoes

1 cup cooked brown rice (see Index)

1 tablespoon chopped fresh parsley

2 large eggs

2 tablespoons freshly grated Parmesan cheese

2 tablespoons Italian bread crumbs (see Index)

salt and black pepper

Preheat oven to 350° F.

Serves four

Slice off the tops of the bell peppers and remove the seeds from inside. Bring 2 quarts of water to a boil in a large pot. Drop the peppers into the water and blanch for 5 to 6 minutes. Remove the peppers from the pot and drain. Melt the butter or margarine in a large skillet and sauté the onion, ground beef, and garlic; cook the mixture for 5 to 10 minutes over medium heat until the meat browns. Add the scallions, Italian seasoning, stock or broth, and tomatoes. Mix well and season to taste with salt and pepper. Fold the rice into the mixture, then add the parsley and eggs. Fill the bell peppers with the beef mixture and sprinkle Parmesan cheese and bread crumbs on top; reserve the remaining beef filling for presentation. Place the peppers upright on a baking sheet and bake in the hot oven about 5 minutes. Divide the remaining beef filling between 4 plates, set a stuffed pepper in the center of each bed of filling, and serve.

Stuffed Cabbage Créole

¼ cup (½ stick) plus 1 tablespoon butter or margarine
1 lb. ground beef
2 lbs. medium raw shrimp, peeled and deveined
1½ lbs. (about 5 medium) chopped tomatoes
3 cups créole sauce (see Index)
2 cups cooked brown rice (see Index)
1 large head of cabbage
Preheat oven to 350° F.

Serves eight

*M*elt 1 tablespoon of the butter or margarine in a large skillet and brown the ground beef. Fold in the shrimp and tomatoes; cook, stirring, until the shrimp turn pink, then add 1½ cups of the créole sauce. Simmer the mixture for 10 minutes, then stir in the brown rice. Set the filling aside while preparing the cabbage.

Fill a large pot with water and add the remaining ¼ cup butter or margarine. Bring the buttered water to a boil. Core the cabbage and drop the head into the boiling water. Cook the cabbage about 20 minutes until the leaves become limp and begin to separate. Remove the cabbage from the pot and drain. When cool enough to handle, peel off 8 large leaves. Place a generous portion of the beef and shrimp filling on the base of each leaf, then roll the leaves, tucking in the sides. Place the cabbage rolls in a shallow baking dish.

Chop the leftover cabbage and combine it with the remaining 1½ cups créole sauce. Pour the cabbage and créole sauce mixture over the stuffed cabbage. Bake in the hot oven for 20 to 25 minutes and serve.

CHAPTER ELEVEN

Grilling and Marinades

Jumbo Shrimp with Lemon Marinade and Vegetable Sauté

1 lb. raw extra large shrimp, about 18, peeled

Citrus Marinade (see Index)

Preheat a grill

Serves six

Vegetable Sauté:

1 tablespoon cooking oil

3 cups vegetables, zucchini, hearts of artichoke, fennel, red bell pepper
cut into ½ inch wide sticks, about 2 inches long

salt and freshly ground black pepper to taste

3 tablespoons balsamic vinegar

*P*repare the marinade. Add the shrimp to the marinade and marinate at room temperature for 3 hours. Warm the oil over medium heat in a sauté pan. Add the vegetables and garlic; stir continuously for 4 minutes. Add the balsamic vinegar and season with salt and pepper. Continue cooking for 1 more minute. Remove the shrimp from the marinade, and grill for 2 minutes on each side. Split the sautéed vegetables among 6 plates, put 3 to 4 shrimp on top. Serve immediately.

Garlic Shrimp

2 lbs. jumbo raw shrimp, peeled

16 large whole garlic cloves

3 large garlic cloves, minced

⅓ cup olive oil

¼ cup tomato sauce

2 tablespoons red wine vinegar

2 tablespoons chopped fresh basil

½ teaspoon salt

½ teaspoon cayenne pepper

6 skewers for shrimp

Preheat a grill

Serves six

B lanch the whole garlic cloves for 3 minutes, drain well and set aside. In a large bowl, stir together the oil, tomato sauce, vinegar, basil, garlic, salt, and cayenne pepper. Add the shrimp and toss to coat evenly. Refrigerate for 30 minutes. Remove the shrimp from the marinade. Reserve the remaining marinade. Thread the shrimp and garlic cloves alternately on the skewers. Place the shrimp on the grill, brushing frequently with the marinade. Turn frequently, grill until the shrimp become pink, about 8 minutes.

Tuna with Spicy Louisiana Butter

4   8 oz. tuna steaks

cooking oil

salt and freshly ground black pepper to taste

Spicy Louisiana Butter (see Index)

Preheat a grill

Serves four

Rub the tuna lightly with oil and sprinkle with salt and pepper. Arrange the fish on the rack. Grill, turning once, for about 10 minutes. Remove the fish to plates. Top each tuna steak with a slice of the spicy butter. Serve immediately.

Seafood Brochette

1 lb. jumbo raw shrimp, peeled

1 lb. sea scallops or thick, firm fish of your choice, cut into cubes

1 lb. fresh button mushrooms, steamed

¼ cup olive oil

2 tablespoons fresh lemon juice

2 tablespoons chopped fresh tarragon

1 clove garlic

½ teaspoon salt

¼ teaspoon freshly ground black pepper

2 lemons, cut into ¼ inch slices

6 skewers for seafood

Preheat a grill

Serves six

Whisk together the oil, lemon juice, tarragon, garlic, salt, and pepper in a large bowl. Add the scallops, shrimp, and mushrooms and coat well. Refrigerate for 30 minutes. Remove the scallops, shrimp, and the mushrooms from the mixture. Reserve the lemon mixture. Alternate the scallops, shrimp, and mushrooms with the lemon slices on 6 skewers. Arrange the skewers on the rack. Grill for 8 minutes, turning frequently and brushing with the mixture, until the scallops and shrimp are cooked through. Serve immediately.

Ginger Lemon Chicken

6 chicken breast halves, skinned and boned
1 cup lemon juice
2 cloves garlic, minced
1 tablespoon grated fresh ginger
1 tablespoon chopped fresh tarragon
½ teaspoon salt
¼ teaspoon freshly ground black pepper

Serves six

In a bowl, stir together the lemon juice, garlic, tarragon, ginger, salt, and pepper. Put the chicken breasts in a baking pan and pour the lemon and ginger mixture over them, coating evenly. Refrigerate for 3 hours. Preheat a grill. Remove the chicken from the mixture and dry with paper towels. Reserve the remaining mixture. Place the chicken on a rack, grill, turning 3 times and brushing with reserved mixture, for about 15 to 25 minutes or until the chicken is no longer pink in the center.

Grilled Chicken with Quick Sautéed Greens

8 boneless chicken breasts
mustard greens, collard or kale
4 tablespoons olive oil
4 cloves garlic, minced
2 cups sliced fresh mushrooms
½ cup chopped red onion
2 cups Eleana's Special Blend Mustard Sauce (see Index)
Preheat a grill

Serves four

*M*arinate chicken breasts in mustard sauce for 2 hours in refrigerator. Clean greens, trimming sharp edges and stems. Chop coarsely with kitchen shears. Heat olive oil in skillet. Add garlic, red onions, and mushrooms. Stir fry until heated. Grill chicken until cooked through, add greens to skillet and stir fry for 5 minutes, until just tender. Serve chicken with greens and top with extra mustard sauce. Serve immediately.

Creole Mustard Quail

8 5 oz. quail

⅓ cup Creole mustard

½ cup dry white wine

⅓ cup olive oil

1 tablespoon chopped fresh thyme

salt and freshly ground black pepper to taste

Preheat a grill

Serves four

Stir the mustard, wine, 3 tablespoons of oil and the thyme, together in a small bowl. Pat the quail dry with paper towels. Coat the quail with the remaining olive oil. Add salt and pepper. Place the quail, breast down, on the rack. Grill for 8 minutes, turning them frequently. Brush the Creole mustard mixture on the quail and grill for about 5 minutes more. Turn them once and brush them with the Creole mustard mixture. The quail meat should remain slightly pink at the bone. Serve immediately.

Grilled Double Veal Chops

2 tablespoons cracked black peppercorns

4 white veal chops, about 16 oz. each

2 tablespoons butter or margarine

¼ cup water

1 tablespoon chopped fresh parsley

Preheat oven to 400° F.

Serves four

Preheat a grill. Press the cracked black peppercorns onto both sides of the veal chops, then sear on the hot grill until scored with grill marks on both sides.

Place the seared chops in a rectangular baking dish and add the butter or margarine and ¼ cup water. Roast the chops in the hot oven for 20 to 30 minutes until medium or well done. Transfer the veal chops to warm plates and add the parsley to the pan drippings; drizzle the drippings over the meat.

If desired, serve the veal chops accompanied by a colorful array of sautéed vegetables.

Butterflied Leg of Lamb

8 lb. butterflied leg of leg

5 large cloves of garlic, peeled

1 cup olive oil

1 tablespoon fresh thyme

¼ cup Creole mustard

¼ cup freshly squeezed lemon juice

3 shallots, finely chopped

1 teaspoon freshly ground black pepper

1 teaspoon salt

Preheat a grill

Serves ten

*B*lend all ingredients, except the lamb in a food processor. Place the lamb in a large container and pour in the marinade. Cover and refrigerate overnight, turning the lamb 2 or 3 times. Allow the lamb to reach room temperature. Grill for about 15 minutes per side for medium doneness. Slice thinly. Serve immediately.

Shish-ka-bob

2 lbs. sirloin tip cut into 2 inch chunks
1 pint cherry tomatoes or 2-3 whole tomatoes cut into 2 inch chunks
1 pint pearl onions or 1-2 onions cut into 2 inch pieces
2 green peppers cut into 2 inch pieces
½ lb. fresh small button mushrooms
1½ cups Italian Dressing (see Index)
6 skewers for grilling

Serves six

*M*arinate meat in Italian dressing overnight or for at least 1 hour. Alternate meat and vegetables on skewers. Place on barbecue pit and grill for approximately 20 minutes turning and basting with marinade on each side. As an alternative, they can be broiled under the oven broiler approximately 10 minutes turning and basting with marinade on each side.

Dijon Mustard Coated Sirloin Steak

8 12 oz. sirloin steaks, well trimmed
2 cups Dijon mustard
⅓ cup olive oil
2 teaspoons dried oregano
2 teaspoons dried thyme
2 teaspoons dried rosemary
2 teaspoons dried basil
4 medium garlic cloves, minced

Serves eight

*C*ombine the mustard with olive oil, herbs, and garlic. Coat the steaks with the mixture and refrigerate for 12 hours. Preheat a grill. Remove from the refrigerator 1 hour before grilling. Grill the steaks over a hot fire, until medium-rare, about 5 minutes on each side. Slice the steaks thinly and serve immediately.

Roasted Eggplant with Tomatoes and Goat Cheese

8 medium eggplant
olive oil
1 bunch chives, finely chopped
¾ lb. goat cheese, cut into ½ inch pieces
Boston lettuce leaves, or other greens
4 large tomatoes, peeled and quartered
salt and black pepper to taste
Prepare a grill.

Serves eight

Dressing:

½ cup extra-virgin olive oil
2 tablespoons balsamic vinegar
salt and black pepper to taste

Cut the eggplant lengthwise into slices about ½ inch thick. Brush with olive oil and grill for 6 to 8 minutes until the eggplant is softened.

Press some chives into each slice of goat cheese. For the dressing, whisk the vinegar and oil together in a small bowl and add salt and pepper.

Arrange a large platter with the lettuce leaves topping with the eggplant, goat cheese slices and tomatoes. Add salt and pepper and drizzle on the dressing. Serve immediately.

Grilled Marinated Vegetables

4 zucchini, cut lengthwise into ¼ inch slices

1 large eggplant, peeled and cut lengthwise into ¼ inch slices

2 large red onions, sliced into discs, but not separated

8 large fresh mushrooms

Thyme and Lemon Marinade (see Index)

Preheat a grill

Serves four

Place the vegetables in the marinade and let them sit for 1 hour at room temperature. Remove the vegetables from the marinade and grill turning frequently for 10 minutes. Serve immediately.

Lemon Marinade

1 cup olive oil

½ cup freshly squeezed lemon juice

2 teaspoons garlic, minced

4 tablespoons green onions, finely chopped

4 teaspoons grated lemon zest

4 teaspoons chopped fresh dill

1 teaspoon salt

1 teaspoon freshly ground black pepper

Yields 2 cups

In a bowl, blend all of the ingredients. Use immediately.

Lemon, Mustard and Herb Marinade

½ cup fresh lemon juice

zest of one lemon

¼ cup Dijon mustard

1 teaspoon fresh basil, finely chopped

1 teaspoon fresh oregano, finely chopped

1 teaspoon fresh parsley, finely chopped

Yields 1 cup

Combine all ingredients in a bowl and mix by hand. Use immediately.

Eleana's Marinade
(Special Mustard Blend Sauce)

1 cup mustard

1 cup cider vinegar

2 or 3 teaspoons salt

1½ oz. regular chili powder

3 cups water

1 tablespoon paprika

Yields 5½ cups

*I*n a bowl, whisk together all ingredients. Place marinated ingredients in a refrigerator for 1 or 2 hours. Grill as desired, basting with reserved sauce. Use as a marinade for pork chops, chicken or seafood.

Note: *Can be used as a barbecue sauce.*

Thyme and
Lemon Marinade

1½ cups olive oil

½ cup freshly squeezed lemon juice

2 tablespoons dried thyme

¼ teaspoon granulated Sweet 'N Low®

salt and pepper to taste

Yields 2 cups

*I*n a bowl, combine all ingredients and mix well. Use immediately.

Steak Marinade

2 tablespoons dried green peppercorns

5 large garlic cloves, minced

5 cups red wine vinegar

1 onion, coarsely chopped

Jalapeno peppers to taste

Yields 5½ cups

*C*ombine all ingredients. Place in a closed container and allow to stand for 2 days.

Note: This is a very good marinade for steak. Marinate the steak for 2 hours.

Red Wine Marinade

1 bottle dry red wine

½ cup olive oil

2 teaspoons Worcestershire sauce

1 onion, finely chopped

4 tablespoons fresh parsley, finely chopped

2 teaspoons garlic, minced

1 tablespoon fresh tarragon, finely chopped

1 teaspoon salt

½ teaspoon freshly ground black pepper

Yields 5 cups

*B*lend all ingredients. Use immediately.

Vegetable Marinade

1 cup olive oil

1 cup balsamic vinegar

1 cup water

1 teaspoon garlic, minced

1 small onion, finely chopped

½ teaspoon thyme

salt and pepper to taste

Yields 3½ cups

*M*ix all ingredients together. Add fresh vegetables and marinate over night.

Dry Meat and Fowl Marinade

2 tablespoons fresh rosemary

2 teaspoons garlic, minced

1½ teaspoons salt

1 teaspoon freshly ground black pepper

1 tablespoon lemon zest, finely grated

Yields 4 tablespoons

*I*n a small bowl, stir together the ingredients. Rub the meat or fowl lightly with olive oil, before coating it with the marinade. This should be done several hours before grilling.

Dry Pork Marinade

2 tablespoons fresh thyme, finely chopped

1 tablespoon fresh sage, finely chopped

2 teaspoons salt

1 teaspoon freshly ground black pepper

¼ teaspoon ground allspice

¼ teaspoon cayenne pepper

2 teaspoons garlic, minced

Yields 4 tablespoons

*I*n a small bowl, stir together the ingredients. Rub pork lightly with olive oil, before coating it with the marinade. This should be done several hours before grilling.

Dry Fish Marinade

2 tablespoons fresh dill, finely chopped

2 teaspoons paprika

1 tablespoon lemon zest, finely grated

1 teaspoon salt

1 teaspoon freshly ground black pepper

¼ teaspoon cayenne pepper

Yields 4 tablespoons

*I*n a small bowl, stir together the ingredients. Rub fish lightly with olive oil, before coating it with the marinade. This should be done several hours before grilling.

Creole Mustard Butter

1 cup softened unsalted butter or margarine

6 tablespoons Creole mustard

1 teaspoon Tabasco®

4 tablespoons green onions, finely chopped

2 tablespoons fresh parsley, finely chopped

4 teaspoons freshly squeezed lemon juice

1 teaspoon salt

½ teaspoon freshly ground black pepper

Yields 1¼ cups

Blend all ingredients until smooth. Chill and serve.

Lime Butter

1 cup softened unsalted butter or margarine

8 tablespoons fresh parsley, finely chopped

4 tablespoons freshly squeezed lime juice

4 teaspoons lime zest, finely grated

2 teaspoons Worcestershire sauce

1 teaspoon salt

½ teaspoon freshly ground black pepper

Yields 1¼ cups

Blend all ingredients until smooth. Chill and serve. Lemon can be substituted.

Spicy Louisiana Butter

1 cup softened unsalted butter or margarine

2 teaspoons chili powder

1 teaspoon Tabasco®

½ teaspoon red pepper flakes

½ teaspoon salt

Yields 1¼ cups

Blend all of the ingredients until smooth. Chill and serve.

Tarragon Butter

1 cup softened unsalted butter or margarine

4 tablespoons fresh tarragon, finely chopped

4 tablespoons fresh parsley, finely chopped

1 teaspoon salt

1 teaspoon garlic, minced

1 teaspoon freshly ground black pepper

Yields 1¼ cups

Blend all of the ingredients until smooth. Chill and serve.

CHAPTER TWELVE

Side Dishes or Vegetarian's Fare

Asparagus Au Gratin

2 lbs. fresh asparagus, cut into 1 inch pieces

2 tablespoons butter or margarine

2 tablespoons stone ground whole wheat flour

1 cup milk

1 cup Colby and Monterey Jack Cheeses, shredded

6 Triscuit®, crushed

2 tablespoons melted butter or margarine

salt and pepper to taste

Preheat oven to 350° F.

Serves six

*W*ash, trim, and cut asparagus. Place in 1 quart casserole dish. Cover and microwave for 8 minutes. While cooking melt butter or margarine in a saucepan, add flour and whisk until blended. Stir in milk and whisk constantly until sauce is a medium thickness. Add cheese and correct seasonings. Mix until cheese is melted. Pour sauce over cooked asparagus. Sprinkle top with Triscuit® crumbs and butter or margarine. Bake for 20 minutes and serve.

Asparagus with Mustard Sauce

½ cup sour cream

1½ tablespoons Dijon mustard

2 teaspoons butter or margarine

½ teaspoon fresh parsley, finely chopped

Dash of salt

24 medium asparagus spears cooked

Serves four

*I*n a small sauce pan, combine all the ingredients except asparagus. Cook over low heat until just warm, stirring occasionally. Arrange asparagus on individual plates. Pour sauce over top. Serve immediately.

Cauliflower and Broccoli Casserole

16 oz. frozen broccoli florets, thawed and drained

16 oz. frozen cauliflower, thawed and drained

1 cup mayonnaise (see Index)

3 tablespoon Dijon mustard

½ teaspoon salt

½ cup grated sharp Cheddar cheese

Preheat oven to 375° F.

Serves six

*C*ombine all ingredients in a large bowl except the cheese, until the vegetables are completely coated. Spray a 1½ quart casserole dish with cooking spray and pour mixture into the dish. Sprinkle with cheddar cheese. Cook for about 30 minutes, until the cheese is a golden brown. Serve immediately.

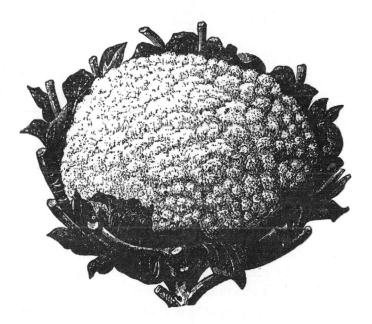

Stewed Cabbage

cooking oil to a depth of 1 inch in a large saucepan (approx. 6 quart size)

1 large head cabbage, cut into large chunks, rinsed, and drained

1 medium white onion, finely chopped

2 to 3 stalks celery, finely chopped

1 teaspoon salt

½ teaspoon black pepper

¼ cup water

Serves eight

*H*eat the oil, then add the cut-up cabbage. Cook the cabbage and keep pressing it down into the pan with a large spoon. When the cabbage is pressed down just below the rim of the pot, add the onion, celery, salt, and pepper. Cook uncovered over medium heat, stirring frequently, until the cabbage begins to brown. Add the water, stir thoroughly, then cover the pan. Lower the heat and cook, uncovering to stir from time to time, until the cabbage looks brown and tastes tender. Serve as is or over brown rice.

Cabbage Noodles

1 medium head cabbage

½ medium onion, thinly sliced

1 cup diced tasso or other seasoning meat

1 tablespoon olive oil or butter

salt, black or hot red pepper

garlic powder to taste

4 oz. whole grain noodles

Serves four to six

*P*repare noodles according to package directions, drain, set aside. Wash and cut cabbage into eighths. Cook over medium heat with salt and black or hot red pepper in very little water in heavy iron skillet, covered on stove. When it begins to soften, uncover and stir in thinly sliced onions, diced tasso or seasoning meat. Raise heat, add olive oil or butter, stirring frequently, until onion is transparent and meat and cabbage begin to brown. Water should have evaporated. Add noodles and stir in skillet with browned cabbage, onion, meat, adding more seasoning to taste.

Broccoli au Gratin

2 bunches fresh broccoli, trimmed

6 tablespoons butter or margarine

¾ cup stone ground whole wheat flour

1 quart milk

1 pint light cream

1 tablespoon salt

¼ teaspoon white pepper

1 cup grated sharp Cheddar cheese

Preheat oven to 350° F.

Serves eight

*C*ut broccoli into 1 inch pieces. Boil in water until slightly tender. Drain and place in a 2 quart shallow baking dish. Melt butter or margarine in a sauce pan over low heat. Add the milk and cream, stir constantly while slowly adding flour. Season with salt and pepper to taste. Pour sauce over broccoli and sprinkle with Cheddar cheese. Bake for 40 minutes or until a golden brown. Serve immediately.

Brussel Sprouts

3 cups fresh brussel sprouts

¼ cup olive oil

½ chopped large onion

1 teaspoon parsley, finely chopped

1 teaspoon garlic powder

¼ teaspoon salt

¼ teaspoon black pepper

½ cup chicken broth or stock (see Index)

Serves four

*C*ook fresh brussel sprouts until tender. Heat oil in a large skillet, sauté the onion, parsley, garlic powder, salt, and pepper until a golden brown. Add the chicken broth or stock to the seasonings and cook for 4 minutes until liquid reduces. Add brussel sprouts, simmer, and serve.

NOTE: *You can substitute chunks of broccoli, cauliflower, or asparagus for the brussel sprouts.*

Eggplant Parmesan

2 medium fried eggplant (see below)

2 cups tomato sauce

3 tablespoons chopped fresh basil

salt and freshly ground black pepper to taste

1½ lbs. Mozzarela cheese, sliced ¼ inch thick

8 tablespoons freshly grated Romano cheese

1 tablespoon olive oil

Preheat oven to 375° F.

Serves six

Spread ⅓ of the tomato sauce in the bottom of a 1½ inch casserole dish and sprinkle with ⅓ of the basil. Layer half the eggplant in the dish. Sprinkle lightly with salt and pepper. Cover the eggplant with a layer of tomato sauce and sprinkle with another ⅓ of the basil. Add a layer of Mozzarela cheese and sprinkle with 2 tablespoons of Romano cheese. Add the remaining eggplant sprinkled with salt and pepper, tomato sauce, and cheeses. Top with olive oil and bake in the oven for 15 minutes or until golden brown.

Fried Eggplant

1 large eggplant (about 1 lb.) peeled

1 tablespoon salt

oil for frying

2 eggs, beaten

¾ cup Italian bread crumbs (see Index)

Serves six

Cut eggplant in ¼ inch thick round slices. Rinse with cool water, drain, and pat dry with paper towels. In a large frying pan heat oil, dip eggplant in eggs, and then in bread crumbs. Fry in hot oil, until golden brown, about 5 minutes. Drain on paper towel. Serve immediately.

Sautéed Green Beans with Garlic and Mushrooms

1 lb. fresh green beans, washed and trimmed

1 teaspoon garlic, minced

1 shallot, finely chopped

1 teaspoon olive oil

¼ cup sliced fresh mushrooms

Serves two

Steam beans for 5 minutes, then immerse them in ice water to stop cooking, drain and set aside. In a medium-sized heavy skillet, sauté the shallots and garlic in olive oil for 2 minutes over medium heat; add mushrooms and sauté for 1 additional minute. Stir in the steamed green beans and cook, stirring until thoroughly heated. Serve immediately.

Green Beans with Dilled Havarti Cheese

8 oz. frozen green beans

2 oz. dilled Havarti cheese, grated

1 medium tomato, diced

½ teaspoon salt

½ teaspoon black pepper

Serves four

In a medium sauce pan, bring 3 cups of water to a boil. Add green beans and simmer for 8 minutes. Drain the beans. Place on plates and top with grated Havarti and diced tomatoes. Salt and pepper to taste. Serve immediately.

String Bean Ragout

1½ lbs. fresh green beans

4 tablespoons cooking oil

2 tablespoons stone ground whole wheat flour

6 strips uncooked bacon

1 chopped onion

2 teaspoons garlic, minced

1 bay leaf

¼ teaspoon thyme

1½ cups water

Tabasco®

salt and pepper

Serves six

*C*lean and cut green beans into bite size pieces. Put in covered bowl and micro-wave on high for 6 minutes. Cook bacon until crisp, drain well, and crumble. Sauté onions, garlic, and seasonings in cooking oil until soft. Add water and bring to a boil. Add beans and bacon and simmer for 15 minutes. Season to taste.

Tomato Green Bean Casserole

¼ cup butter or margarine

¼ cup stone ground whole wheat flour

¾ teaspoon salt

⅛ teaspoon black pepper

½ teaspoon Dijon mustard

¼ teaspoon paprika

2 cups milk

½ cup sharp Cheddar cheese

2   14 oz. cans cut green beans, drained

3 sliced tomatoes

salt and pepper to taste

Preheat oven to 350° F.

Serves eight

*I*n a sauce pan, melt the butter, mix in the flour, salt, pepper, mustard, and paprika. Stir in milk until it boils and thickens. Add cheese, stir to melt. Mix in the green beans and put into 2 quart casserole. Arrange tomato slices over top. Sprinkle with salt and pepper. Bake, uncovered, in oven for about 30 minutes. Serve immediately.

Southern Greens

2 lbs., fresh or frozen, Collard, Mustard or Turnip Greens, cut into 1 inch strips.

4 tablespoons butter or margarine

3 teaspoons garlic, minced

3 teaspoons onion, finely chopped

½ teaspoon dried red pepper

1 lb., ham bone (preferably the butt)

½ cup chicken broth or stock (see Index)

salt and pepper to taste

Serves four to six

*W*ash the cut greens well under cold water and drain. In a large cooking pot, sauté the garlic and onion in the butter or margarine until soft. Add the greens, and sauté for about 5 minutes over medium heat. Add the ham bone, chicken broth or stock and red pepper flakes. Bring the mixture to a boil and cook for about 15 minutes until greens are tender. Salt and pepper to taste and serve immediately.

Fresh Mushrooms in Sour Cream

¼ cup butter or margarine

1 cup onion, finely chopped

1 lb. sliced fresh mushrooms

1 cup sour cream

1 teaspoon dill weed

¼ teapoon garlic powder

salt and pepper to taste

Serves four

*I*n a frying pan, melt the butter or margarine and the onions and sauté until soft. Add mushrooms and sauté until lightly brown. Add remaining ingredients. Continue stirring until all ingredients are heated through. Add salt and pepper. Serve immediately.

Creamed Spinach

¾ cup (1½ sticks) butter or margarine

10 oz. fresh spinach leaves, washed, stemmed, and chopped

1½ cups onion, finely chopped

¼ cup stone ground whole wheat flour

2 cups scalded milk

1 teaspoon salt

Pinch of white pepper

Pinch of nutmeg

Serves four

Melt ½ cup butter or margarine in a large sauté pan; add the spinach and cook over medium heat a few minutes until wilted.

In a large saucepan, melt the remaining ¼ cup butter or margarine. Add the onion and cook over medium heat until tender. Using a whisk, blend the flour into the mixture, then gradually pour in the milk. Stir until smooth, then add the spinach. Season with salt, white pepper, and nutmeg. When the mixture is thick and warmed through, remove it from the heat and serve.

Mint Peas

2 cups shelled fresh peas

2 tablespoons unsalted butter or margarine

2 tablespoons fresh mint leaves, finely chopped

¼ teaspoon granulated Sweet 'N Low®

salt and freshly ground black pepper to taste

Serves four

In a small sauce pan, bring lightly salted water to a boil. Add the Sweet 'N Low® and peas. Reduce the heat to low, cover, and simmer for 10 minutes. When the peas are a bright green, drain, and place in a serving bowl. Combine the peas, butter or margarine, salt, pepper, and chopped mint. Serve immediately.

Spinach Artichoke Casserole

2 10oz. bags of fresh spinach

1 box frozen artichoke hearts, thawed and cut small

8 green onions, thinly sliced

4 tablespoons butter or margarine

1 teaspoon thyme

8 oz. cream cheese, room temperature

8 oz. Monterey Jack cheese, shredded

1 tablespoon Worcestershire sauce

1 teaspoon Tabasco®

⅛ teaspoon cayenne pepper

salt to taste

Serves eight

*C*ut spinach and microwave 8 minutes. Drain spinach on 3 folded paper towels. Sauté green onions in butter or margarine with thyme until soft. Add artichoke hearts and heat until cooked. Add all other ingredients, except spinach and blend together. Squeeze out as much water as possible from the spinach and add to mixture. Mix thoroughly and put into a casserole dish sprayed with cooking oil. Refrigerate several hours or overnight. Bake uncovered for 20-30 minutes in a 350° F. preheated oven.

Stewed Okra

⅓ cup cooking oil

2 lbs., fresh or frozen okra, cut into ½ inch slices

1 ham steak (about 1 lb. in weight), boned and diced ½ inch thick

1 medium white onion, finely chopped

2 stalks celery, finely chopped

½ green pepper, finely chopped

2 medium-size cloves garlic, minced

4 sprigs fresh parsley, finely chopped

2   8oz. cans tomato sauce

¼ cup water

¾ teaspoon salt

¼ teaspoon black pepper

2 bay leaves

Serves eight

Heat the oil in a large skillet or sauté pan just until warm. Add the okra, ham, and remaining vegetables. Cook, stirring from time to time to keep the vegetables from sticking to the pan, until the okra begins to get soft. Then add the tomato sauce and the water. Stir, then add the salt, pepper, and bay leaf. Turn the heat to very low and cover the pan. Cook until the okra is tender to taste, uncovering to stir frequently.

Tomato Concasse

1 tomato

Yields 1 cup

Remove the stem of a tomato, trying not to break into the seed pockets. Immerse the tomato into boiling water for 3 to 5 seconds, then immerse in ice bath. Remove peel, cut the tomato in half, horizontally, taking one half of the tomato in hand and gently squeezing the seeds out to discard. Repeat the process with the second half. Dice the seeded tomato pulp into ½ inch pieces.

Tomatoes Stuffed with Mushrooms

8 medium-sized tomatoes

½ cup (1 stick) butter or margarine

1¼ lbs. sliced fresh mushrooms

1 cup sour cream

4 teaspoons stone ground whole wheat flour

1½ oz. Stilton cheese, room temperature

1 teaspoon chopped parsley

salt and pepper to taste

Dash of Worcestershire sauce

8 teaspoons ground almonds

paprika

Preheat oven to 375° F.

Serves eight

Slice off the tops of the tomatoes and spoon out the soft insides. Turn the tomatoes upside down to drain. Melt the butter or margarine, in a pan and sauté mushrooms until moisture has vaporized. Combine the sour cream and flour and cook over low heat until thick and bubbly. Add Stilton and stir until there are no more lumps in the mixture. Add the remaining ingredients and let cool. Stuff the tomatoes with the mixture, top with the almonds, and sprinkle with paprika. Bake for about 20 minutes and serve.

Tomato Zucchini Au Gratin

¼ cup butter or margarine

½ cup chopped green onion

3 small zucchini, unpeeled and sliced

2 sliced tomatoes

2 tablespoons grated Parmesan cheese

¼ teaspoon salt

⅛ teaspoon black pepper

3 tablespoons grated Parmesan cheese

Serves four

In a frying pan, melt the butter, add the onion and zucchini. Sauté for about 5 minutes. Add tomato, 2 tablespoons Parmesan cheese, salt and pepper to taste. Pour into serving bowl, sprinkle with 3 tablespoons Parmesan cheese and serve immediately.

Grilled Tomatoes

2 large ripe tomatoes

½ cup freshly grated Parmesan cheese

Preheat oven to 375° F. or light a grill

Serves four

Cut a thin slice off the stem and base ends of the tomatoes, then slice them in half crosswise. Bake on a greased baking sheet or grill the tomatoes until soft. Sprinkle with Parmesan cheese, then broil until the cheese melts.

Zucchini and Squash Casserole

4 zucchini

4 squash

½ cup (1 stick) butter or margarine, melted

¼ cup vegetable seasoning

salt and pepper to taste

Serves eight

*C*lean and slice zucchini and squash and put in a large covered bowl. Microwave high for 8 minutes. Drain any liquid. Sprinkle with salt and pepper and Creole vegetable seasonings. Pour butter or margarine on vegetables and toss to coat. Cover and cook 2 more minutes on high in the microwave.

Barbara's Spaghetti Squash

1 large squash

Serves six to eight

*B*ake squash for 10 minutes, or microwave for 2-3 minutes, to soften skin. Cut squash along length and remove seeds.

Bake: Place cut side down on pan and bake 45 minutes at 350° F. Turn and bake until tender.

OR

Microwave: Cook 5 minutes cut side down in ¼ cup water in a dish, covered with clear wrap.

When done, pull out vegetable strands with fork. Toss with salt and pepper, spices, bacon bits, Parmesan cheese, white sauce or spaghetti sauce.

Roasted Asparagus

1 lb. medium asparagus, tough ends removed

2 tablespoons extra-virgin olive oil

salt and freshly ground black pepper to taste

1 tablespoon chopped fresh parsley

2 lemons, halved

Preheat oven to 400° F.

Serves four

*P*lace the asparagus in a baking dish. Toss to coat very well with the olive oil, salt and pepper. Make sure the asparagus are in a single layer. Cover with aluminum foil and roast in the center of the oven for 10 minutes. Remove the foil and roast for another 10 minutes. Sprinkle with parsley and squeeze lemons over asparagus. Serve immediately.

Roasted Garlic

1 pod or bulb garlic

½ teaspoon olive oil

Preheat oven to 325° F.

Yields one head garlic

*S*lice the top off the pod or bulb of the garlic and trim the roots even with the base of the bulb without cutting into garlic cloves. Remove some of the papery skin from the outside of the bulb, but do no seperate the cloves. Place the garlic in a small baking dish, drizzle with ½ teaspoon of olive oil and cover with foil. Bake for 10 to 15 minutes or until the garlic begins to soften. Cool briefly and peel or squeeze garlic from each clove. The garlic will keep refrigerated for 5 to 7 days.

Roasted Vegetables

1 lb. small button mushrooms

1 pint pearl onions

1 green, red, and yellow bell peppers, cut into bite-size pieces

1 large eggplant, sliced and cut into 1½ inch cubes

1 bunch of asparagus, cut into 1½ inch pieces

½ cup (1 stick) butter or margarine, melted

½ cup olive oil

2 tablespoons garlic, minced

salt and pepper to taste

Preheat oven to 400° F.

Serves four to six

Spray roasting pan with cooking spray. Add all vegetables, season with salt and pepper and mix well. Combine butter or margarine, oil and garlic. Pour sauce over vegetables, toss until vegetables are coated. Roast in the oven for about 1 hour turning vegetables occasionally.

Roasted Sweet Potatoes

3 sweet potatoes, peeled and cubed

½ cup (1 stick) butter or margarine, melted

1 tablespoon garlic, minced

salt and pepper to taste

Preheat oven to 350° F.

Serves six

Peel and cube sweet potatoes. Place in a roasting pan sprayed with cooking spray. Salt and pepper potatoes. Combine butter or margarine and garlic and pour over potatoes. Toss potatoes to thoroughly coat with sauce. Bake for 1 - 1½ hours turning potatoes periodically.

Sweet Potatoes with Lime

4 sweet potatoes, cooked

½ stick butter or margarine, melted

2 teaspoons fresh lime juice

¼ teaspoon lime zest

¼ teaspoon granulated Sweet 'N Low®

salt to taste

Serves four

Scoop out the inside of the cooked sweet potatoes. Mash by hand. Add fresh lime juice, lime zest, melted butter or margarine and a little salt to taste. Mash until smooth and serve hot or very warm. Lemon can be substituted.

Mashed Sweet Potatoes

2 large sweet potatoes

1 stick (½ cup) butter or margarine

½ teaspoon salt

¼ teaspoon Sweet & Low® Brown

¼ cup hot milk

Dash of cinnamon

Dash of nutmeg

¼ cup chopped pecans

Preheat oven to 350° F.

Serves six

Scrub sweet potatoes, prick and oil skins. Place on roasting pan sprayed with cooking spray. Place in oven. Cook for about 1 hour. Remove from oven. Skin sweet potatoes. Cut up potatoes and place in bowl with butter or margarine, salt, hot milk, Sweet & Low® Brown, nuts, and spices. Mash with potato masher until fluffy. Pour in a baking dish and reheat for about 10 minutes. Serve immediately.

Mashed Sweet Potatoes with Garlic

2 large sweet potatoes
1 pod or bulb garlic
1 tablespoon olive oil
1 cup (½ stick) butter or margarine
salt and pepper to taste
Preheat oven to 350° F.

Serves six

Scrub sweet potatoes, prick and oil skins. Place on roasting pan sprayed with cooking spray. Cut off top of the pod of garlic. Place in garlic roaster or on foil. Pour olive oil over the garlic and cover roaster or wrap in foil. Place in oven with sweet potatoes. Cook for about 1 hour. Remove from oven. Skin sweet potatoes and push garlic cloves out of their skins. Cut up potatoes and place in bowl with garlic and butter or margarine. Mash with potato masher until fluffy. Add salt and pepper.

Brabant Sweet Potatoes

2 large sweet potatoes, peeled and cubed
¼ cup butter or margarine
1 tablespoon garlic, minced
Pinch of paprika
Pinch of salt
1 tablespoon fresh parsley, finely chopped

Serves four

Place the potatoes in a large sauce pan and add water to cover; boil the potatoes until tender, about 15-20 minutes. Drain the potatoes and set aside.

Melt the butter or margarine in a large skillet and cook the garlic a few minutes over medium heat. Add the potatoes, paprika, salt, and parsley. Cook briefly, stirring, until the potatoes are well coated with the seasonings. Serve hot.

Skillet Sweet Potatoes

1 large sweet potato (about 1 lb), peeled and cut crosswise into 12 slices, each about ¼ inch thick

1 tablespoon unsalted butter or margarine

1 tablespoon cooking oil

½ cup water

¼ teapoon salt

Serves two

*I*n a very large skillet, place the potatoes in one layer. Add the remaining ingredients. Bring to a boil and cover, boiling gently over high heat for 5 minutes. Once the potatoes become soft continue to cook, uncovered, over medium heat. Turn the slices until each side is a golden brown. Serve immediately.

Fried Sweet Potatoes

4 fresh sweet potatoes

cooking oil

salt to taste

Serves eight

*C*ut up sweet potatoes and deep fry in about 2 inches of very hot cooking oil, until golden brown. Add salt.

Aproximate cooking times:
Cottage Fries: 8 minutes
Shoestrings: 6 minutes

Sweet Potato Chips

6 large sweet potatoes, peeled

cooking oil

salt to taste

Serves twelve

*W*ith a sharp knife, cut the potatoes into round slices, as thin as possible. Heat cooking oil to 350° F. Deep fry small batches of potato slices, turning often until golden brown, about 1 minute. Drain on paper towels and add salt. Serve immediately.

Oyster Dressing

½ cup (1 stick) butter or margarine

½ cup onion, finely chopped

½ cup celery, finely chopped

½ cup green pepper, finely chopped

2 tablespoons garlic, minced

1 large bay leaf

Pinch of thyme

1 tablespoon Worcestershire sauce

24 shucked oysters

1 large egg

2 cups bread crumbs (see index)

1 tablespoon parsley, finely chopped

salt and black pepper to taste

Yields 3 cups

*M*elt the butter or margarine in a large skillet and sauté the onion, celery, green pepper, and garlic. When the vegetables are tender, add the bay leaf, thyme, Worcestershire, and oysters, along with any oyster water. Cook for 2 to 3 minutes, until the edges of the oysters begin to curl. Season the mixture with salt and pepper, then working quickly, stir in the egg. Fold in the bread crumbs and parsley and cook for 1 to 2 minutes longer until the mixture is heated through. Refrigerate until use.

Baked Macaroni and Cheese Annie

2 quarts water
1 lb. whole grain macaroni
12 eggs
2 cups cream or evaporated milk
salt and white pepper to taste
1 lb. sharp Cheddar cheese, cubed plus extra sliced Cheddar for top of the casserole
½ cup (1 stick) butter or margarine
Preheat oven to 400° F.
Serves eight

Bring 2 quarts of water to a boil. Add the macaroni and cook approximately 10 minutes until tender, stirring frequently. Drain the macaroni in a colander.

In a large mixing bowl, beat the eggs slightly, then add the cream. Season the mixture with salt and pepper. Stir in the cheese, then add the macaroni and toss.

Slice the butter or margarine and place the pats in the bottom of a 13x9x2 inch baking dish. Pour the macaroni into the baking dish and, top with slices of cheese. Place the baking dish in a larger pan containing ½ inch of water and bake until set and lightly browned, 35 to 45 minutes.

Whole Grain Fettuccine with Sun-Dried Tomatoes and Garlic

2 tablespoons garlic, minced

1 tablespoon green peppercorns

¼ cup sun-dried tomatoes, not packed in oil, dehydrated and julienned

1 tablespoon olive oil

½ cup chicken broth or stock (see Index)

4 cups whole grain fettuccine, cooked al dente

½ cup frozen green peas, defrosted

⅓ cup fresh basil, julienned

4 teaspoons grated Parmesan cheese

Serves four

In a medium-sized, heavy sauce pan, sauté the garlic, peppercorns, and sun-dried tomatoes in olive oil over medium-low heat, being careful not to brown the mixture. Add the chicken broth or stock and cook for 1 minute over medium-high heat. Add the fettuccine, tossing well. Heat thoroughly and add the peas and half the basil. To serve, garnish each serving with the remaining basil and sprinkle with the Parmesan cheese.

Rice and Asparagus Au Gratin

2 lbs. fresh aspargus, cleaned, trimmed, and cut into 1 inch pieces

2 cups cooked brown rice, cooled

¼ teaspoon salt

¼ teapoon cayenne pepper

⅓ cup sour cream

⅔ cup milk

2 cups grated sharp Cheddar cheese

Preheat oven to 350° F.

Serves eight

*I*n a large pot of boiling water, cook the asparagus about 10 minutes, until tender crisp. In a medium-size bowl, combine half of the cheese and the remaining ingredients except the asparagus. Spoon ½ of the rice mixture, into a 9 inch square baking pan that has been coated with cooking spray. Arrange the asparagus on top, then spread the remaining rice mixture over the asparagus. Bake for 20 minutes. Sprinkle the remaining cheese over the top. Bake for 5 minutes or until golden brown. Serve immediately.

Wild Rice

1 cup wild rice

1 tablespoon butter or margarine

⅓ cup chopped scallions

½ cup ham, finely chopped

⅓ cup chopped pecans

¼ cup fresh parsley, finely chopped

1 tablespoon white wine

½ teaspoon white pepper

salt to taste

Serves four

*C*ook the wild rice until tender according to the package directions. Melt the butter or margarine in a large skillet and sauté the scallions, pecans, and ham until the ham is lightly browned. Add the remaining ingredients and cook over medium heat, stirring, for 5 minutes. Fold in the wild rice and serve.

Rice Stuffed Peppers

4 large green peppers

2 tablespoons olive oil

1 chopped small onion

3 cloves garlic, minced

1 cup uncooked brown rice

2 tablespoons tomato paste

1   14oz. can tomatoes, drained and coarsely chopped

2 tablespoons chopped fresh parsley

1 teaspoon dried oregano

1 teaspoon salt

¼ teaspoon freshly ground black pepper

2 cups water

Preheat oven to 350° F.

Serves four

*T*rim off the tops of the peppers and set aside. Scoop out the cores, ribs, and seeds. Be very careful not to puncture the peppers. Heat the oil, over medium-high heat in a medium sauce pan. Add the onion and garlic and sauté for 3 minutes. Add the rice and stir for 1 minute. Add the remaining ingredients and simmer for 3 minutes. Arrange the peppers in a baking dish and fill each pepper with the rice mixture. Divide the water among the peppers and filling as needed to just cover the rice. Do no over fill. Replace the tops, bake for about 1 hour or until the rice is tender.

Fiesta Rice Casserole

1 cup cooked brown rice

3 medium zucchini, sliced

1   7 oz. can chopped green chiles

12 oz. grated Monterey Jack cheese

2 large tomatoes, thinly sliced

2 cups sour cream

1 teaspoon oregano

1 teaspoon garlic salt

¼ cup chopped green pepper

¼ cup chopped green onion

2 tablespoon chopped fresh parsley

Preheat oven to 350° F.

Serves six

*I*n a large buttered casserole, layer the cooked rice, chopped chiles, ½ of the cheese, zucchini, and tomato slices. In a bowl, combine the sour cream, oregano, garlic salt, green pepper, and green onions. Spoon this mixture over the tomatoes and sprinkle on the rest of the cheese. Bake for 45 minutes. Sprinkle with fresh parsley and serve immediately.

Brown Rice

1 cup brown rice

2¼ cups water

salt and black pepper to taste

Serves four

*P*lace the rice in a saucepan and add 2¼ cups of water. Bring the mixture to a boil over high heat. Stir the rice, then reduce the heat to low and cover the pan. Simmer for 30 to 40 minutes, remove the pan from the heat and let the rice sit, covered, for a few minutes in the pan. Just before serving, fluff the rice with a fork and season with salt and pepper.

Rose's Rice

1½ cups brown rice

5½ oz. chicken broth or stock (see Index)

15½ oz. beef broth or stock (see Index)

1 large sliced onion

¼ cup plus ½ cup butter or margarine

1 cup sliced fresh mushrooms, sautéed and drained (optional)

Preheat oven to 350° F.

Serves four to six

In a pan, sauté the onions in ¼ cup butter or margarine, until golden brown. Add chicken broth or stock and 5½ oz. beef broth or stock. Let simmer for 15 to 20 minutes. In a 8x8x3½ inch Pyrex dish, combine the onion mixture and all remaining ingredients, except mushrooms. Bake in the oven for 1-1½ hours. Take the casserole dish out of oven and, if desired, stir in fresh mushrooms. Serve immediately.

Seafood Rice

3 cups chicken stock or broth (see Index)

¼ cup white wine

10 medium raw shrimp, peeled and deveined

8 oz. sea scallops, drained

1 small onion, finely chopped

1 clove garlic, minced

1 cup brown rice

½ tablespoon parsley, finely chopped

black pepper to taste

1 tablespoon Parmesan cheese

thin lemon slices

whole leaves of Italian parsley

Serves four

*I*n a medium sauce pan, bring one cup of chicken broth or stock and ¼ cup white wine to a boil. Add the shrimp and scallops and poach for 3 to 5 minutes. Remove the seafood and reserve the poaching liquid. Heat the olive oil in a large, heavy sauce pan. Add the onion and garlic and sauté for 2 to 3 minutes, until the onion clarifies. Add the brown rice and cook 1 to 2 minutes. Stir in 1 cup of the reserved poaching liquid and cook, stirring gently and continuously, until the liquid is absorbed. Continue to stir, add additional liquid ½ cup at a time until it is absorbed and the rice is tender. This may take 20 to 30 minutes.

When the rice is cooked, add the poached seafood and heat thoroughly. Stir in parsley and pepper to taste and sprinkle with Parmesan cheese. Garnish with sliced lemon and whole parsley leaves, and serve on warmed dinner plates.

Curried Rice

5 tablespoons cooking oil

1 bunch green onions, sliced on an angle, about ¼ inch thick

2 teaspoons curry powder

¼ teaspoon garlic powder

2 teaspoons salt

8 cups cooked brown rice

Serves eight

*H*eat the oil, in a large sauce pan. Add the green onions and sauté quickly until warm. Stir in the remaining ingredients; cook just until heated through.

Spinach-Herbed Rice

2 cups chicken broth or stock (see Index)

1 teaspoon unsalted butter or margarine

¼ cup onion, finely chopped

½ cup spinach, cut into strips

½ teaspoon fresh oregano

½ teaspoon fresh thyme

1 bay leaf

½ tomato concasse (see Index)

1 cup brown rice

Serves four

*I*n a medium sized heavy sauce pan, heat the butter or margarine and sauté the onion until transluscent. Add the spinach and herbs and stir for 1 minute. Add the concasse, brown rice, and chicken broth or stock. Cover and bring to a boil. Reduce heat and simmer for 20 minutes or until done. Remove bay leaf. Serve immediately.

CHAPTER THIRTEEN

Just Desserts

Almond Lemon Cookies

½ cup plus 2 tablespoons butter or margarine

¼ cup plus 1 tablespoon sugar-free syrup

1 tablespoon liquid artificial sweetener

1 egg yolk

1 teaspoon almond extract

½ teaspoon vanilla extract

2½ teaspoons lemon extract

1 cup stone ground whole wheat pastry flour

½ teaspoon baking soda

⅛ teaspoon salt

½ cup crushed almonds

Preheat oven to 300° F.

Serves six to eight

*I*n a bowl, beat the butter or margarine with an electric mixer at medium speed. Add artificial sweetener and syrup, beat well. Add egg yolk and extracts; beat well. Mix the flour, almonds, baking soda and salt; add to creamed mixture, beating well. Shape dough into 1 inch balls; place 2 inches apart on nonstick cookie sheets. Press down to flatten. Bake for 20 minutes or until edges begin to turn a golden brown. Remove cookies to wire racks and let cool completely.

Oatmeal Chocolate Chunk Cookies

1½ cups oatmeal

¾ cup stone ground whole wheat pastry flour

½ teaspoon ground cinnamon

½ teaspoon baking soda

½ teaspoon salt

2 sticks unsalted butter or margarine

1 tablespoon sugar free syrup

1 egg

1½ teaspoons vanilla extract

½ cup chopped Lindt chocolate (70% cocoa content)

Preheat oven to 350° F.

Serves six

In a medium bowl, combine the oats, flour, cinnamon, baking soda and salt; set aside. In a large bowl, mix roughly the butter and syrup. Beat in the egg and vanilla extract. Stir in the dry ingredients until mixture is well blended. Add the chunks of chocolate and mix. On a greased cookie sheet drop the dough by tablespoons. Bake 8 to 10 minutes or until lightly browned. Cool on a wire rack.

Crêpes Bridget

1 lb. cream cheese, room temperature
5 tablespoons sour cream
1 teaspoon liquid artificial sweetener
1 tablespoon vanilla extract
16 crêpes (see Index)
½ cup sliced almonds
2 cups hot fudge sauce (see Index)
2 cups whipping cream

Serves eight

*I*n a mixing bowl, combine the cream cheese, sour cream, artificial sweetener and vanilla. Beat the mixture until smooth. Place 3 tablespoons of the cream cheese filling on one end of each crêpe; roll the crêpes, then refrigerate them until serving.

Spread the almonds on a baking sheet and toast in a preheated 300° F. oven for 5 to 10 minutes. Let cool.

Place 2 crepes on each plate and spoon the hot fudge sauce over the crepes. Top with whipping cream and toasted almonds.

Hot Fudge Sauce

1 teaspoon liquid artificial sweetener

3.5 oz. Lindt chocolate (70% cocoa content)

1½ cups whipping cream

1 teaspoon vanilla extract

½ stick butter or margarine

*M*elt chocolate, butter or margarine, whipping cream, vanilla, and artificial sweetener in a sauce pan. Bring mixture to a rolling boil, whisking constantly. Remove from the heat whisking as it cools. It will thicken. Refrigerate after it cools. To use, heat in a sauce pan or in a microwave, whisk and serve.

Optional: Add mint extract for Mint Chocolate Sauce.

Crêpes

3 large eggs

1 cup milk

½ cup stone ground whole wheat flour

melted butter or margarine for brushing

Yields 16 crêpes

*I*n a medium bowl, beat the eggs with the milk. Add the flour and whisk until smooth. Strain the batter to remove any lumps.

Preheat a 5 inch crêpe pan or skillet, and brush it lightly with melted butter or margarine. Pour about 2 tablespoons batter into the pan and tilt the pan to spread the batter evenly over the bottom of the pan. Cook the crêpe over medium heat until golden brown, about 30 seconds, then turn the crêpe and brown the other side.

Repeat the procedure with the remaining batter, making about 16 crêpes in all. The crêpes can be sealed in plastic wrap and frozen for several weeks.

Double Chocolate Brownie Supreme

1½ cups stone ground whole wheat flour

½ cup unsweetened cocoa

¼ teaspoon salt

3½ teaspoons granulated Sweet 'N Low®

9 tablespoons sugar free syrup

1½ teaspoons baking soda

2 eggs, beaten

¾ cup milk

¾ cup butter or margarine, melted

4 oz. cream cheese, at room temperature

1 tablespoon vanilla extract

¼ teaspoon almond extract

1 cup chopped nuts

1.75 oz. chopped Lindt chocolate (70% cocoa content)

Preheat oven to 400° F.

Serves twelve

In a large bowl, combine the flour, cocoa, Sweet 'N Low®, baking soda and salt; mix well. Add the eggs, milk, butter, syrup, vanilla extract and almond extract; mix well with a spoon. Add the cream cheese and mash in until combined well. Add the chocolate chips and the chopped nuts, mix just until combined. Coat a 8x8 inch pan with nonstick cooking spray and fill the pan with the mixture. Bake for 15 to 20 minutes. Remove from oven and let cool at room temperature. Cut into serving size pieces and serve immediately.

Optional: Serve vanilla ice cream atop brownie with hot fudge sauce.

Cream Puffs

Shells:

1 cup water

½ cup (1 stick) butter or margarine

1 cup stone ground whole wheat pastry flour

1 teaspoon baking soda

⅛ teaspoon salt

4 eggs

Preheat oven to 450° F.

Serves four to six

Boil water and add butter or margarine until it melts. Add flour, baking soda and salt all at once. Lower the fire and stir vigorously with a wooden spoon until batter forms a thick smooth ball that follows the spoon around the pan. Remove from heat. Put the ball of batter in a mixer and beat in the eggs 1 at a time for 1 minute each until the batter is smooth. Divide the batter into sixths. Place on a greased cookie sheet and bake in oven for 15-25 minutes, until puffed and golden.

Cream Sauce:

4 tablespoons butter or margarine

4 tablespoons stone ground whole wheat pastry flour

3 teaspoons granulated Sweet 'N Low®

6 egg yolks

½ teaspoon salt

4 cups milk

½ teaspoon vanilla

In a small sauce pan, melt butter or margarine and blend with salt and flour. Add milk and egg yolks stirring constantly until mixture thickens. Remove from stove and add vanilla and Sweet 'N Low®. Continue to mix until thoroughly blended. Refrigerate until chilled.

Cut tops off shells and fill with cream.

Bread Pudding

2 sticks unsalted butter or margarine

3½ teaspoons granulated Sweet 'N Low®

½ teaspoon nutmeg

3 eggs

1½ cups evaporated milk

5 cups stone ground whole wheat bread, coarsely chopped

1 cup chopped nuts

2 teaspoons vanilla extract

4 egg whites

Preheat oven to 300° F.

Serves eight

Vanilla Hard Sauce:

2 teaspoons stone ground whole wheat pastry flour

2 teaspoons granulated Sweet 'N Low®

2 eggs

3 cups evaporated milk

2 teaspoons vanilla extract

*M*elt butter or margarine in a 8x8x3 inch sized pyrex dish. Gradually beat in the 3 eggs, until creamed. Add evaporated milk, nutmeg, vanilla, and Sweet 'N Low®. Fold in the bread and allow the mixture to be absorbed. Add the chopped nuts. Beat egg whites until they form stiff white peaks. Gradually fold in egg whites. Bake for 1 hour.

For the hard sauce, in a small bowl, mix the evaporated milk with the 2 eggs and vanilla. Warm the mixture in a sauce pan and gradually add the flour stirring constantly. After it has come to a slow boil, remove the mixture from the stove and allow to stand for 10 minutes. Add the Sweet 'N Low® and strain, for a smooth consistency.

In individual bowls, serve the bread pudding with a desired amount of vanilla sauce on top.

Brown Rice Pudding

½ cup brown rice

4 cups whole milk

3 tablespoons vanilla extract

½ teaspoon ground cinnamon

1½ cups heavy cream

1 tablespoon liquid artificial sweetener

1 tablespoon granulated Sweet 'N Low®

Serves six to eight

In a heavy pot, combine milk, 2 tablespoons vanilla extract, and ¼ teaspoon of cinnamon. Slowly bring the mixture to a boil over medium heat, being careful not to scorch the milk. Reduce the heat to low. Add the rice, and cook at a low simmer for 2 hours, covered and stirring occasionally or until the rice is cooked thoroughly and creamy. Remove from the heat and refrigerate until completely cold.

Whip the heavy cream into stiff peaks with an electric mixer, adding the Sweet 'N Low® gradually. Add the remaining cinnamon, 1 tablespoon liquid sweetener, and 1 tablespoon vanilla extract. Using a spatula, fold the cream into the chilled pudding. Spoon into pudding cups, and serve immediately or refrigerate until ready.

Butterscotch Custard

8 eggs

2 tablespoons vanilla extract

1 tablespoon granulated Sweet 'N Low®

2 12 oz. cans evaporated milk

20 Sweet 'N Low® Butterscotch hard candies, crushed

Preheat oven to 375° F.

Serves eight

In a bowl, beat the eggs well, gradually add the vanilla extract, Sweet 'N Low®, and evaporated milk, until it reaches a smooth consistency. Spray an 8x11.5x2 inch pyrex dish with cooking spray. Pour in the mixture. Place the dish inside a larger dish filled with water and bake for 1 hour. Sprinkle the crushed Butterscotch candies over the custard and bake for another 15 to 20 minutes until candies are melted. Let cool for about an hour and serve.

Chocolate Mousse

2 cups whipping heavy cream

8 oz. Lindt chocolate (70% cocoa content)

1 teaspoon vanilla extract

¼ teaspoon almond extract

1½ teaspoons liquid artificial sweetener

Serves four

*P*our 1 cup heavy cream into a sauce pan bring just to a boil and remove from heat. Whisk in 8 oz. of finely chopped chocolate until smooth. Add extracts. Beat 1 cup heavy cream with liquid sweetener until soft peaks form. Whip chocolate mixture to lighten about 2 minutes. Fold the whipped cream into the chocolate mixture. Refrigerate for several hours and serve.

Mocha Mousse

2 eggs yolks, seperated

1   12 oz. can evaporated milk

1 tablespoon unsweetened cocoa

1 tablespoon instant coffee granules

1 tablespoon gelatin

1 tablespoon water

1½ teaspoons granulated Sweet 'N Low®

1 cup whipping cream, whipped

1 teaspoon vanilla extract

Serves four

*B*eat egg yolks. Place them in a saucepan with milk, cocoa, coffee, and vanilla. Mix until smooth. Stir constantly and warm the mixture over medium heat. Do not allow to boil. Remove from heat and cool. Sprinkle gelatin over hot water and dissolve or microwave on medium for 10 seconds. Cool slightly. Stir into mixture. Add sweetener. Fold whipping cream into chocolate mixture. Pour into serving dishes. Cover and refrigerate overnight.

Lime Mousse

1½ cups heavy cream

2 teaspoons granulated Sweet 'N Low®

¼ cup freshly squeezed lime juice

1 teaspoon lime extract (lemon can be substituted)

2 dashes green food coloring (optional)

Freshly grated lime zest for garnish

Serves four

Beat together all ingredients except the lime zest. When the mixture begins to softly mound, spoon into individual dishes and serve with lime zest garnish. Lemon can be substituted for a Lemon Mousse dessert.

Frozen Lemon Cream

2 cups half and half

2 teaspoons granulated Sweet 'N Low®

2 teaspoons finely grated lemon zest

½ cup fresh lemon juice

6 large lemons

Serves twelve

Combine half and half, Sweet 'N Low®, lemon juice, and grated lemon zest and whisk until completely blended. Pour into a shallow pan and freeze. Cut lemons in half, lengthwise, and remove the pulp. Place shells in freezer. Remove the frozen lemon cream, place in a food processor, and mix until smooth. Spoon into frozen shells and keep frozen until ready to serve.

Key Lime Pie

Basic Pie Crust (see Index)

Filling:

8 egg yolks

1 cup (2 sticks) butter or margarine, room temperature

3½ teaspoons plus ½ teaspoon granulated Sweet 'N Low®

6 tablespoons lime juice

3 teaspoons grated lime zest

2 cups whipping cream

1 teaspoon vanilla extract

Serves eight

Beat egg yolks until light. Add butter or margarine and beat until soft. In a double boiler heat mixture over medium-high heat, until the mixture begins to coat the sides of the pot or until the back of the spoon begins to coat. Remove from stove and add 3½ teaspoons Sweet 'N Low®, lime juice, and zest into egg yolk mixture and beat until creamy. In a separate bowl, whip cream with ½ teaspoon Sweet 'N Low® and vanilla extract until stiff. Fold whipped cream into lime cream mixture. Fill pie shell and refrigerate for at least two hours before serving.

Lemon Meringue Pie

Basic Pie Crust (see Index)

Filling:

8 egg yolks

1 cup (2 sticks) butter or margarine, room temperature

3½ teaspoons plus ½ teaspoon granulated Sweet 'N Low®

6 tablespoons lemon juice

3 teaspoons grated lemon zest

4 egg whites

2 drops lemon juice

Preheat oven to 400° F.

Serves eight

B eat egg yolks until light. Add butter and beat until soft. In a double boiler heat mixture over medium-high heat, stirring constantly, until the mixture begins to coat the sides of the pot or until the back of the spoon begins to coat. Remove from stove and add 3½ teaspoons Sweet 'N Low®, 6 tablespoons lemon juice, and zest into egg yolk mixture and beat until creamy. Fill pie shell and let set. In a separate bowl beat the egg whites until fluffy but not dry. Add the remaining Sweet 'N Low® and lemon juice. Beat until peaks form at the ends of the mixer. Spoon the topping over the filled pie and even it out with a spatula. If desired, form decorative swirls. Place the pie in the oven and bake until the meringue is golden brown. Remove from oven and allow to cool before serving.

Chocolate Mousse Torte

Chocolate Crunch Crust (see Index)

1.75 oz. Lindt chocolate (70% cocoa content)

1 pint whipping cream

3 eggs whites

1 teaspoon liquid artificial sweetener

Serves six to eight

*M*elt chocolate in a double boiler. Beat the whipping cream over ice, until stiff. Add sweetener while beating the cream. Whip the egg white until stiff peaks form. Mix half the cream into the chocolate, folding carefully then fold in the rest of the whipped cream. Fold in half of the egg whites with the rest of the mixture until blended and fold in the remaining egg whites. Spread the mousse into the Chocolate Crunch Crust. Refrigerate for up to 2 hours and serve immediately.

Cheese Cake

Triscuit® Cracker Crust (see Index), in a 9 inch spring form pan

3 eggs

2   8oz. packages cream cheese, room temperature

1 teaspoon vanilla extract

3 teaspoons granulated Sweet 'N Low®

Sour Cream Topping:

1 pint sour cream

1 teaspoon vanilla extract

2 teaspoons granulated Sweet 'N Low®

Preheat oven to 375° F.

Serves eight to ten

*B*eat cream cheese for 2 to 3 minutes, add vanilla, and gradually beat in the Sweet 'N Low®. Add the eggs to the mixture, one by one. Pour the mixture in a 9 inch pan and bake for 20 minutes. Remove from oven and let stand for 15 minutes. Reset temperature of oven to 475° F. While the cake is cooling, mix the sour cream topping. In a bowl, combine the vanilla, Sweet 'N Low®, and sour cream. Spread over cake and bake for 10 more minutes. Remove and let cool at room temperature.

Chocolate Angel Pie

Meringue Crust (see Index)

Chocolate Filling:

1 cup whipping cream

½ cup (1 stick) butter or margarine

3 teaspoons granulated Sweet 'N Low®

2 packets 2 oz. unsweetened chocolate, melted

2 eggs

Topping:

2 cups whipping cream

1 teaspoon vanilla extract

½ teaspoon granulated Sweet 'N Low®

Serves six to eight

*W*hip 1 cup cream until stiff. Put in refrigerator. In a separate bowl cream the butter or margarine and Sweet 'N Low®. Stir in chocolate and add eggs one at a time. Beat mixture until light and fluffy. Fold in whipped cream and fill pie crust.

Whip 2 cups cream with Sweet 'N Low®. Add vanilla and beat until stiff peaks form. Fold on top of pie.

Meringue Crust

3 egg whites
4 teaspoons granulated Sweet 'N Low®
12 low sodium Triscuit®, crushed
½ teaspoon baking soda
½ cup chopped pecans
1 teaspoon vanilla extract

Preheat oven to 320° F.

*B*eat egg whites with Sweet 'N Low® until stiff peaks form. Add baking soda and vanilla. Fold in crushed crackers and nuts. Place in a greased 9 inch pie pan and bake for 20 minutes in the oven. Pie crust will rise while baking and fall while cooling.

Chocolate Crunch Crust

1 cup crushed low sodium Triscuit®
1 cup pecans, finely chopped
2 oz. Lindt chocolate, melted (70% cocoa content)
¼ cup melted butter or margarine

Preheat oven to 350° F.

*M*ix together and lay out on a 9 inch pan. Bake for 10 minutes.

Basic Pie Crust
(1 pie shell - 9 inch)

1½ cups stone ground whole wheat pastry flour

¼ teaspoon salt

1½ sticks butter or margarine, room temperature

4 tablespoons cold water

Preheat oven to 425° F.

*M*ix flour and salt together, add butter or margarine, and work into the flour by hand or with a pastry blender until the mixture resembles bread crumbs. Sprinkle water on dough, 1 tablespoon at a time, stirring lightly with a fork. Form dough into a cake. Roll out on a lightly floured surface until the crust is about ⅛ inch thick and 2 inches larger than your inverted pan. Trim and crimp the edges. Prick pie shell all over to prevent puffing and swelling while baking. Bake in oven for 6 minutes with edges covered with foil and 4 to 6 minutes with the foil removed.

Triscuit ® Cracker Crust

1 cup crushed low sodium Triscuit®

1½ teaspoons granulated Sweet 'N Low®

¼ cup softened butter or margarine

*M*ix all ingredients together and place in a lightly greased 9 inch pan.

Vanilla Ice Cream

6 eggs

2   12 oz. cans evaporated milk

4 teaspoons granulated Sweet 'N Low®

1 tablespoon plus 2 teaspoons vanilla extract

3 tablespoons sugar-free syrup

¼ teaspoon salt

1 cup whipping cream

Serves six

*I*n a bowl, beat the eggs, evaporated milk, salt, and vanilla extract. Pour the mixture in a sauce pan and heat on a low-medium fire, until the sides of the pan begin to coat with the mixture or the mixture begins to bubble. Pour the mixture in the ice cream maker and add the whipping cream to the mixture. The ice cream should take approximately 30 minutes to 1 hour depending on the temperature of the mixture and your machine. Once the ice cream begins to harden add the syrup and the Sweet 'N Low®. Let the ice cream finish processing. Serve immediately or freeze for another time.

Optional: For coconut flavored ice cream, coconut extract can be substituted for the vanilla extract.

Praline Parfait

½ cup (1 stick) salted butter or margarine

¾ cup sugar free maple syrup

½ cup chopped pecans

½ cup chopped walnuts

1 tablespoon vanilla extract

2 pints vanilla ice cream (see Index)

Serves four

*B*lend the butter or margarine, syrup, pecans, walnuts, and vanilla in a small pot to make the praline sauce. Over a medium-high fire bring mixture to boil, immediately remove. Let sit for 5 to 7 minutes. Fill 4 stemmed glasses with praline sauce and ice cream, layering the 2 ingredients. Finish with praline sauce and serve. Top with whipped cream and chopped pecans.

Note: Praline Sauce can be used as a topping for other ice creams and desserts.

Chocolate Ice Cream

6 eggs

3.5 oz. Lindt chocolate, finely chopped (70% cocoa content)

2   12 oz. cans evaporated milk

¼ teaspoon butter extract

1 tablespoon plus 2 teaspoons vanilla extract

¼ teaspoon salt

1 cup whipping cream

4 teaspoons granulated Sweet 'N Low®

3 tablespoons sugar free syrup

Serves six

*M*elt chocolate in a microwave for approximately 15-20 seconds, until the chocolate is fully melted. In a bowl, beat the eggs, add the evaporated milk, butter extract, vanilla extract, and salt. Pour the mixture in a sauce pan and heat on a low-medium fire, until the sides of the pan begin to coat with the mixture or the mixture begins to bubble. Pour the mixture in the ice cream maker and add the whipping cream to the mixture. The ice cream should take approximately 30 minutes to 1 hour depending on the temperature of the mixture and your machine. Once the ice cream begins to harden add the syrup and the Sweet 'N Low®. Let the ice cream finish processing. Serve immediately or freeze for another time.

Coffee Ice Cream

6 eggs

2 12 oz. cans evaporated milk

4 teaspoons granulated Sweet 'N Low®

5 tablespoons concentrated coffee

3 tablespoons sugar free syrup

¼ teaspoon salt

1 tablespoon vanilla extract

1 cup whipping cream

Serves six

*I*n a bowl, beat the eggs, add the coffee, evaporated milk, salt, and vanilla extract. Pour the mixture in a sauce pan and heat on a low-medium fire, until the sides of the pan begin to coat with the mixture or the mixture begins to bubble. Pour the mixture in the ice cream maker and add the whipping cream to the mixture. The ice cream should take approximately 30 minutes to 1 hour depending on the temperature of the mixture and your machine. Once the ice cream begins to harden add the syrup and the Sweet 'N Low®. Let the ice cream finish processing. Serve immediately or freeze for another time.

Peppermint Ice Cream

6 eggs

½ cup crushed peppermints, sugar free

2   12 oz. cans evaporated milk

4 teaspoons granulated Sweet 'N Low®

1 tablespoon vanilla extract

2 teaspoons mint extract

3 tablespoons sugar free syrup

¼ teaspoon salt

1 cup whipping cream

Serves six

In a bowl, beat the eggs, evaporated milk, vanilla extract, mint extract, and salt. Pour the mixture in a sauce pan and heat on a low-medium fire, until the sides of the pan begin to coat with the mixture or the mixture begins to bubble. While mixture is warming, crush the peppermints in a ziplock bag and pound a rolling pin on them, until the peppermints are in chunks. Pour the mixture in the ice cream maker, add the whipping cream to the mixture, and ¼ cup of crushed peppermints. The ice cream should take approximately 30 minutes to 1 hour depending on the temperature of the mixture and your machine. Once the ice cream begins to harden add the syrup, Sweet 'N Low®, and remaining peppermints. Let the ice cream finish processing. Serve immediately or freeze for another time.

Strawberry Ice Cream

6 eggs
2   12 oz. cans evaporated milk
4 teaspoons granulated Sweet 'N Low®
1 tablespoon strawberry extract
2 teaspoons vanilla extract
3 tablespoons sugar free syrup
¼ teaspoon salt
1 cup whipping cream
red food coloring

Serves six

In a bowl, beat the eggs, evaporated milk, vanilla extract, strawberry extract, salt, and 2 to 3 drops of red food coloring. Pour the mixture in a sauce pan and heat on a low-medium fire, until the sides of the pan begin to coat with the mixture or the mixture begins to bubble. Pour the mixture in the ice cream maker and add the whipping cream to the mixture. The ice cream should take approximately 30 minutes to 1 hour depending on the temperature of the mixture and your machine. Once the ice cream begins to harden add the syrup and the Sweet 'N Low®. Let the ice cream finish processing. Serve immediately or freeze for another time.

Alana's Mile High Pie

1 pint vanilla ice cream (see Index)

1 pint chocolate ice cream (see Index)

1 pint peppermint ice cream (see Index)

Meringue Crust (see Index)

Hot Fudge Sauce (see Index)

Serves six to eight

Layer the slightly softened ice cream in the pie shell. Vanilla first, chocolate second, and peppermint on the top. Freeze the pie for 2 to 3 hours. Cut serving size pieces and top with hot fudge sauce. Serve immediately.

Mud Pie

Chocolate Crunch Crust (see Index)

2 quarts coffee ice cream (see Index)

1½ cups hot fudge sauce (see Index)

2 cups almonds, slivered

Serves eight

Cover the pie crust with coffee ice cream. Put into freezer until the ice cream is firm. Slice Mud Pie into 8 portions and serve on a chilled dessert plate. Top with hot fudge sauce, whipped cream and slivered almonds.

Maude's Peanut Butter Ice Cream Pie

Chocolate Crunch Crust (see Index)

1 quart vanilla ice cream (see Index)

1 cup crunchy peanut butter

¼ cup chopped unsalted nuts

Serves six to eight

P lace the Chocolate Crunch Crust in a 9 inch pie pan. In a non-metallic bowl, combine the ice cream and peanut butter; work quickly, mixing the ingredients either by hand or using an electric mixer set on medium speed.

Pour the ice cream mixture into crust, smooth the top and sprinkle with chopped nuts. Freeze the pie overnight or until solid, then serve.

Lemon Ice

2 teaspoons lemon zest, finely grated

4 cups water

¼ teaspoon salt

¾ cup lemon juice

8 teaspoons granulated Sweet 'N Low®

Serves eight

B oil the lemon zest in the water and salt for 5 minutes. Cool and add lemon juice and Sweet 'N Low® until thoroughly blended. Place in ice cube trays and freeze. To serve, remove from ice cube trays and break up into shallow dishes. Lime zest and juice may be used in place of the lemon for a Lime Ice.

CHAPTER FOURTEEN

Breads and Bread Crumbs

Stone Ground Whole Wheat Bread

3 cups stone ground whole wheat pastry flour

1 cup buttermilk, warmed

½ cup water, warm to touch from faucet

2 teaspoons dry yeast

1 tablespoon butter or margarine, room temperature

½ teaspoon granulated Sweet 'N Low®

2 teaspoons salt

Preheat oven to 350° F.

*W*arm milk; add warmed water and yeast and mix. Let stand for a minute until dissolved. Place 2 cups flour, butter or margarine, Sweet 'N Low®, and salt in mixing bowl and beat vigorously with flat beater. Replace flat beater with dough hook. Incorporate additional flour by flicking the machine on and off to take the stickiness out of dough. Scrape the side of the bowl and knead the mixture at a medium speed for 6–8 minutes. Continue adding flour periodically until the dough is completely bound and comes clean from the mixing bowl. Place in a large greased bowl, cover, and let rise until double in size. Punch down the dough and place in a greased 8½ inch loaf pan. Cover and let it rise again to double in size. Bake 40–50 minutes. Remove when done and cool before slicing.

Cheese Bread

½ cup buttermilk, warmed

½ cup water, warm to touch from faucet

2 teaspoons dry yeast

½ teaspoon granulated Sweet 'N Low®

¾ cup Colby and Monterey Jack cheese, shredded

1 teaspoon salt

2½ cups stone ground whole wheat pastry flour

Preheat oven to 350° F.

*M*ix buttermilk, water, and yeast thoroughly. Let stand for 1 minute until dissolved. Place 2 cups flour, Sweet 'N Low®, salt, and cheese in mixing bowl and beat vigorously with flat beater. Replace flat beater with dough hook. Incorporate additional flour by turning the machine on and off to take the stickiness out of the dough. Scrape the side of the bowl and knead the mixture at a medium speed for 6 to 8 minutes. Continue adding flour periodically until the dough is completely bound and comes clean from the mixing bowl. Place in a large greased bowl, cover, and let rise until double in size. Punch down the dough and place in a greased 8½ inch loaf pan. Cover and let rise again to double in size. Bake for 40 to 50 minutes. Remove when done and cool before slicing.

Onion Bread

½ cup buttermilk, warmed

½ cup water, warm to touch from faucet

2 teaspoons dry yeast

½ teaspoon granulated Sweet 'N Low®

3 tablespoons butter or margarine

½ cup onions, finely chopped

1 teaspoon salt

3 cups stone ground whole wheat pastry flour

Preheat oven to 350° F.

*I*n a microwave sauté onions in butter or margarine approximately 3 minutes. Mix buttermilk, water, and yeast. Let stand for 1 minute until dissolved. Place 2½ cups flour, Sweet 'N Low®, salt, and sautéed onions in a mixing bowl and beat vigorously with flat beater. Replace flat beater with dough hook. Incorporate additional flour by turning the machine on and off to take the stickiness out of the dough. Scrape the side of the bowl and knead the mixture at a medium speed for 6 to 8 minutes. Continue adding flour periodically until the dough is completely bound and comes clean from the mixing bowl. Place in a large greased bowl, cover, and let rise until double in size. Punch down the dough and place in a greased 8½ inch loaf pan. Cover and let rise again to double in size. Bake for 40 to 50 minutes. Remove when done and cool before slicing.

Rye Bread

½ cup buttermilk, warmed
½ cup water, warm to touch from faucet
½ teaspoon granulated Sweet 'N Low®
1 teaspoon dry yeast
1 teaspoon salt
1 tablespoon caraway seeds
1 cup whole grain stone ground rye flour
1½ cups stone ground whole wheat pastry flour

Preheat oven to 350° F.

*M*ix buttermilk, water, and yeast. Let stand for 1 minute until dissolved. Place 1 cup rye flour and 1 cup wheat flour, Sweet 'N Low®, salt, and caraway seeds in a mixing bowl and beat vigorously with a flat beater. Replace flat beater with a dough hook. Incorporate additonal flour by turning the machine on and off to take the stickiness out of the dough. Scrape the side of the bowl and kneed the mixture at a medium speed for 7 to 8 minutes. Continue adding flour periodically until the dough is completely bound and comes clean from the mixing bowl. Place in a large greased bowl, cover, and let rise until double in size. Punch down the dough and place in a greased 8½ inch loaf pan. Cover and let it rise again to double in size. Bake for 40 to 50 minutes. Remove when done and cool before slicing.

Spinach Bread

½ cup buttermilk, warmed

½ cup water, warm to touch from faucet

2 teaspoons dry yeast

½ teaspoon granulated Sweet 'N Low®

5 oz. fresh spinach, chopped and cooked

1 teaspoon salt

3 cups stone ground whole wheat pastry flour

Preheat oven to 350° F.

*C*ut spinach into small pieces, wash, drain, and microwave for approximately 6 to 8 minutes. Drain again on paper towels squeezing out as much liquid as possible. Mix buttermilk, water, and yeast. Let stand for 1 minute until dissolved. Place 2½ cups flour, Sweet 'N Low®, salt, and cooked spinach in a mixing bowl and beat vigorously with flat beater. Replace flat beater with dough hook. Incorporate additional flour by turning the machine on and off to take the stickiness out of the dough. Scrape the side of the bowl and knead the mixture at a medium speed for 6 to 8 minutes. Continue adding flour periodically until the dough is completely bound and comes clean from the mixing bowl. Place in a large greased bowl, cover, and let rise until double in size. Punch down the dough and place in a greased 8½ inch loaf pan. Cover and let rise again to double in size. Bake for 40 to 50 minutes. Remove when done and cool before slicing.

Whole Wheat Dinner Rolls

2 cups stone ground whole wheat pastry flour

½ teaspoon granulated Sweet 'N Low®

¾ cup buttermilk

4 tablespoons butter or margarine

1 egg

1 teaspoon yeast

2 egg whites, beaten

Preheat oven to 350° F.

Place the kneading blade in a bread pan, with all ingredients except yeast. Insert pan securely into machine. Close the top lid and fill the yeast dispenser with the dry yeast. Select the dough setting and press the start button. When kneading is completed, place the dough into a greased bowl. Cover the bowl with plastic wrap and let rest for 20 minutes. Divide the ball by 2 until you have 24 small balls. Roll balls and place 3 balls together in each greased muffin cup. Cover and let rise until almost doubled, approximately 30-50 minutes. Brush rolls with beaten egg whites. Bake for 10-15 minutes or until golden brown. Remove the rolls from the baking pan and serve warm. Recipe makes 8 rolls.

Bran Muffins

2½ cups unprocessed wheat bran

1⅓ cups stone ground whole wheat flour

1½ teaspoons granulated Sweet 'N Low® Brown

1½ teaspoons baking soda

2 eggs, beaten

1 cup buttermilk

½ cup (1 stick) butter or margarine, softened

⅔ cup maple sugar free syrup

Preheat oven to 425° F.

Combine bran, flour, Sweet 'N Low® Brown, baking soda in a large mixing bowl and whisk until well blended. Add eggs, buttermilk, butter or margarine and syrup until blended into a moist batter. Spray muffin cups with cooking spray. Spoon mixture into muffin cups to about ⅔ filled. Bake for approximately 15 minutes.

Stone Ground Whole Wheat Bread
(Bread Machine Recipe)

4 tablespoons stone ground whole wheat flour

2 cups stone ground whole wheat pastry flour

½ teaspoon granulated Sweet 'N Low®

1 cup milk

1 teaspoon salt

1 tablespoon butter or margarine

1½ teaspoons yeast

*P*lace all ingredients, except yeast in a bread machine. Put yeast in top dispenser and start the bread machine.

Stone Ground Whole Wheat Buttermilk Bread
(Bread Machine Recipe)

1½ teaspoons salt

1½ cups stone ground whole wheat flour

2 cups stone ground whole wheat pastry flour

1 extra large egg

½ teaspoon granulated Sweet 'N Low®

1 cup buttermilk

1 tablespoon yeast

*P*lace all ingredients, except the yeast in the bread machine. Add the yeast to the dispenser and start the bread machine.

Whole Wheat Pizza Crust
(Bread Machine Recipe)

2 cups stone ground whole wheat pastry flour

½ teaspoon granulated Sweet 'N Low®

1 teaspoon salt

1 teaspoon butter or margarine

1 cup milk

½ teaspoon yeast

*P*lace all ingredients except the yeast in the bread machine and add the yeast to the dispenser. Use the dough setting. When complete, place dough in a greased bowl and allow to rest for 20-30 minutes. Then place the dough on a greased pizza pan. Cover with favorite toppings and bake in a preheated 400° F. oven for 15-20 minutes.

Bread Crumbs

1 box Triscuit®

1 cup stone ground whole wheat flour

2 tablespoons dried parsley flakes

Yields 3 cups

Place Triscuit® in food processor and pulverize to crumbs. Add parsley and mix until well blended.

Italian Bread Crumbs

1 box Triscuit®

1 cup stone ground whole wheat flour

½ cup grated Parmesan cheese

2 tablespoons dried parsley flakes

1 tablespoon Italian seasonings

2 tablespoons garlic powder

Yields 3½ cups

Place the Triscuit in a food processor and pulverize to crumbs. Add all other ingredients and mix until well blended.

Suggested Red Wine List

Compiled by wine expert and connoisseur, James C. Brennan

Brennan's Restaurant of New Orleans boasts of a 35,000 bottle wine cellar with 3,000 different selections. In recognition of its excellence, Brennan's has received the Oscar of wine cellar awards, the *Wine Spectator Grand Award*, for fifteen consecutive years. Such an outstanding cellar is largely attributable to the expertise and passion for wine of Jimmy Brennan, Ted's brother and a co-owner of Brennan's Restaurant. In the wine list that follows, Jimmy shares his knowledge and understanding of affordable fine, young red wines (three to five years old), rich in tannins that are acceptable within the *Sugar Bust For Life!* guidelines.

Cabernet Sauvignon

Benziger
Cafaro, Napa
Cakebread Cellars
Caymus, Napa
Chalk Hill, Sonoma
Chateau St. Jean, Sonoma
Chateau Montelena
Chateau Saint Michelle, Washington State
Clos Du Val, Napa
B.R. Cohn, Sonoma
Cuvaison, Napa
DeLoach, Russian River
Dry Creek
Eberle, Paso Robles
Far Niente, Napa
Frog's Leap, Napa
Geyser Peak, Alexander Valley
Grgich Hills, Napa
Gundlach-Bundshu, Sonoma
Hess Collection, Napa
Iron Horse, Sonoma
Jordan, Alexander Valley

Cabernet Sauvignon (cont.)

Kunde, Sonoma
Robert Mondavi, Napa
Niebaum-Coppola, "Rubicon"
Shafer
Stelzner, S.L.D., Napa
Stag's Leap Wine Cellars, Napa
Sullivan Vineyards, Napa
Swanson, Napa

Merlot

Cafaro, Napa
Ferrari Carano, Sonoma
Fetzer
Kendall-Jackson Vintner's Reserve
Kenwood, Sonoma
Kunde, Sonoma
MacRostie, Carneros
Matanzas Creek, Sonoma
Rabbit Ridge, North Coast
St. Francis, Estate Bottled
Duckhorn
Jekel

Pinot Noir

Bouchaine, Carneros Napa
David Bruce, Vintner's Select, Sonoma
Davis Byrum, Russian River
Byron, Santa Barbara County
Cambria, Julia's Vineyard, Santa Maria
DeLoach, Sonoma
Domaine Drouhin, Oregon
Domaine Serene, Willamette Valley, Oregon
Elk Cove Vineyards, Oregon
Kalin Cellars
Robert Mondavi
Rex Hill, Oregon
Robert Sinskey, Los Carneros, Napa
Willamette, Valley Vineyards, Reserve

Zinfandel

Gary Farrell, Russian River, Sonoma
Ravenswood, Sonoma
Seghesio, Old Vines, Sonoma
Rodney Strong, Old Vines, Sonoma
Sutter Home, Reserve
Turley

California Cabernet Franc

Benziger
Dry Creek, Dry Creek Valley, Sonoma
Gundlach-Bundschu, Sonoma
Whitehall Lane, Napa

California Mourvedre

Bonny Doon, "Old Telegram"
Bonny Doon, "Grahm Crew"
Joseph Phelps, Vin du Mistral, "Le Mistral"

California Sangiouese

Cambria, Tepusquet Vineyard

Syrah/Shiraz
California and Australia

Eberle, Syrah, Paso Robles, California
Fess Parker, Reserve, Calfornia
C. Henschke, Keystone Estate, Australia

Italian Reds

Barolo
Chianti Classico
Sangiovese
Barbera

"To Market, To Market!" Brand Name Guide

$\mathcal{A}$t the grocery avoiding refined sugar and other high glycemic ingredients in food products is impossible to do without taking the time to read labels. Learning to read a label is your only safeguard against sinister ingredients in foods that, oftentimes, appear to be healthy. Taking the necessary time to read a label creates an awareness of just how much sugar or comparably evil ingredients are in the foods we eat.

Always remember that fresh should be your first choice. Frozen food products should be your second choice. Canned foods, although many in our guide are not preserved in any type of sugar, should be chosen third.

Many people ask, "How many grams of sugar am I allowed per meal?" The answer is, "As few as possible." Keep in mind, once again, that this is a low sugar dietary concept, not a no sugar dietary concept. You are already consuming natural sugar in fruit and vegetables as well as dairy products.

In other words, knowing how to read a label is a must. The amount of sugar per serving identified on the label of an acceptable food item should not exceed 1 gram. This means two things.

First, as serving sizes vary depending on the food item be certain that you understand just how much a serving size is and only eat one or two servings. Second, take into consideration that if a serving size is diluted by another ingredient such as water you may eat more than one or two servings depending upon the degree of dilution. As always, moderation is the key.

CAUTION! Inspection of a food product does not end at reading the number of sugar grams per serving. Reading the detailed list of ingredients is a must. This is where the "hidden sugars" and other unacceptable ingredients are found.

"Hidden Sugars" Include:

Beet Juice	High Fructose Corn Syrup
Beet Sugar	Honey
Brown Rice Syrup	Maltodextrin
Brown Sugar	Maltose
Cane Juice	Maple Syrup
Cane Syrup	Molasses
Corn Syrup	Raisin Juice
Dextrose	Sugar, Raw and Refined
Glucose	Sucrose

Other Unacceptable Ingredients Include:

Barley Malt

Cornstarch

Flour: Corn, Enriched Wheat and White

Malted Barley

Modified Food Starch

Modified Tapioca Starch

Potato Starch

Don't be confused! Fructose in fruit and lactose in milk are acceptable natural sugars. Interestingly, certain sources believe maltodextrin to have a glycemic index or response as high as refined sugar and recommend the use of only small amounts of this popular artificial sweetener. We chose artificial sweeteners for our recipes and products for our brand name guide which are void of maltodextrin as over-consumption could prove unsafe.

Most other artificial sweeteners such as aspartame, saccharin, acesulfame-K and the newly FDA approved sucralose as well as the sugar alcohols isomalt, maltitol, mannitol, sorbitol and xylitol are slowly absorbed inducing a low glycemic response. However, all are carbohydrates and should be used in moderation.

Variety in the usage of artificial sweeteners is an important consideration. Alternating the use of different sweeteners will reduce the ingestion of significant amounts of any one kind — thus diminishing the risk of potential side effects.

Unfortunately, most people do not have the time required to avidly read labels in maintaining a truly healthful lifestyle. We understand this challenge and have applied our acquired knowledge in compiling a list of brand names to choose. If we are unable to recommend a food item that you need, check our recipe section for possible sugar free substitutions.

Our guide predominantly notes brand names void of anything unacceptable. We recommend very few products containing even traces of "hidden sugars" and other unacceptable ingredients so as not to create confusion although ingredients listed in accordance with FDA guidelines at the bottom of a label can be insignificant.

Equally as insignificant can be small amounts of "forbidden" foods, "hidden sugars" or other unacceptable ingredients spread throughout large quantities of food. For example, the small amounts of Worcestershire sauce in some of our recipes should be inconsequential.

Beyond the Greater New Orleans area sugar free whole grain breads are limited and difficult to find. Our homemade bread recipes provide a viable solution. Contacting one of the two New Orleans bakeries mentioned in the Brand Name Guide provides another option. As a third alternative, a store bought whole grain bread with minimal amounts of hidden sugar listed at the bottom of a label could be consumed in extreme moderation.

Our extensive list of acceptable brand names is based on the inventories of approximately 20 grocery, health food and specialty stores in the New Orleans and Dallas-Ft. Worth areas. There is the possibility that we have failed to include certain appropriate brand names of which we are, simply, unaware. Occasionally, store shelves and freezers were incompletely stocked. In any event, we urge you to share with us any additional items that we may have inadvertently excluded. We will include them in our next printing.

Our brand name guide should expedite your grocery shopping and contribute to the ease of your low sugar lifestyle. Once again, we have taken the guesswork out of making wise choices. *Sugar Bust For Life!* has revealed an easy road to a healthful life for you!

Anchovies
Giovanni Anchovy Paste
Haddon House Anchovy Fillets
King Oscar Anchovies
Musette Anchovy Fillets
Reese Anchovy Paste
Reese Anchovies
Roland Anchovy Paste
Roland Anchovies

Baking Soda
Arm & Hammer Brand

Beans, Canned
Bean Salad
Westbrae Natural Bean Salad
Black Beans
Goya Black Beans
Green Giant Black Beans
Progresso Black Beans
Trappey's Black Beans
Westbrae Black Beans
Westbrae Natural Black Beans
Butter Beans
Stubbs Butter Beans
Fava Beans
Progresso Fava Beans
Great Northern Beans
Green Giant Great Northern Beans
Westbrae Natural Great Northern
  Beans
Green Beans
America's Choice Green Beans
Delchamps Green Beans
Del Monte Fresh Cut Green Beans
Del Monte Fresh Cut Seasoned Green
  Beans
Double Luck Green Beans
Food Club Green Beans
Good Day Green Beans
Green Giant Green Beans

Jack and the Bean Stalk Green Beans
Libby Green Beans
Le Sueur Green Beans
Pride Green Beans
Prestige Green Beans
Shur Fine Green Beans
S&W Cut Green Beans
The Allens Italian Green Beans
Thrifty Maid Green Beans
Lentils
Westbrae Lentils
Westbrae Natural Lentils
Lima Beans
America's Choice Lima Beans
Thrifty Maid Lima Beans
Del Monte Fresh Cut Lima Beans
Trappey's Baby Green Lima Beans
Valu Time Lima Beans
Pinto Beans
Trappey's Navy Pinto Beans
Red Kidney Beans
Progresso Red Kidney Beans
Van Camp's New Orleans Style Red
  Kidney Beans
Westbrae Red Kidney Beans
Westbrae Natural Red Kidney Beans
Salad Beans
Westbrae Natural Salad Beans
Soy Beans
Westbrae Soy Beans
Westbrae Natural Soy Beans
Soup Beans
Westbrae Natural Soup Beans
Black-Eyed Peas
Bush's Black-Eyed Peas
Green Giant Black-Eyed Peas
Shur Fine Black-Eyed Peas
Trappey's Black-Eyed Peas with
  Jalapenos
Trappey's Black-Eyed Peas

Field Peas
Bush's Field Peas with Snaps
The Allens Sunshine Field Peas
Trappey's Field Peas

Garbanzo Beans/Chick Peas
Casa Fiesta Garbanzo Beans
La Lechonera Chick Peas/Garbanzo
    Beans
Old El Paso Garbanzo Beans
Progresso Chick Peas/Garbanzo Beans
Westbrae Garbanzo Beans
Westbrae Natural Garbanzo Beans

Pinto Beans
Casa Fiesta Pinto Beans
Old El Paso Pinto Beans
Westbrae Pinto Beans

Wax Beans
America's Choice Cut Wax Beans
Del Monte Wax Beans
Shur Fine Wax Beans

Beans, Dried
All Brands

Beans, Refried
Bearitos (Vegetarian) Refried Beans -
    Spicy with Green Chilies
Old El Paso Fat-Free Refried Beans
Old El Paso Refried Beans
Old El Paso Refried Black Beans
Ortega Refried Beans
Rosarita Refried Beans
San Carlos Refried Beans
Shari's Refried Black Beans
Taco Bell Refried Beans

Beverages
Coffee
Diet Colas
Any Brand Unsweetened Tea
Community Diet Iced Tea
Snapple Diet Drinks - All Flavors

Bread
Finn Crisp Thin Crisp Rye Bread
French Meadow Whole Grain Rice Bread
Katrina's Sugar Free Baked Goods,
    New Orleans, Louisiana
La Louisiane Sugar Free Baked Goods,
    Kenner, Louisiana
Mestemacher Pumpernickel
Pepperidge Farms Pumpernickel Bread
Pepperidge Farms Rye Bread
Pepperidge Farms Party Dark
    Pumpernickel Bread
Pepperidge Farms Party Jewish Rye Bread
Rudolph's 100% Rye Bread with Whole
    Grain
Ryvita Tasty Dark Rye Whole Grain
    Crisp Bread
Ryvita Toasted Sesame Rye Whole
    Grain Crisp Bread

Cakes, Brown Rice
Konriko Brown Rice Cakes
Lundberg Family Farms Brown Rice Cakes

Candy
Eda's Naturally Sweeetened Sugar Free
    Hard Candies
Estee Sugar Free Hard Candies
Fifty 50 Sugar Free Hard Candy
Sweet 'N Low Sugar Free Hard Candies

Capers
Cento Capers
Crosse & Blackwell Capers
Fancifood Capers
Haddon House Capers
Haddon House Imported Non-Pareil
    Capers
Reese Capers
Roland Capers
San Marc Capers

Victoria Capers
Zatarain's Capers

Cereals, Whole Grains
Kellogg's Extra Fiber All Bran
Arrowhead Mills Pearled Barley
Quaker Barley
Arrowhead Mills Steel Cut Oats
Arrowhead Mills Oat Bran
Mother's 100% Natural Hot Cereal
    Whole Wheat/Rolled Wheat
Hodgson Mills Oat Bran Hot Cereal
Quaker Oat Bran Hot Cereal
Arrowhead Mills Old Fashioned
    Oatmeal
John McCann's Irish Oatmeal (not
    instant)
Quaker Oatmeal (not instant)
Scottish Oatmeal
Food Club Old Fashioned Oats
Kountry Fresh Old Fashioned Oats
Quaker Oats
Kashi, The Breakfast Pilaf
Puffed Kashi
Puffed Kashi Seven Whole Grain and
    Sesame
Bob's Red Mill Stone Ground Cracked
    Wheat Hot Cereal
Bob's Red Mill Seven Grain Hot Cereal
Bob's Red Mill Stone Ground Whole
    Wheat Farina Hot Cereal
America's Choice Shredded Wheat
Barbara's Shredded Wheat
Nabisco Shredded Wheat
Post Shredded Wheat

Chips
Chifles Plantain Chips
Terra Sweet Potato Chips

Chocolate
Baker's Unsweetened Chocolate Squares
Cuana Chocolate
Ghirardelli Premium Unsweetened Cocoa
Hershey's Unsweetened Baking
    Chocolate
Hershey's 100% Cocoa
Hershey's European Style Dutch
    Processed Cocoa
LeNoir American Chocolate
Lindt 70% Cocoa Chocolate Bar
Nestle Unsweetened Baking Chocolate
Orinico Chocolate
Valvrona Chocolate

Chocolate Mix
Carnation No Sugar Added Hot Cocoa
    Mix
Food Club Hot Cocoa Mix, No Sugar
    Added
Swiss Miss Diet Hot Chocolate

Cooking Oils
Basil Oil
Lorina Basil Flavored Oil
Canola Oils
America's Choice Canola Oil
Astor Canola Oil
Crisco Puritan Canola Oil
Food Club Canola Oil
Lorina Canolive Oil
Lou Ana Canola Oil
Mazola Canola Oil
Mrs. Tucker's Canola Oil
Shur Fine Canola Oil
Spectrum Naturals Canola Oil
Wesson Canola Oil
Whole Food Canola Oil
Chili Oil
Stonewall Kitchen Hot Chili Oil

Corn Oil
America's Choice Corn Oil
Crisco Corn Oil
Delchamp's Corn Oil
Food Club Corn Oil
Mazola Corn Oil
Mrs. Tucker's Corn Oil
Shur Fine Corn Oil
Wesson Corn Oil

Garlic Oil
Lorina Garlic Flavored Oil
Stonewall Kitchen Roasted Garlic Oil

Peanut Oil
Astor Peanut Oil
Duke's Peanut Oil
Food Club Peanut Oil
Lorina Peanut Oil
Lou Ana Peanut Oil
Shur Fine Peanut Oil

Safflower Oil
Hain Safflower Oil
Hollywood Safflower Oil
Lou Ana Safflower Oil
Wesson Safflower Oil

Vegetable Oil
America's Choice Vegetable Oil
Blue Plate Vegetable Oil
Chef Way Vegetable Oil
Crisco Vegetable Oil
Food Club Vegetable Oil
Lou Ana Vegetable Oil
Mrs. Tucker's Vegetable Oil
Shur Fine Vegetable Oil
Wesson Vegetable Oil

Walnut Oil
Hain Walnut Oil

Cooking Sprays
Baker's Joy Cooking Spray
Crisco Cooking Spray
Mazola Cooking Spray
Naturally Canola Cooking Spray
Naturally Garlic Cooking Spray
Naturally Olive Oil Cooking Spray
Pam Cooking Spray
Shur Fine Cooking Spray
Savor's Choice Cooking Spray
Spectrum Naturals Skillet Spray Canola Oil
Spectrum Naturals Skillet Spray Super Canola
Spectrum Naturals Skillet Spray Olive Oil
Sunola Canola Cooking Spray
Tryson House Butter Cooking Spray
Tryson House Garlic Cooking Spray
Tryson House Olive Cooking Spray
Weight Watcher's Canola Cooking Spray
Wesson Cooking Spray

Cooking Wines
Reese Maitre Jacques Burgundy Cooking Wine
Reese Maitre Jacques Vintage Cooking Wine
Regina Sherry Cooking Wine

Crackers
Bran a Crisp
Konriko Brown Rice Cakes
Lundberg Family Farms Brown Rice Cakes
Wasa Fiber Rye
Wasa Light Rye
Wasa Sourdough Rye
Hol Grain Brown Rice Crackers
San-J Sesame Brown Rice Crackers
San-J Tamari Brown Rice Crackers
Edward and Sons Brown Rice Snaps, Onion Garlic
Edward and Sons Brown Rice Snaps, Tamari Seaweed

Edward and Sons Brown Rice Snaps, Unsalted Sesame
Finn Crisp Dark
Finn Crisp Dark with Caraway
Kavli All Natural Whole Grain Crispbread Crispy Thin and Hearty Thick
Nabisco Triscuit Original
Nabisco Triscuit Low Sodium
Ryvita Whole Grain Crisp Bread, Tasty Light Rye
Ryvita Whole Grain Crisp Bread, Tasty Dark Rye

Dips & Spreads

Guiltless Gourmet Bean Dip, Mild and Spicy
Whole Food Pinto Bean Dip
Baba Ganoush Eggplant and Tahini Spread
Colavita Peppazza Hot Pepper Spread
Sun Fix Roma Italia Spread

Evaporated Milk

Carnation Evaporated Milk
Pet Evaporated Milk

Extracts

McCormick Extracts: Almond, Banana, Butter, Coconut, Lemon, Mint, Orange, Strawberry, Vanilla, Black Walnut
Shur Fine Lemon Extract
Trader's Choice Pure Lemon Extract
Zatarain's Root Beer Extract
Melipone Mexican Vanilla
Shur Fine Vanilla
Valu Time Vanilla
Zatarain's Vanilla

Flours

Arrowhead Mills Brown Rice Flour
Hodgson Mill Brown Rice Flour
Bob's Red Mill Fava Bean Flour
Bob's Red Mill Stone Ground Garbanzo Bean Flour
Hodgson Mill Oat Bran Blend Flour
Hodgson Mill Whole Grain Stone Ground Whole Wheat Pastry Flour
Hodgson Mill Whole Grain Stone Ground Whole Wheat Flour
Bob's Red Mill Stone Ground Dark Rye Flour
Arrowhead Mills Whole Grain Rye Flour
Hodgson Mill Whole Grain Rye Flour

Fruit, Canned

All Brands Canned Fruit Packed in Water or Natural Juices
Lucky Leaf Sliced Apples
America's Choice Unsweetened Old Fashioned Applesauce
Leroux Creek Apple-Apricot Sauce
Leroux Creek Apple-Berry Sauce
Leroux Creek Apple-Cherry Sauce
Leroux Creek Apple-Cinnamon Sauce
Lucky Leaf Old Fashion Natural Applesauce
Vermont Village Apricot Applesauce
Vermont Village Cranberry Applesauce
Whole Food Organic Unsweetened Applesauce
S&W Natural Style Mandarin Orange Sections
America's Choice Lite Peaches
Del Monte Fruit Naturals Sliced Peaches
Food Club Peaches
Shur Fine Peaches, in Natural Juices
Thrifty Maid Peaches

America's Choice Lite Pears
Astor Lite Pears
Del Monte Pear Halves
Food Club Pears
Shur Fine Pears, in Natural Juices
Thrifty Maid Pears

Fruit, Frozen
Food Club Whole Blackberries
Stilwell Blackberries
Cascadian Farms Blueberries
Food Club Whole Blueberries
Stilwell Blueberries
Food Club Honey Dew and Cantaloupe
    Melon Balls
Food Club Sliced Peaches
McKenzie's Peaches
Southern Sliced Peaches
Cascadian Farms Strawberries
Food Club Whole Strawberries
Southern Whole Strawberries
Stilwell Strawberries

Fruit, Juice
Flavorite Lemon Juice
Real Lemon Lemon Juice
Real Lime Lime Juice

Fruit, Spreads
American Spoon Spreadable Fruit,
    "Spoon Fruit"
Bionaturae 100% Fruit
Community Kitchens Fruit Spread
Dickerson's Purely Fruit
Estee Fruit Spread
Fifty 50 Fruit Spread
Fiordi Frutta 100% Fruit
La Don's Fancy Fruit Spread
Polaner All Fruit
R. W. Knudsen All Natural Fancy Fruit
    Spread

Smucker's Simple Fruit
Sorrell Ridge 100% Fruit
St. Dalfour 100% Fruit
The New Organic Co. - Conserve -
    Golden Apple, Mediterranean, Red
    Orange, Raspberry, Strawberry
Whole Food Market "365" 100% Fruit

Gelatin
Jell-O Sugar Free Low Calorie Gelatin
    Snacks
Knox's Unflavored Gelatin

Horseradish
Horse Shoe Prepared Horseradish
Kraft Horseradish, Prepared
Silver Spring Horseradish, Prepared
Sophia Clikas Horseradish, Prepared
Zatarain's Horseradish, Prepared

Hot Sauces
All Cajun Food Co. Andre's Rouge
    Spiced Pepper Sauce
Cajun Chef Green Hot Sauce
Chef Prudhomme's Pepper Sauce
CheRith Valley Gardens Hot Pepper
    Sauce
Colavita Classic Hot Sauce
Crystal Classic Cayenne Garlic Sauce
Crystal Classic Cayenne Pepper Sauce
Crystal Hot Sauce
El Fenix Hot Sauce
Gardens-by-the-Bay Hot Chile Oil
Louisiana Hot Sauce
"Louisiana" The Perfect Hot Sauce
Louisiana Gold Hot Sauce
Louisiana Gold Pepper Hot Sauce
Melinda's Hot Sauce
Tabasco Hot Sauce
Trappey's Louisiana Hot Sauce

Hummus

Choice of Vermont Hummus
Fantastic Foods Hummus
Maranatha Hummus
Melissa's Black Bean Hummous
Melissa's Red Pepper Hummous
Out to Lunch Hummus
Swan Gardens Hummus

Ice Cream

Brown's Velvet Ice Cream - No Sugar
    Added

Ketchup

Estee Sugar Free Ketchup
Westbrae Unsweetened Un-Ketchup

Marinades and Sauces

California Harvest Artichoke Tapenade
California Harvest Green Olive
    Tapenade
Olivier Napa Valley Mediterranean
    Kalamata Olive Sun-Dried Tomato
    Tapenade
California Harvest Portabello
    Mushroom Tapenade
Cherchies Champagne Sauce for All
    Seasons, Marinade or Seafood Pasta
Postilion Bordeaux Wine Marinade

Mayonnaise

Consorzio Basil Flavored Olive Oil
    Mayonnaise
Consorzio Roasted Garlic Flavored
    Olive Oil Mayonnaise
Whole Food Canola Oil Mayonnaise

Meat, Canned

Hormel Canned Chicken
Hormel Breast of Chicken

Swanson's Canned Chicken
Swanson's White Chicken
Swanson's Chunk Chicken
Swanson's White Chicken in Water
Swanson's Premium Chunk Chicken
    Breast
Swanson's Premium White and Dark
    Chicken
Sweet Sue Canned White Chicken
Valley Fresh White Chicken
Valley Fresh Chunk Chicken
Underwood Liverwurst Spread
Hormel Canned Turkey
Hormel White Turkey
Swanson's Canned Turkey

Meat, Sausage and Salami

D'Antonio's Hot Beef Patties
D'Antonio's Hot Links
D'Antonio's Italian Sausage with Beef
Hormel Genoa Salami
Manda Supreme Deli Style Sausage
Martin's Country Smoked Andouille
    Sausage
Martin's Pork Tasso
Martin's Smoked Sausage, Mild and
    Hot
Shelton's Italian Sausage
Shelton's Turkey Franks
*Note: Most Store-Made Sausage Is
    Acceptable*

Mustards

Dry
Colman's Dry Mustard
Maille Dry Mustard with Horseradish
Brown & Creole
Arnaud's Sauce - Original Creole
    Remoulade
Ba-Tampte Delicatessen Style Mustard
Creole Delicacies Creole Mustard

Cottage Delight English Mustard with Horseradish
French's Bold & Spicy Mustard
French's Hearty Deli Mustard
Grey Poupon Peppercorn Mustard
Horseshoe Creole Mustard
Luzianne Creole Mustard
McIlhenny Farms Mustard Coarse Ground
Crystal Brown Mustard, Pure Prepared
Crystal Spicy Brown Mustard
Grey Poupon Spicy Brown Mustard
Guilden's Spicy Brown Mustard
Jack Daniel's Spicy Brown Mustard
McIlhenny Farms Spicy Brown Mustard
Nathan's Deli Style Mustard
Rex Creole Mustard
Temeraire Green Peppercorn Mustard
Temeraire Old-Fashioned Mustard
Westbrae Natural Stoneground Mustard
Zatarain's Creole Mustard

Yellow
Crystal Yellow Mustard
French's Classic Yellow Mustard
All Cajun Food Co. T-Loui's Chow Chow
Horseshoe Chow Chow Mustard
Horseshoe French Style Mustard
Hunt's Gourmet Mustard
Zatarain's Chow Chow

Dijon
Amora Dijon
Danish Blue Dijon Blend
Don's Mountain Herb Dijon Mustard
French's Dijon Mustard
Grey Poupon Country Dijon
Grey Poupon Dijon Mustard
Jack Daniel's Dijon Mustard
La Don's Gourmet Mustard
Maille Dijon Mustard with Horseradish

Moutarde de Lion Pommery Extra Strong Mustard
Temeraire Dijon Mustard
Westbrae Natural Dijon Style Mustard
Flavored Mustards
Champ's Tarragon Mustard
Champ's Mustard with Fennel
Champ's Mustard with Herbs

Nuts
Blue Diamond Almonds, Roasted and Plain
Blue Diamond Pistachios
Clement Faugier Whole Chestnuts
Energy Club Assorted Nuts
Fisher Nuts
Food Club Nuts
Hubs Peanuts
John Macadam Macadamia Nuts
Mauna Loa Macadamia Nuts
Maranatha Brand Almonds, Butternuts, Cashews, Macadamia, Pistachio Nuts & Sunflower Seeds
Planters Assorted Nuts, Roasted, Salted, Unsalted
Roddenbery's Peanut Patch Green Boiled Peanuts
Shur Fine Assorted Nuts
Sun Flower Kernels
Sunshine Country Peanuts
Sunshine Country Pecans
Sunshine Country Pistachios
Sunshine Sunflower Seeds

Olives
All Brands Black, Green, Stuffed
America's Choice Olives
Olivies Napa Valley Mediterranean Green Olive Salad
Progresso Olive Salad
Peloponnese Kalamato Olives

Domaine de Provence Olives
Haddon House Olives
Krino's Kalamata Olives
Lindsay Olives
Mario Olives
Miss Scarlett's Olives
Reese Olives
Tabasco Manzanilla Spanish Olives
Zatarain's Olives

Olive Oils

All Brands
Alessi Olive Oil
Bella Cucina Extra Virgin Olive Oil
Berio Olive Oil
Bertolli Olive Oil
Bionaturae Olive Oil
Boscoli Olive Oil
Carapelli Olive Oil
Casteluetrano Olive Oil
Colavita Olive Oil
Consorzio Basil Flavored Olive Oil
Consorzio Rosemary Flavored Olive Oil
Da Vinci Olive Oil
Filippo Berrio Olive Oil
Gardens-by-the-Bay Herbed Olive Oil
Goya Olive Oil
Greek Gourmet Olive Oil
Grey Poupon Olive Oil
James Plagriol Olive Oil
Kirlangic Lizma Zeytinyagi Olive Oil
Loriva Olive Oil
Master Choice Olive Oil
Melina's Olive Oil
Morea Olive Oil
Olio Santa Extra Virgin Olive Oil
Perfecto Herbed Olive Oil
Prestigio Olive Oil
Pompeian Olive Oil
Progresso Olive Oil
San Marc Olive Oil

Sasso Olive Oil
Spectrum Naturals Olive Oil
Ti'Amo Herbed Olive Oil
Vigo Olive Oil
Whole Food Olive Oil
Whole Food Market "365" Extra
    Virgin Olive Oil
Zuppardo Bros. Olive Oil

Pasta

Bionaturae Pasta
De Cecco Whole Durum Wheat Pasta
Eden Organic Golden Amber Durum
    Wheat Kamut Spirals Whole Grain
Eden Organic Golden Amber Durum
    Wheat Parsley Garlic Ribbons
Eden Organic Golden Amber Durum
    Wheat Pesto Ribbons
Fresina Pasta Co., Baton Rouge,
    Louisiana
Hodgson Mill Stone Ground Whole
    Wheat Pasta
Mendocino Pasta Co. Italian Herb
    Linguine
Mendocino Pasta Co. Garlic Basil Angel
    Hair
Mendocino Pasta Co. Garlic Basil
    Fettuccine
Mendocino Pasta Co. Garlic Basil
    Penne
Mendocino Pasta Co. Tomato Basil
    Fettuccine
Pritikin Whole Durum Wheat Pasta
Westbrae Natural 100% Whole Durum
    Wheat Pasta
Whole Food Organic Durum Whole
    Wheat Pasta

Peanut Butter and Other Flavored Butters

Peanut Butter

Arrowhead Mills Organic Peanut Butter
Fifty 50 No Sugar Added Peanut Butter
Masters Choice All Natural
    Peanut Butter
Smuckers All Natural Peanut Butter
Whole Food Organic Peanut Butter

Other Flavored Butters

Maranatha Almond Butter
Maranatha Cashew Butter
Maranatha Macadamia Butter
Maranatha Pistachio Butter
Maranatha Sunflower Butter
Whole Food Organic Almond Butter
Whole Food Organic Cashew Butter

Peppers

Casa Fiesta Whole Green Chilies
Food Club Green Chilies
Old El Paso Green Chilies
Herdez Chilpotles
Pelloponnese Rainbow Peppers
Casa Fiesta Nacho Sliced Jalapenos
Goya Jalapeno Peppers
McIlhenny Farms Jalapeno Nacho
    Slices
Mezzetta Pickled Peppers
Mission Jalapeno Peppers
Old El Paso Jalapeno Slices
Old El Paso Jalapeno Relish
Progresso Cherry Peppers
Progresso Tuscan Peppers
Mrs. Renfro's Jalapeno Peppers

Pickles

America's Choice Dill Pickles
America's Choice Dill Pickle Slices
Ba-Tampte Garlic Dill Pickles
Bubbies Kosher Dill Pickles

Ma Brown Pickles
CheRith Valley Gardens Dill Pickles
CheRith Valley Gardens "Hot 'n Spicy"
    Dill Pickles
Clausen's Dill Pickles
Cosmic Cukes Dill Pickles
Food Club Dill Pickles
Mt. Olive Dill Chips
Rainbo Dill Pickles
America's Choice Hamburger Slices
Deep South Hamburger Dill Pickles
Food Club Hamburger Dill Slices
Shur Fine Hamburger Dills
Valu Time Hamburger Dill Slices
Vlasic Hamburger Dill Chip Pickles
Amercia's Choice Kosher Pickles
Clausen's Kosher Dill Pickles
Deep South Kosher Dill Spears
Shur Fine Kosher Dills
Valu Time Kosher Dills
Vlasic Snack' MMs - Kosher Dill Pickles
Shur Fine No Garlic Dill Pickles
Deep South Whole Dill Pickles

Pimentos

Dromedary Slice Pimentos
Goya Pimentos

Pine Nuts

Imported Alessi Pignoli Pine Nuts
Haddon House Imported Alessi Pignoli
    Pine Nuts
Haddon House Pine Nuts

Relish

Bubbies Pure Kosher Dill Relish
Cascadian Farms Dill Relish
Mt. Olive Dill Relish
Rainbo Dill Relish
Vlasic Dill Relish

Rice, Brown, Brown Basmati, & Wild

Not Instant - All Brands Long Grain Brown Rice
America's Choice Brown Rice
Arrowhead Mills Brown Rice
Fantastic Food Brown Basmati Rice
Cache River Brown Basmati Rice
Konriko Brown Rice
Lundberg Wehani Brown Rice
Mahatma Brown Rice
Nutra-Farmed Lundberg Family Farms California Brown Basmati Rice
Nutra-Farmed Tilda Brown Basmati Rice
S&W Long Grain Brown Rice
Texmati Brown Basmati Rice
Uncle Ben's Brown Rice
California Harvest Wild Rice with Shitake Mushrooms
Haddon House Extra Fancy Cultivated Wild Rice
Lake 100% Wild Rice

Salad Dressings

Annie's Naturals Caesar Dressing
Annie's Naturals Famous Garlic and Herb Salad Dressing
Annie's Naturals Green Garlic Salad Dressing
Annie's Naturals Shitake and Sesame Vinaigrette
B. Felice and Sons Garlic Herb and Dill Dressing
Briana's Real French Vinaigrette
Cardini's Herb Dressing & Marinade
Cardini's Italian Dressing & Marinade with Extra Virgin Olive Oil
Cardini's Lime Dill Dressing & Marinade
Cardini's Original Caesar Dressing

Cardini's Zesty Garlic Dressing & Marinade
Chef Crozier Caesar Salad Dressing
Chef Crozier Vinaigrette
Isabella & Rae's Lemony Olive Dressing
Jardine's Green Olive Vinaigrette
la Madeleine la Vinaigrette Caesar Salad Dressing
La Martinque Bleu Cheese
La Martinque True French Vinaigrette
Martin Bros. Classic Caesar
Martin Bros. Garlic Mustard Dressing
Naturally Fresh Italian Herb Vinaigrette
Naturally Fresh Lite Ranch
All Natural Newman's Own Olive Oil & Vinegar
The Perfect Caesar
Postilion Anchovies Vinaigrette
Postilion Moutarde Forte de Dijon Vinaigrette
Postilion Roquefort Fresh Creamy Vinaigrette
Sal and Judy's Italian Dressing
Sal and Judy's Bleu Cheese
The Silver Palate Julie's Caesar Salad Splash
The Silver Palate Pesto Garden Mustard Dressing
Stonewall Kitchen Lemon Peppercorn Vinaigrette
Stonewall Kitchen Roasted Red Pepper Vinaigrette
Timpone's Fresh Sicilian Dressing & Marinade
Whole Food Sesame Garlic Dressing

Sauces, Barbecue

M. Eleana's Bar-Be-Que Sauce, Special Family Recipe, see recipe page or to order: (804) 282-7523

Sauces, Pasta

Dell Amore Artichoke and Capers Pasta Sauce

San Remo Artichoke Heart Sauce

Del Amore Fresh Basil and Garlic Pasta Sauce

Muir Glen Organic Tomato Basil Pasta Sauce Fat Free

Pritikin Tomato Basil Pasta Sauce

Sinatra's Tomato Basil and Parmesan Cheese Pasta Sauce

Tommaso's Tomato Basil Pasta Sauce

Dell Amore Eggplant and Marinara Pasta Sauce

Jacques Pepin's Kitchen Champagne Sauce

Jacques Pepin's Kitchen Pasta Sauce

Jacques Pepin's Kitchen Tomato Provencale Sauce

Elena's Funghi Pepe Verde Pasta Sauce

Millina's Finest Fat Free Organic Garlic Pasta Sauce

Millina's Finest Fat Free Organic Hot 'n Spicey Pasta Sauce

Millina's Finest Fat Free Organic Marinara Sauce

Millina's Finest FF Organic Sweet Pepper and Onion Pasta Sauce

Millina's Tomato and Mushroom Pasta Sauce

Classico Roasted Peppers and Onion Pasta Sauce

Lagniappe Gourmet Roasted Sweet Red Pepper Sauce

Muir Glen Organic Cabernet Marinara Pasta Sauce Fat Free

Colavita Marinara

Colavita Marinara Classic Hot

Dell Amore Marinara Pasta Sauce

Dell Amore Spicey Marinara Sauce

Patsy's Marinara Sauce

Sinatra's Milano Marinara Sauce

Sinatra's Mushroom Marinara Sauce

Thunder Bay Zucchini Marinara Sauce

Dell Amore Porcini Mushroom Pasta Sauce

Whole Foods Organic Pasta Sauce Fat-Free

Whole Foods Organic Pasta Sauce

Muir Glen Organic Garlic and Onion Pasta Sauce Fat Free

Classico Roasted Garlic Pasta Sauce

Muir Glen Organic Roasted Garlic Pasta Sauce Fat Free

Thunder Bay Garlic and Pepper Pasta Sauce

Tommaso's Pasta Sauce Arrabbiata

Coyote Cocina New Mexico Red Chile Pasta Sauce

Coyote Cocina Yellow Chile Pasta Sauce

Patsy's Puttanesca Sauce

Tommaso's Puttanesca Sauce

Whole Food Apulian Sauce Diavoliccino, Hot

Whole Food Roman Puttanesca with Olives, Capers and Anchovies

Hunt's Homestyle Spaghetti Sauce - No Sugar Added

Hunt's Homestyle Flavored Meat Spaghetti Sauce - No Sugar Added

Hunt's Homestyle Garlic and Herb Spaghetti Sauce - No Sugar Added

Hunt's Homestyle Spaghetti Sauce with Mushrooms - No Sugar Added

Mom's Spaghetti Sauce

Timpone's Classic Spaghetti Sauce

Newman's Own Tomato Diavolo Spicy Sauce for Pasta, Chicken, etc.

Muir Glen Organic Sun-Dried Tomatoes Pasta Sauce Fat Free

Elena's Bread Dipping Sauce - Spicey Tomato and Herb

Sauces, Pesto

Bella Cucina Olivada Olive Pesto
Bella Cucina Sun-Dried Tomato Pesto
Cardine's Pesto Sauce with Basil and
   Extra Virgin Olive Oil
Fox's Fine Foods Arugula, Roasted
   Garlic and Artichoke Pesto
Fox's Fine Foods Fine Roasted
   Vegetable Pesto
Fox's Fine Foods Roasted Onion Pesto
   with Lemon and Rosemary
Fox's Fine Foods Yellow Sun-Dried
   Tomato Pesto with Fennel and Basil
Master Choice Red Pepper Pesto Sauce
Master Choice Sun-Dried Tomato
   Pesto Sauce
Melissa's Sun-Dried Tomato Pesto
Sanremo Pesto
Sonoma Pesto
The Grower's Co. Nouvelle Garni
   Selection Pesto Basil Sauce and
   Seasoning Concentrate
Tex France Pesto
Tex France Sun-Dried Tomato Pesto

Sauces, Pizza

Gold Whisk Pizza Sauce
Muir Glen Organic Pizza Sauce
Whole Foods Apulian Sauce
   Diavoliccino, Hot

Sauces, Salsa & Picante

Salsa

Arribe Mexican Green Salsa
Del Monte Thick and Chunky Salsa
El Paso Chile Co. Salsa
El Paso Chile Co. Mild Salsa Primera
El Paso Chile Co. Snake Bite Salsa Hot
Food Club Thick and Chunky Salsa
Garden of Eatin Hot Habanero Fiery
   Salsa

Garden Valley Naturals Black Bean Salsa
Garden Valley Naturals Roasted Garlic
   Salsa, Mild or Hot
Guiltless Gourmet Tomato Salsa
Guiltless Gourmet Roasted Pepper Salsa
Guiltless Gourmet Salsa
Herdez Salsa Casera
Herdez Salsa Ranchera
Herdez Salsa Verde
La Mexicana Salsa
Marie's Roasted Garlic Salsa
Newman's Own Mild Salsa - Not
   Medium
Old El Paso Garden Pepper Salsa
Old El Paso Thick-N-Chunky Salsa
Ortega Salsa
Rose Timpone's Recipe Salsa Muy Rica
Rose Timpone's Salsa
Simply Zinful Salsa

Picante

Food Club Mexican Style Picante Sauce
Old El Paso Picante Sauce
Pace Picante Salsa
Pace Picante Sauce
The New Organics Co. Authentic
   Mexican Picante

Sauces, Soy

Kikkoman Soy Sauce
Shoyu Soy Sauce
Tabasco Soy Sauce
Tamari Soy Sauce
Tamari Soy Sauce Natural
Tamari Soy Sauce Wheat Free

Seafood, Canned

Clams and Clam Juice

Cento Minced Clams
Chicken of the Sea Baby Clams
Chicken of the Sea Clams
Crown Prince Baby Clams
Doxee Minced Clams

Orleans Clams
Orleans All Natural Clam Juice
Progresso Minced Clams
Reese Smoked Baby Clams
Reese All Natural Clam Juice
Roland Baby Clams
Snow's Chopped Clams

Crabmeat
Chicken of the Sea Crabmeat
Crown Prince Crabmeat
Orleans Canned Crabmeat
Reese Crabmeat

Fish
Chicken of the Sea Jack Mackeral
Reese Naturally Smoked Fillets of
Kippered Herring

Mussels and Oysters
Reese Mussels in Red Sauce
Ty Ling Smoked Mussels
Chicken of the Sea Canned Smoked
Oysters
Chicken of the Sea Oysters
Crown Prince Smoked Oysters
Empress Whole Oysters
Geesha Whole Oysters
Orleans Canned Whole Oysters
Orleans Smoked Oysters
Reese Smoked Oysters
Reese Whole Boiled Oysters

Salmon
America's Choice Salmon
Chicken of the Sea Salmon
Chicken of the Sea Pink Salmon
Chicken of the Sea Red Salmon
Double Q Pink Salmon
Food Club Salmon
Master Choice Salmon
Miramonte Pink Salmon
Pillar Rock Salmon
Pink Beauty Salmon

Reese Whole Pink Salmon
Roland Salmon

Sardines
Brunswick Holmes Sardines, Spring
Water or Soybean Oil & Seasoned
with Peppers
Crown Prince Sardines
Haddon House Sardines
Holmes Sardines
King Oscar Sardines
Port Clyde Sardines
Reese Sardines in Garlic Sauce
Roland Sardines
Underwood Sardines
Vigo Sardines

Shrimp
Chicken of the Sea Shrimp
Orleans Canned Shrimp
Reese Tiny Shrimp

Snails
Reese Pre-Cooked Snails

Tuna
America's Choice Tuna
Breast o' Chicken Tuna
Bumble Bee Tuna
Chicken of the Sea Tuna
Dave's Solid White Albacore Tuna
Food Club Tuna
Hormel Tuna
Master Choice Tuna
Miramonte Tuna
Shur Fine Tuna
Star Kist Tuna
Swanson's Tuna
Tree of Life Tongol Tuna
Whole Food Chunk Light Tongol Tuna
Whole Food Solid White Albacore Tuna

Seasonings, Spices, Herbs

Seasonings

Accent Flavor Enhancer
McCormick Flavor Enhancer
All Cajun Food Co. Bruce's Blend
  Sydeco Seasoning
Arise's Seasoning
Andy Roo's Cajun Jambalaya Creole
  Seasoning
Applewood Herb Farm Premium Blend
  Seasonings
Chef Paul Prudhomme's Majic
  Seasoning Blends
Delaune's Cajun – All Seasoning
Johnny's Seasoning Salt
La Spice All Purpose Seasoning
Bayou Bang Cajun Seasoning
Cajun Classique Cajun Seasoning
Cajun Land Cajun Seasoning with
  Green Onions
Louisiana Cajun Seasoning
Tony Chachere's Cajun More Spice
  Seasonings
Chef Hans Louisiana Creole Seasoning
Konriko Creole Seasoning
Tony Chachere's Creole Seasoning
McCormick Barbecue Seasoning
Rex Barbecue Seasoning
The Spice Hunts Hickory Barbecue
The Spice Hunts Mesquite
Mediterranean Inspirations Marinated
  Garlic
Spice World Garlic and Pepper
  Seasoning Salt
Spice World Lemon and Pepper
  Seasoning Salt
Tone's Lemon-Pepper
Durkee's Herb Seasoning
Durkee's Italian Seasoning
Great Shakes Italian Seasoning
McCormick Italian Seasoning

Rex Italian Seasoning
Sonoma Sun Dried Italian Seasoning
Spice World Italian Seasoning
Tone's Italian Seasoning
Trader's Choice Italian Seasoning
Great Shakes Peppercorn Medley
Great Shakes Pizza Seasoning
McCormick Classic Pizza Seasoning
McCormick Spicy Pizza Seasoning
Cajun Land Poultry Seasoning
McCormick Grill Mates Chicken
McCormick Herb Chicken Seasoning
McCormick Gourmet Spice Poultry
  Seasoning
McCormick Poultry Seasoning
McCormick Rotisserie Chicken
  Seasoning
Rex Poultry Seasoning
Spice Island Poultry Seasoning
The Spice Hunts Poultry
The Spice Hunts Poultry Grill and Broil
Cajun Land Meat Seasoning
Durkee's Steak Sauce
McCormick Grill Mates Montreal Steak
Only in New Orleans Brisket Rub
Great Shakes Grilled Steak Seasoning
Miss Ruth's All Natural Seasoning
Pico de Gallo Mexican Seasoning
The Spice Hunts Fajita Seasoning
The Spice Hunts Vegetable Seasoning
The Spice Hunts Stir Fry Ginger
Spice Island Lemon Herb Seasoning
Spike All Purpose Natural Seasoning
Tabasco 7-Spice Chili Recipe
Instant India Authentic Curry Paste
Thai Kitchen Green Curry Paste
Thai Kitchen Red Curry Paste
Tony Chachere's Extra-Lite
Cajun Classiques Blackened Seasoning
Cajun King Lemon Butter Amandine
  Seasoning

Frank Davis strictly N'Awlins Seasoning: "Bronzing," "Sprinkling Spice," "Seafood"

The Spice Hunts Fish Seasoning

Rex Blackened Seasoning

Zatarain's Blackened Fish Seasoning

Andy Roo's Louisiana BBQ Shrimp Creole Seasoning

Cajun King Barbecued Shrimp Seasoning

McCormick Cajun Quick Spicy Shrimp Seasoning

Shrimp Mosca Seasoning Blend

Cajun Land Crab Boil

Louisiana "Fish Fry Products" Crab Boil

New Orleans Crawfish, Shrimp and Crab Boil

Rex Crab Boil

Zatarain's Crab Boil

Zatarain's Gumbo Filé

Talko's Texas Liquid Smoke

Wright's Natural Hickory Seasoning Liquid Smoke

The Essence of Emeril Southwest Spice

The Essence of Emeril Rustic Rub

McCormick Chinese S Spice

McCormick Fine Herbs

Mrs. Dash Extra Spicy Onion and Herb

Tony Chachere Special Herb Blend

Salt Free

Bayou Bang Gourmet Cajun Spices – Salt Free, All Natural Ingredients

Captain Mike's Seasoning No Salt and Extra Spicey

Estee Sodium Free Salt It

Frank Davis strictly N'Awlins seasonings "No Salt"

McCormick Saltless

McCormick Salt Free All Purpose Seasoning

McCormick Salt Free Garlic and Herb Seasoning

McCormick Salt Free Lemon and Pepper Seasoning

Spices: The spices listed are acceptable in the brands that follow:

Allspice

Anise

Basil, Whole Sweet Basil

Bay Leaves, Select Whole Bay Leaves, Ground Bay Leaves

Dehydrated Bell Pepper, Green Bell Pepper Flakes

Celery Flakes, Celery Salt, Celery Seed

Mild and Hot Chili Powder, Dark Chili Powder

Chives

Cilantro

Cinnamon, Ground Cinnamon, Cinnamon Sticks

Cloves, Ground Cloves

Coriander

Cumin

Curry Powder

Dill Weed

Fennel, Fennel Seed

Crushed Garlic, Garlic Powder, Garlic Salt, Granulated Garlic, Minced Garlic, Parsleyed Garlic Salt

Ginger

Gumbo Filé

Marjoram

Mint, Mint Leaves

Mustard, Ground Mustard, Mustard Seed, Yellow Mustard Seed

Nutmeg, Minced Nutmeg

Chopped Onion, Instant Diced Onions, Minced Onion, Onion Powder, Onion Salt, Chopped Green Onions, Onion Juice

Oregano, Oregano Leaves, Oregano
   Seeds
Paprika, Fancy Paprika
Parsley, Parsley Flakes, Italian Parsley
Black Pepper, Black Peppercorns,
   Ground Red (Cayenne) Pepper,
   Crushed Red Pepper, White Pepper
Pickling Spice
Poppy Seed
Rosemary
Sage, Ground Sage
Salt
Sesame Seeds
Tarragon
Thyme, Whole Thyme Leaves
Tumeric
Brand Names:
Astor
Breaux Mart
Deep South
Durkee
Food Club
Lawry's
Master Choice
McCormick
Old Bay
Rex
Shur Fine
Spice Island
Spice World
The Spice Hunter
Tone's
Trader's Choice
Valu Time
Zatarain's

Also:
Aux Anysetiers Du Roy Ground Pepper
   with Herbs of Provence
Bush's Chili Magic Traditional Style
La Don's Chinese Red Pepper

McCormick California Style Blend
   Garlic Powder and Minced Garlic
San Marc Italian Style Granulated
   Garlic
McCormick California Style Blend
   Onion Powder and Minced Onion
McCormick Salt 'n Spice
Mexene Chili Powder

Soups

Bootsie's South Louisiana Cooking Ten
   Bean Soup
 Mills Choice Bean Soup
Swanson's Beef Broth
Sweet Sue Beef Broth
Health Valley Fat-Free Beef Flavored
   Broth
Health Valley Chicken Broth
Da Vinci Escarole in Chicken Broth
   Canned Soup
Shelton's Chicken Broth
Arrowhead Mills Mushroom Broth
Da Vinci Lentil Canned Soup
Progresso Lentil Soup
Taste Adventure Curry Lentil Soup
Taste Adventure Golden Pea Soup

Syrup

Cary's Sugar Free Syrup
Vermont Sugar Free Maple Syrup

Tomatoes

Bella Cucina Sun-Dried Tomatoes
Boscoli Sun-Dried Tomatoes
Gilroy Farms Marinated Sun-Dried
   Tomatoes
Melissa's Sun-Dried Tomatoes
Moshe Pupik and Ali Mishmunken's
   Sun-Dried Tomatoes (Kosher)
Sonoma Marinated Dried Tomatoes

America's Choice Crushed Tomatoes
America's Choice Whole Tomatoes
Contadina Whole Tomatoes
Delchamps Whole Tomatoes, Peeled, Diced
Del Monte Fresh Cut Tomatoes
Food Club Diced Tomatoes
Food Club Whole Peeled Tomatoes
Hunt's Plain Diced Tomatoes
Hunt's Whole Tomatoes
L'Esprit de Compagne Virginia Sun-Ripened Tomatoes
Luigi Vitelli Italian Peeled Tomatoes
Master Choice Whole Tomatoes
Millina's Finest Tomatoes
Muir Glen Organic Diced Tomatoes with and without Seasonings
Muir Glen Organic Ground Peeled Tomatoes
Muir Glen Organic Peeled Tomatoes
Pomi Chopped Tomatoes
Pomi Strained Tomatoes
Pomodora Fresca Solo Fresh Plum Tomatoes - Cayenne Hot
Pomodora Fresca Solo Fresh Plum Tomatoes Preserved in Own Juices with Vinegar
Progresso Peeled Tomatoes with Basil
Progresso Peeled Tomatoes
Progresso Crushed Tomatoes
Roberts Big R Tomatoes
Rotel Mild Whole Tomato and Green Chilies
Rotel Extra Hot Whole Tomatoes and Green Chilies
Rotel Diced Tomatoes and Green Chilies
S&W Tomatoes
Shur Fine Diced Tomatoes
Shur Fine Whole Peeled Tomatoes
Thrifty Maid Tomatoes
Thrifty Maid Diced Tomatoes

Thrifty Maid Whole Tomatoes
Whole Food Whole Peeled Organic Tomatoes

Tomato - Sauces, Paste, Puree

Sauces

The Grower's Co. Nouvelle Garni Selection Dried Tomato Sauce and Seasoning Concentrate
America's Choice Tomato Sauce
Barilla Tomato Sauce - Sweet Pepper and Garlic
Cento Tomato Sauce
Delchamps Tomato Sauce
Millina's Finest Tomato Sauce
Food Club Tomato Sauce
Muir Glen Organic Chunky Tomato Sauce
Patsy's Tomato Sauce with Olives and Capers
Pomodoro Fresca ANA Fresh Plum Tomatoes and Seasonings
Rustichella D'Abruzzo Tomato Sauce
Sal and Judy's Original Recipe Tomato Sauce
Shur Fine Tomato Sauce
Thrify Maid Tomato Sauce

Paste and Puree

America's Choice Tomato Purée
Amore Concentrated Sun-Dried Tomato Paste
Amore Concentrated Sun-Dried Tomato-Garlic Paste
Centro Tomato Paste
Contadina Tomato Paste
Del Monte Tomato Paste
Muir Glen Organic Tomato Paste
Progresso Tomato Paste
Progresso Tomato Puree
Thrifty Maid Tomato Paste
Whole Food Puree Organic Tomatoes

Tomato Relish

Pelloponnese Sun-Dried Tomato Relish
Sonoma Muffaletta Dried Tomato and
  Olive Relish
Sun Fix Roma Italia Spread

Vegetables, Canned

Cora Mia Artichoke Hearts
Cohevi Artichoke Hearts
Del Destino Hearts of Artichoke
Haddon House Artichoke Bottoms
Haddon House Artichoke Hearts
Pesto Artichokes
Prestige Artichoke Hearts
Progresso Artichoke Hearts
Reese Artichoke Hearts
Reese Artichoke Salad
Roland Artichoke Hearts
Romanina Artichoke Hearts
Romanina Artichoke Hearts, Quartered
Vigo Artichoke Hearts
Del Monte Asparagus Spears
Del Monte Fresh Cut Asparagus Tips
Food Club Asparagus
Green Giant Asparagus Spears
Le Sueur Asparagus Spears
Pepita Moreno Asparagus
Pride Asparagus
Pride Asparagus Spears
Reese Asparagus
Reese Asparagus Spears
Shur Fine Asparagus
Thank You Asparagus Spears
Thrifty Maid Asparagus
Walla Walla Asparagus
Whopper Walla Walla Colossal Extra
  Long White Asparagus
La Choy Sliced Bamboo Shoots
Port Arthur Bamboo Shoots
La Choy Bean Sprouts
Ty Ling Bean Sprouts

La Choy Water Chestnuts
Port Arthur Water Chestnuts
Ty Ling Water Chestnuts
Bush's Chopped Collard Greens
Stubb's Harvest Collard Greens
Bush's Mustard Greens
Stubb's Harvest Mustard Greens
The Allen's Sunshine Turnip Greens
Bush's Turnip Greens
Food Club Turnip Greens
Stubb's Harvest Turnip Greens
Bosco Garlic
CheRith Valley Gardens Hearts of Palm
Haddon House Hearts of Palm
Reese Hearts of Palm
Regency Hearts of Palm
Roland Hearts of Palm
Stubb's Kale
America's Choice Mushrooms
B in B Mushrooms
DaVinci Marinated Mushrooms
Epicurean Specialty Gourmet Dried
  Mushrooms and Peppers
Flavorite Mushrooms
Food Club Mushrooms
Green Giant Mushrooms
Kame Straw Mushrooms
Roland Mushrooms
Thrifty Maid Mushrooms
Ty Ling Stir Fry Mushrooms
Stubbs Cut Okra
Trappey's Cut Okra
Trappey's Cut Okra and Tomato
America's Choice Sauerkraut
Bubbies Sauerkraut
Cascadian Farms Sauerkraut
Clausen's Sauerkraut
Del Monte Sauerkraut
Vlasic Sauerkraut
The Allens Popeye Brand Chopped
  Spinach

America's Choice Leaf Spinach
Del Monte Fresh Cut Whole Leaf
  Spinach
Fresh Cut Spinach
Pesto Spinach
Bruce's Sliced Squash
CheRith Valley Gardens Sunburst
  Squash
Witt's Vegetable Garnish

Vegetables, Frozen

Bird's Eye Frozen Foods
Cascadian Farm Frozen Vegetables:
  Broccoli, Cut Green Beans, Organic
  Garden Peas, Chopped Spinach
Green Giant Frozen Foods
Janet Lee Brand
Pic Sweet Frozen Foods
Whole Food Market "365" Green Peas
Whole Food Market "365" Cut Green
  Beans
Haddon House Artichoke Hearts and
  Bottoms
Dixiana Asparagus Spears
Astor Butter Beans
Dixiana Butter Beans
McKenzie's Butter Beans
America's Choice Green Beans
Bird's Eye Side Orders Green Beans
  with Almonds
Dixiana Green Beans
Food Club Green Beans
Shur Fine Green Beans
Sno Pac Green Beans
Thrifty Maid Green Beans
America's Choice Lima Beans
Astor Lima Beans
Food Club Lima Beans
McKenzie's Lima Beans
Thrifty Maid Lima Beans
America's Choice Broccoli

Astor Broccoli
Cascade Farms Broccoli
Dixiana Broccoli
McKenzie's Broccoli
Shur Fine Broccoli
Thrifty Maid Broccoli
America's Choice Brussel Sprouts
Astor Brussel Sprouts
McKenzie's Brussel Sprouts
Thrifty Maid Brussel Sprouts
Astor Cauliflower
Dixiana Collard Greens
Food Club Collard Greens
Dixiana Mustard Greens
McKenzie's Mustard Greens
Dixiana Turnip Greens
Food Club Turnip Greens
McKenzie's Turnip Greens
Dixiana Chopped Green Peppers
Food Club Chopped Green Peppers
America's Choice Okra
Dixiana Okra
Food Club Okra
McKenzie's Okra
McKenzie's Okra, Tomatoes and
  Onions
Thrifty Maid Okra
Dixiana Onions
Dixiana Black Eyed Peas
McKenzie's Black Eyed Peas
Astor Peas
Cascade Farms Peas
Dixiana Peas
Food Club Crowder Peas
Food Club Green Peas
McKenzie's Petite Peas
McKenzie's Peas
Shur Fine Green Peas
Sno Pac Green Peas
La Choy Snow Pea Pods
Thrifty Maid Peas
Dixiana Seasonings

Chef's Seasonings
McKenzie's Seasoning Blend
America's Choice Spinach
Astor Spinach
Cascade Farms Spinach
Food Club Spinach
McKenzie's Spinach
Shur Fine Spinach
Sno Pac Spinach

Vegetables, Pickled

Boscoli Asparagus
Mezzetta Pickled Broccoli
Mezzetta Pickled Brussel Sprouts
Pickled Cauliflower
Porter's Pick a Dilly Farmstyle Dilly
  Beans
Porter's Pick a Dilly Farmstyle Dilly
  Beans - Great Garlic
Porter's Pick a Dilly Farmstyle Dilly
  Beans - Mild
Wickland Farms Blue Lake Spiced
  Beans
Boscoli Garlic
CheRith Valley Gardens Pickled Garlic
Mezzetta Pickled Crushed Garlic
Boscoli Green Beans
Boscoli Italian Olive Salad
CheRith Valley Gardens Pickled Okra
Tiffe's Pickled Okra
Mezzetta Pickled Olives
Boscoli Onions
Holland Pickled Onions
Reese Pickled Onions

Vinegar

Antica Acetaia Dei Carandini Balsamic
  Vinegar of Modena
Belle Cucina Cabernet Vinegar
Blue Runner Vinegar
Candoni Balsamic Vinegar
Cento Garlic Flavored Wine Vinegar
DaVinci Vinegar
De Nign's Wine Vinegar
Eden Selected Red Wine Vinegar
Food Club Vinegar
Grey Poupon Imported Balsamic
  Vinegar of Modena
Heinz Distilled White Wine Vinegar
Herbs de Provence Provencal Vinegar
Master Choice Vinegar
Monari Federzoni Red Wine Vinegar
Monari Federzoni White Wine Vinegar
Pastene Imported Balsamic Vinegar of
  Modena
Progress's White Wine Vinegar
Reese Garlic Flavored Wine Vinegar
Reese Maitre Jacques Garlic Wine Vinegar
Regina Red Wine Vinegar
Regina Red Wine Vinegar with Garlic
Regina White Wine Vinegar
Regina White Wine Vinegar with
  Tarragon
Spice Island Vinegar
Stonewall Kitchen Chili Chive Vinegar
Whole Food Champagne Vinegar
Whole Food Red Wine Vinegar
Zatarain's White Wine Vinegar

Yogurt

Breyers Yogurt, Sugar Free
Brown Cow Farm Yogurt, Sugar Free
Dannon Yogurt, Sugar Free
Horizon Yogurt, Sugar Free
Natural Alta Dena Select Yogurt, Sugar
  Free

CHAPTER SEVENTEEN

Index

RECIPE INDEX

A

APPETIZERS, HORS D'OEUVRES AND SNACKS

Artichoke Spread, 45
Asparagus and Crabmeat Mousseline, 26
Boiled Shrimp with Choice of Sauces, 34
Buffalo Wings, 31
Buster Crab Bernaise, 28
Cajun Pecans, 48
Cerviche, 40
Chicken Liver Pate, 33
Crabmeat Mariniere, 27
Crawfish Mold, 36
Cream Cheese and Salmon Spread, 38
Creole Crabmeat Spread, 37
Creole Spicy Pecans, 49
Cucumber Dill Dip, 42
Deviled Eggs, 39
Endive with Smoked Salmon, 39
Fresh Vegetables with Dill and Garlic Dip, 42
Fresh Dill Dip, 43
Fresh Salsa, 40
Fresh Tomato Dip, 43
Gorgonzola Spread with Walnuts, 46
Guacamole, 41
"Hot" Crabmeat, 37
Italian Barbecued Shrimp, 29
Marinated Mushrooms, 47
Mexican Layer Dip, 41
Mussels Vinaigrette, 31
Oysters Rockefeller, 30
Parmesan Crackers, 50
Roasted Pecans, 48
Smoked Salmon Mousse, 38
Sardine Mousse with Curry, 36
Shrimp Lafitte, 35
Shrimp Paradis, 28
Shrimp Royale, 35
Spiced Shrimp Manchac, 34
Spinach and Artichoke Dip, 44
Spinach Curry Dip, 45
Steak Tartare Anastasia, 32
Stilton Cheese Ball, 46
Tomato Bruschetta, 50

ARTICHOKE

Artichoke Spread, 45
Chicken and Artichoke Rice Casserole, 188
Cream of Artichoke Soup, 60
Eggs Sardou, 150
Red Snapper au Gratin, 179
Shrimp Stuffed Artichoke Vinaigrette Salad, 130
Spinach and Artichoke Casserole, 263
Spinach and Artichoke Dip, 44
Veal Kottwitz, 213

ASPARAGUS

Asparagus and Crabmeat Mousseline, 26
Asparagus au Gratin, 254
Asparagus in Mustard Vinaigrette, 120
Asparagus with Mustard Sauce, 254
Crabmeat and Asparagus Salad, 128
Creole Shrimp Salad, 131

Rice and Asparagus au Gratin, 276
Roasted Asparagus, 268
Roasted Vegetables, 269

AVOCADO

Avocado and Shrimp Salad, 131
Broccoli and Avocado Salad, 121
Cerviche, 40
Cobb Salad, 111
Garden District Salad, 115
Guacamole, 41
Mexican Layer Dip, 41

B

BEANS

Black Beans
  Black Bean Soup, 68
  Southwestern Bean Soup, 69
  Southwestern Chicken Salad, 108
  Wild Rice Stuffed Tomatoes, 118
Garbanzo Beans
  Bean Salad, 123
  Green Bean Salad, 123
Green Beans
  Beef Salad Vinaigrette, 106
  Beef Vegetable Soup, 55
  Green Beans with Dilled Havarti Cheese, 259
  Green Bean Salad, 123
  Sauteed Green Beans with Garlic and Mushrooms, 259
  String Bean Ragout, 260
  Tomato Green Bean Casserole, 260
Lentil Beans
  Lentil and Ham Soup, 70
Lima Beans
  Beef Vegetable Soup, 55
  Red Snapper Provencale, 178
Northern Beans
  Chicken and Bean Chili, 190
Pinto Beans
  Southwestern Bean Soup, 69
Red Kidney Beans
  Bean Salad, 123
  Beef and Bean Chili, 224
  Bertha's Red Beans and Rice, 187
  Red Bean Soup, 71
  Southwestern Bean Soup, 69
Refried Beans
  Mexican Layer Dip, 41

BEEF

Barbecue Oven Smoked Brisket, 226
Beef and Bean Chili, 224
Beef and Sweet Potato Pepperpot Soup, 54
Beef Salad Vinaigrette, 106
Beef Stew, 224
Beef Stock, 79
Beef Tenderloin with Garlic and Tarragon, 228
Beef Vegetable Soup, 55
Bolognese Sauce, 99
Chateaubriand Bouquetiere, 231
Dijon Mustard Coated Sirloin Steak, 243
Filet Brennan, 229
Glazed Tenderloin, 227
Hamburger Brennan, 217

Hamburgers Stuffed with Sharp Cheddar Cheese, 218
Lasagne, 222
Louisiana Hamburgers, 218
Maude's Spaghetti and Meatballs, 220
Maude's Steak Diane, 232
Meatloaf, 219
Medallions of Beef with Stilton Cheese, 230
New Orleans Roast Beef, 227
Roast Tenderloin of Beef, 228
Roasted Brisket of Beef, 226
San Antonio Beef, 225
Shish-Ka-Bob, 243
Steak au Poivre, 229
Steak Tartare Anastasia, 32
Stuffed Bell Peppers, 233
Stuffed Cabbage Creole, 234
Stuffed Sirloin Steak, 231

BREAD

Bran Muffins, 313
Bread Crumbs, 316
Cheese Bread, 309
Italian Bread Crumbs, 316
Onion Bread, 310
Rye Bread, 311
Spinach Bread, 312
Stone Ground Whole Wheat Bread, 308
Stone Ground Whole Wheat Bread, 314
  (Bread machine recipe)
Stone Ground Whole Wheat Buttermilk Bread, 315
Whole Wheat Dinner Rolls, 313
Whole Wheat Pizza Crust, 315

BREAKFAST AT BRENNAN'S

Basic Omelette, 146
Calves' Liver with Sauteed Onions, 156
Cheddar and Ham Omelette, 146
Crabmeat Omelette, 147
Eggs Benedict, 149
Egg Casserole, 148
Eggs Ellen, 151
Eggs Sardou, 150
Eggs Hussarde, 150
Eggs St. Charles, 151
Florentine Omelette, 147
French Toast, 153
Grillades, 157
Italian Cheese Frittata, 155
Italian Pancakes, 155
Mame's Pancakes, 154
Pecan Oatmeal Waffle, 154
Poached Eggs, 149
Quiche Lorraine, 152
Quiche Pie Crust, 153
Russian Omelette, 148
Texas Breakfast Rice, 156

BROCCOLI

Broccoli and Avocado Salad, 121
Broccoli and Cauliflower Salad, 121
Broccoli and Cheese Soup, 61
Broccoli au Gratin, 257
Broccoli Bleu Cheese Sauce, 102
Broccoli Vinaigrette, 120
Cauliflower and Broccoli Casserole, 255
Cream of Broccoli Soup, 60

347

- Appleton, Nancy, PhD., *Lick The Sugar Habit,* Santa Monica, Avery Publishing Group, 1996.

- http://www.anndeweesallencom/
  (Ann de Wees Allen, N.D., Glycemic Research Institute)

- http://www.caloriecontrol.org
  (Calorie Control Council)

- http://www.cdc.gov/nccdphp/ddt/facts.html
  (Diabetes)

- http://www.geocities.com/HotSprings/4582/
  (Marcel Bovy, The Montignac Method, Food for Thought)

- Guyton, Arthur C., M.D., John E. Hall, Ph. D., *The Textbook on Medical Physiology,*
  Philadelphia: W.B. Saunders, 1996.

- http://www.lanr.unl.edu/pubs/foods/g1030.htm
  (University of Nebraska NebGuide, "Sweeteners")

- http://lifelines.com/libry2.html
  (Lifelines Health Science and Research Library)

- http://www.mendosa.com/glfactor.html
  (The GI Factor)

- http://www.montignac.com/en/gindex.html
  (Glycaemic Index Table)

- Montignac Michel, *Dine Out and Lose Weight,* Paris: Artulen, 1991.

- Montignac, Michel, *Eat Yourself Slim,* Paris: Artulen, 1991.

- http://www.smartbasic.com/glos.news/3glyc.index.dec93.html
  (Smart Basic Intelliscope)

- Steward, Bethea, Andrew, Balart, *SugarBusters!™ Cut Sugar to Trim Fat,* Metairie: 1995.

- http://www.sunflower.org/~cfsdays/nutrasweet.html
  ("The Not So Sweet News About NutraSweet")

- http://www.tiac.net/users/mgold/aspartame2/adverse-new.txt
  (Aspartame Toxicity Information Center)

- Tordoff MG, Alleva AM, Effect of drinking soda sweetened with aspartame or high-fructose, corn syrup on food intake and body weight. *American Journal of Clinical Nutrition,* 1990;51:963-969.

- http://wctc.net/~tbart/NutraSweet.html
  (Untitled)

Order Form

Please send

_____ copies of *Sugar Bust For Life!...*
With The Brennans at $14.95 each $_____

plus $3.75 postage and handling for one copy $_____

add $1.50 postage for each additional book $_____

Orleans Parish residents add $1.35 each
(9% city and state sales tax) $_____

Louisiana state residents add $0.60 each
(4% state sales tax only) $_____

TOTAL $_____

Mail *Sugar Bust For Life!...With The Brennans* book(s) to:

Name:

Address:

City/State/Zip:

Phone:

Make checks payable to: *Sugar Bust For Life!/Shamrock Publishing*
Charge to
(check one): ☐ VISA   ☐ MasterCard   ☐ American Express   ☐ Discover

Account Number: Expiration Date:

Signature:

Mail to: Sugar Bust For Life!...With The Brennans
c/o Shamrock Publishing
P.O. Box 15439
New Orleans, LA 70175-5439

Phone Orders: 504-897-6770 or
Fax: 504-897-6770

E-mail: SBforL@aol.com

SUGAR BUST FOR LIFE!...
WITH THE BRENNANS,
PART II

Available in April 2000

Turn Page For Order Form...

SUGAR BUST FOR LIFE!...
WITH THE BRENNANS, PART II

AVAILABLE APRIL 2000

Order Form

Please send

_____ copies of *Sugar Bust For Life!...With The Brennans,*
Part II at $14.95 each $_____

plus $3.75 postage and handling for one copy $_____

add $1.50 postage for each additional book $_____

Orleans Parish residents add $1.35 each
(9% city and state sales tax) $_____

Louisiana state residents add $0.60 each
(4% state sales tax only) $_____

TOTAL $_____

Mail *Sugar Bust For Life!...With The Brennans, Part II* book(s) to:

Name: _____

Address: _____

City/State/Zip: _____

Phone: _____

Make checks payable to: *Sugar Bust For Life!/Shamrock Publishing*
Charge to
(check one): ☐ VISA   ☐ MasterCard   ☐ American Express   ☐ Discover
Account Number: _____ Expiration Date: _____

Signature: _____

Mail to:	Sugar Bust For Life!...With The Brennans
	c/o Shamrock Publishing
	P.O. Box 15439
	New Orleans, LA 70175-5439
Phone Orders:	504-897-6770 or
	Fax: 504-897-6770
E-mail:	SBforL@aol.com

SUGAR BUST FOR LIFE!...
WITH THE BRENNANS,
PART II
Available in April 2000